C000230854

LINGERIE AND LEISUREWEAR

WITH YOUR OVERLOCKER

LINETTE MARITZ

NH
NEW HOLLAND

SUPPLIERS' ADDRESSES

UNITED KINGDOM
Retail:
JOHN LEWIS
Oxford Street
London W1
Tel: (071) 499 1977
(branches throughout the UK)

Manufacturers:
ELNA
41-45 Southwalk Bridge Road
London SE1 9HH
Tel: (071) 403 3011

BROTHER
Shepley Street
Audenshaw
Manchester M34 5EX
Tel: (061) 330 6531

NEW HOME
Janome Centre
South Side
Bredbury
Stockport
Cheshire SK6 25P
Tel: (061) 430 6011

NEW ZEALAND
BERNINA SEWING CENTRE
St Lukes Shopping Centre
St Lukes Square
Auckland
Tel: (09) 849 4610

JANOME SEWING MACHINE AND OVERLOCKER SPECIALISTS
336 Remuera Road
Remuera
Auckland 5
Tel: (09) 520 0496

Also at:
Lynmall City
Great North Road
New Lynn
Auckland
Tel: (09) 827 7043

AUSTRALIA
A.A. ALL APPLIANCE RENTALS PTY LTD
146 Liverpool Road
Enfield NSW 2170
Tel: (02) 744 3838

BERNINA AUSTRALIA
15 Carrington Road
Castle Hill NSW 2154
Tel: (02) 899 1188

PFAFF
Head Office
Unit 1, 13 Hoyle Avenue
Castle Hill NSW 2154
Tel: (02) 894 6311
(outlets also located in most suburbs)

OVERLOCKER ADVICE SERVICE & SALES
20 Memorial Avenue
Liverpool NSW 2170
Tel: (02) 602 8144

OVERLOCKERS GALORE
325 Belmore Road
Riverwood NSW 2210
Tel: (02) 534 1690

Also at:
53065 Westfield Shopping Plaza
Miranda NSW 2228
Tel: (02) 540 2578

For your nearest stockist please contact any of the manufacturers used above.

First published in the UK in 1994 by
New Holland (Publishers) Ltd
37 Connaught Street, London W2 2AZ

ISBN 1 85368 343 4

Editor: Glynne Williamson
Designer: Darren McLean
Design assistant: Petal Palmer
Cover design: Darren McLean
Photographer: Juan Espi
Stylists: Elaine Levitte and Nancy V Richards
Colour illustrations: Nicci Page
Line drawings: Jacques le Roux

Typesetting: Struik DTP
Reproduction: Hirt & Carter (Pty) Ltd
Printed and bound by: Tien Wah Press (Pte.) Ltd

CONTENTS

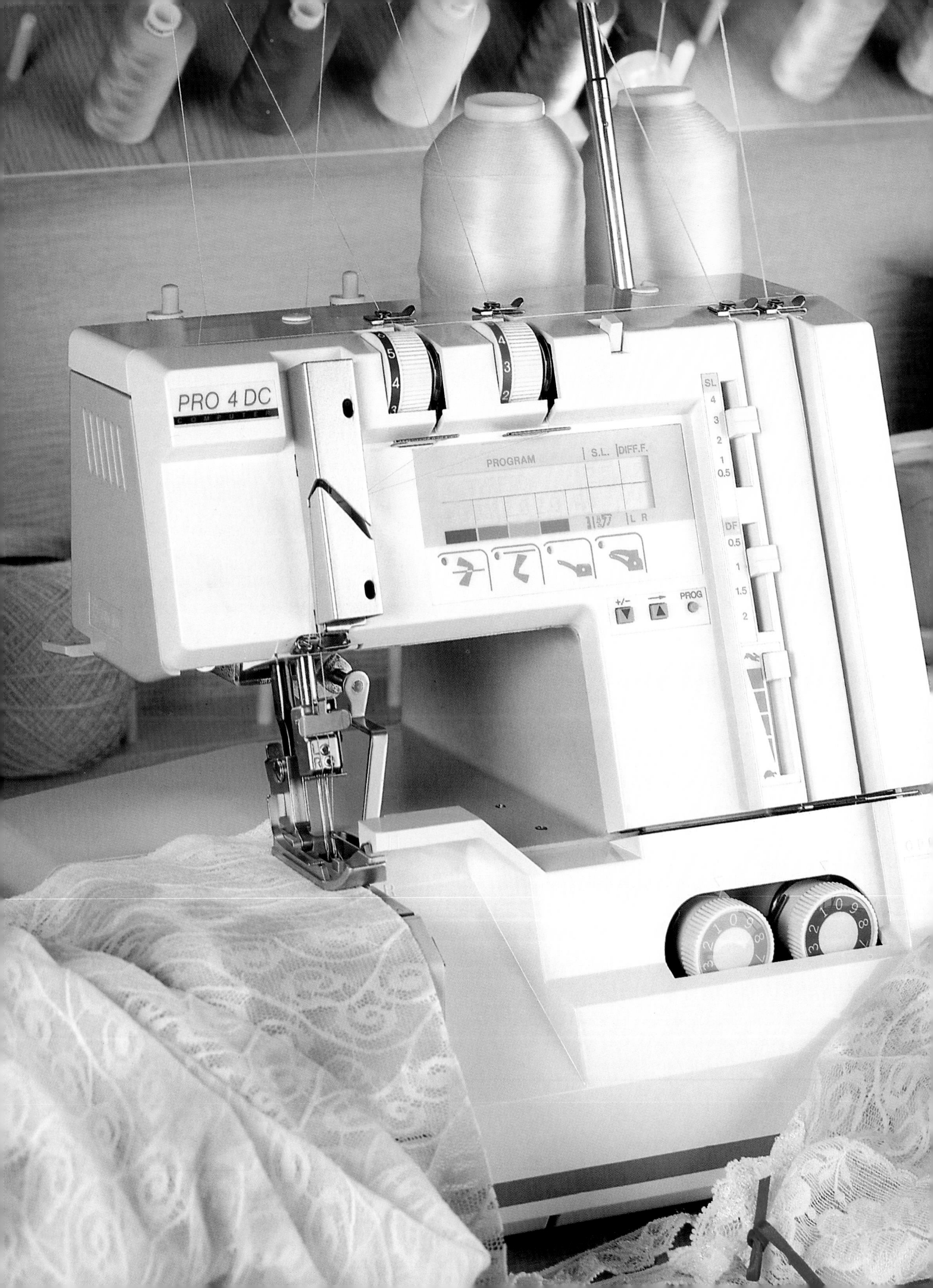
PRO 4 DC
COMPUTER
PROGRAM
S.L.
DIFF.F.
SL
DF
+/–
PROG

INTRODUCTION

Buying lingerie and underwear has become increasingly expensive, and it's no wonder that more and more people are beginning to design and make their own. This book will inspire those wishing to make personalised and original lingerie, underwear and leisurewear the easy and inexpensive way!

With a little know-how and a lot of enthusiasm, use your overlocker and sewing machine to create silky camisoles and French knickers, flattering briefs, and colourful gym-wear using fabric and designs of your choice, and decorate them with pretty lace and elastic.

I hope you will have as many hours of fun sewing special lingerie and leisurewear for yourself and your family as I did while putting this book together!

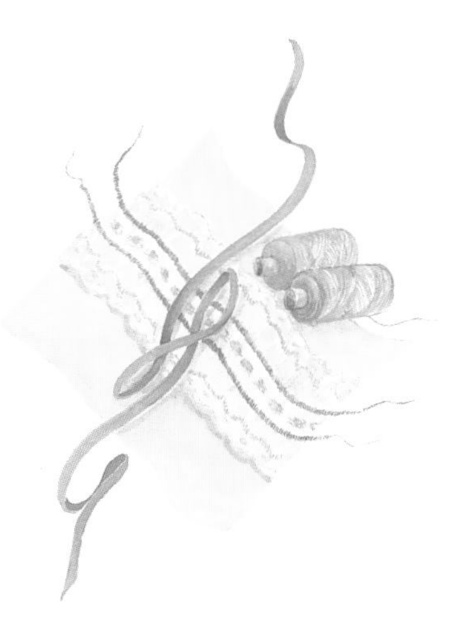

NEEDLES

Selecting the correct needle for both your overlocker and sewing machine when sewing lingerie and leisurewear is important. The type and size of needle you choose will depend on the fabric used.

- Universal needles are suitable for polyester, cotton and linen.
- Ballpoint needles are suitable for thin fabrics such as satin, silk, rayon, and crêpe de Chine.
- Stretch needles are suitable for T-shirt fabric and Lycra.
- Twin needles: 2.5 mm or 4.0 mm (⅛ in) twin needles are available specifically for use on stretch fabric. They can be used for decorative topstitching on lingerie, underwear and leisurewear. Twin needles can only be used on sewing machines.

THREADS

- Mercerised cotton has a silky, lustrous appearance and must only be used on a sewing machine. A sewing machine is designed to allow for stretch when using stretch or overlock stitches such as zig-zag or overcasting. Inferior cotton can cause problems with tension and may damage your sewing machine.
- Always use a good quality polyester cotton thread on your overlocker. Polyester cotton thread consists of cotton-wrapped polyester strands, and can be used in loopers and needles. As your overlocker sews at high speeds, the thread must be able to stretch, irrespective of the type of fabric used. Make sure that the different reels you are using on your overlocker are all the same brand, and that the cotton is evenly wound on the reel, so as to avoid adjusting the tension frequently.
- Floss can only be used on an overlocker in the loopers. Floss is a superstretch thread and is made from bulked nylon. It forms attractive, regular satin stitches and is suitable for overlocking seams or as decorative stitching on underwear and leisurewear. It is soft but strong and stretches with the fabric. Floss is available in two ply (thin) and four ply (thick).

Decorative threads

- Embroidery thread or crochet cotton is a thick thread used on the loopers for decorative stitching and is available in different thicknesses. Only the no. 8 or no. 12 thread is suitable for use on an overlocker. Similar threads, for example, ribbon thread, can also be used. Always test that the thread can be threaded through the eye of the looper. If the thread is too thick, it will damage your overlocker.
- Metallic thread is a strong, decorative thread, for example, Madeira, DMC or Metler, and is available in plain, gold and silver, or variegated colours. It can be used on your sewing machine or overlocker in the needles or loopers.

TENSION

When threading your overlocker, keep the thread pulled tightly to ensure that it is properly inserted into the tension spring on the tension knob. If the thread is not inserted properly, the overlocking stitch will form loops on the front of the article. The tension settings on a four-thread overlocker are as follows:

LEFT NEEDLE

This is the outside needle. Of the four tension settings on your overlocker, the tension setting for this needle must always be the highest, as this controls the thread which holds the seam together and prevents it from pulling open.

RIGHT NEEDLE

This is the inside needle and is also known as the mock safety stitch. The tension setting for this needle must always be lower than that of the outside needle, as this controls the thread which supports the outside thread. If the tension is set too high, the seam will pucker.

UPPER LOOPER

This needle controls the thread which lies across on top of the stitching. The tension setting must always be as low as possible to prevent the seam from pulling open.

LOWER LOOPER

This needle controls the thread which lies across the bottom of the stitching. The tension setting must always be as low as possible to prevent the seam from pulling open.

> NOTE: On an overlocker, 0 signals a very low setting and 9 a very high tension setting.

STITCH LENGTH

The stitch length is the distance between the stitches and the loops formed. The desired stitch length will depend on the thickness of the fabric and the finish required. A short stitch length is used on thin fabrics, for example, silk or viscose, as it prevents the fabric from puckering, and for sewing a narrow or rolled hem. A long stitch length is suitable for heavier or thicker fabrics, for example denim or wadding, and for gathering.

PRESSURE KNOB

The pressure knob is used to increase or decrease the pressure of the sewing foot on the fabric. For thin fabrics, increase the pressure to prevent puckering. For thick fabrics, decrease the pressure to prevent the fabric from bunching and knits from stretching.

MOVING AND FIXED BLADE

There are two blades on an overlocker which will cut the edge of the fabric before it is overlocked.

Moving blade: Depending on the make and model of your overlocker, this blade is usually made of strong steel and need not be replaced. On some models the moving blade can be locked when sewing thick fabrics, or disengaged for decorative sewing.

Fixed blade: Depending on the make and model of your overlocker, this blade is usually made of soft steel and must be replaced when it no longer cuts cleanly and leaves edges frayed. The fixed blade controls the cutting width, which can be adjusted, depending on the fabric used.

DIFFERENTIAL FEED

Most overlockers are equipped with a differential feed for perfect fabric control. This means that the overlocker has two sets of 'feed dogs'. The purpose of the feed dog is to feed the fabric through from the bottom. The speed of the feed dogs can be controlled by adjusting the differential feed knob.

When the differential feed knob is set on 0.5-0.7, the front feed dog is set to feed the fabric through at a slower speed to prevent thin fabrics, such as silk, viscose or net, from puckering.

When the differential feed knob is set on 1.0, the front and back feed dogs feed the fabric through at the same speed. This is the normal setting, used when sewing cotton, polyester cotton, linen or tracksuiting.

When the differential feed knob is set on 1.5, the front feed dog will feed the fabric through faster than the back feed dog. This setting, therefore, is suitable for sewing on thicker fabrics, such as woven tracksuiting, and can also be used to facilitate sewing when joining seams or sewing over seams.

When the differential feed knob is set on 2.0, the front feed dog will feed the fabric through faster than at a setting of 1.5 and prevents knits from waving or stretching. It also prevents thick fabrics from bunching up. Use this setting when sewing very thick fabrics such as denim or leather, or when applying rib trim.

This setting can also be used to gather fabrics, as described under DECORATIVE FINISHES USING THE OVERLOCKER on page 10.

OVERLOCKING STITCHES

The overlocking stitch is formed around a stitch tongue with the use of loopers and needles. The type of stitching depends on the number of needles and loopers used.

THREE-THREAD OVERLOCKING

This stitch is formed around the stitch tongue with the use of one needle and two loopers. This is the most basic stitch formed on an overlocker. The three-thread stitch is 5 mm (3/16 in) wide and can be used on its own if, for example, it is used for a seam that is not under stress, or to prevent unnecessary bulk on lingerie and underwear. For normal sewing it is usually used in conjunction with a sewing machine to finish an edge.

All decorative finishing, for example flatlocking and narrow hemming (pages 10-13), is always done with three threads.

FOUR-THREAD OVERLOCKING

This stitch is formed around the stitch tongue with the use of two needles and two loopers. It is also known as the mock safety stitch.

The four-thread stitch is 6-7 mm (approximately 1/4 in) wide and is used for seams. This stitch is particularly suitable for the seams of stretch fabrics. The overlocker can also be converted to a three-thread stitch by removing the left needle to form a narrow stitch, or by removing the right needle to form a wide stitch.

FIVE-THREAD OVERLOCKING

The five-thread overlocker has many possibilities as it operates with two needles and three loopers. On some models, the five-thread overlocker can also be used as a four-thread overlocker by changing the needles, or by inserting a special double needle to obtain a mock safety stitch finish suitable for sewing stretch fabrics. It also forms a two-thread chain stitch which functions as a conventional straight stitch and is mainly used for decorative purposes. Five-thread overlocking is suitable for woven fabrics.

OVERLOCKER ACCESSORIES

Consult your dealer or agent for more information about many different accessories and attachments available.

A VARIETY OF PRODUCTS USED IN THE PROJECTS

ROLLED HEM PLATE OR ATTACHMENT

This is a standard accessory supplied with all three-, four- or five-thread overlockers. It can form an integral part of the overlocker, or can be an optional plate or attachment which can be fitted onto the machine. This plate or attachment produces a narrow stitch, as the stitches are formed around a narrower stitch tongue, which is ideal for sewing narrow or rolled hems.

A narrow hem gives a decorative finish to viscose, polyester, cotton and viscose. The fabric is rolled while the stitches are being formed, but the tension locks at the edge of the fabric.

A rolled hem is very narrow and is used on net, organza and thin, silky fabrics. Used with gut, on wedding dresses for example, it gives a scalloped edge. When the stitches are formed, the fabric as well as the tension roll over and lock at the back.

ELASTIC GATHERER ATTACHMENT

This optional attachment can be fitted onto a three-, four- or five-thread overlocker and is used to gather elastic and sew it onto the fabric in one operation, or to sew on cord or ribbons using three-thread overlocking.

- Attach the elastic gatherer attachment onto your overlocker. To attach the elastic, thread the elastic through under the attachment, and depending on the width of the elastic you are using, use either the right or the left needle.
- To sew on cord or ribbon, thread the ribbon or the cord through the hole in the attachment and, depending on the width of the ribbon or cord, use either the left needle or the right needle, ensuring that the elastic is completely covered by the stitches.

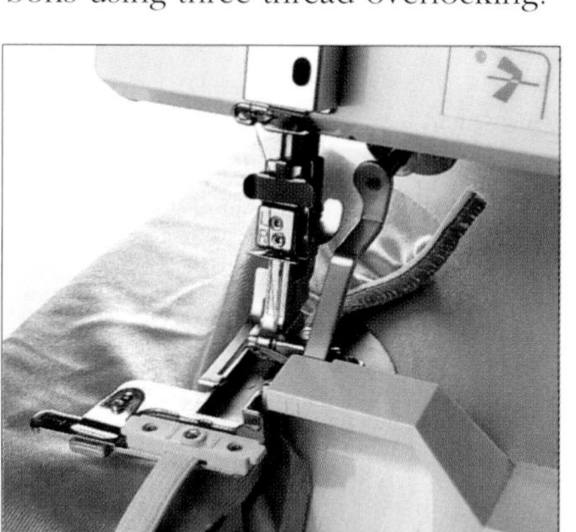

NEEDLE	THREAD	TENSION
Left/right needle	polyester cotton thread	balanced
Upper looper	polyester cotton thread or floss	balanced
Lower looper	polyester cotton thread or floss	balanced

Stitch length: 3-3½
Differential feed: 1.0
- The moving blade must be in the cutting position

BLIND HEM ATTACHMENT

This attachment can be fitted onto a three-, four- or five-thread overlocker. You can cut and overlock while hemming, using three-thread overlocking. Depending on the make and model of overlocker, use either the right or left needle. Test on a scrap of fabric before sewing; adjust the guide on the attachment so that the needle catches one or two fibres on the fold.

- Attach the blind hem attachment onto the overlocker. Fold the hem back the desired width to the wrong side, then fold it back towards the right side of the article, leaving a 1 cm (½ in) raw edge.
- Place the fabric under the blind hem attachment, with the folded edge on top against the guide and sew, using three-thread overlocking.

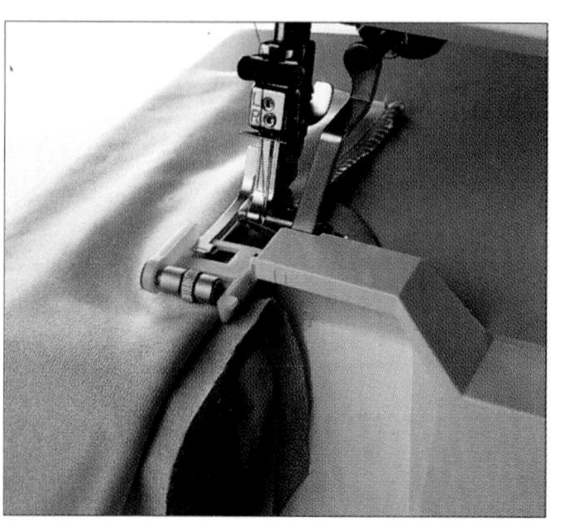

NEEDLE	THREAD	TENSION
Left/right needle	polyester cotton thread	2 - 3 (loosen)
Upper looper	polyester cotton thread or floss	balanced
Lower looper	polyester cotton thread or floss	balanced

Stitch length: 3 - 3½
Differential feed: 1.0
- The moving blade must be in the cutting position

QUARTER PIN MARKING

Quarter pin marking is a term used throughout the book, describing how to pin elastic or fabric in quarters:

Elastic: Fold the elastic in half on the seam, and mark the other half of the elastic with a pin. Open out the elastic, and fold the seam and side pin on top of each other; mark the two fold lines with pins. The elastic is now divided into quarters (Fig. 1).

Fabric: The two side seams divide the fabric in half. Place the two side seams on top of each other; on the fold lines, mark the centre front and cantre back fold with pins. The fabric is now divided into quarters.

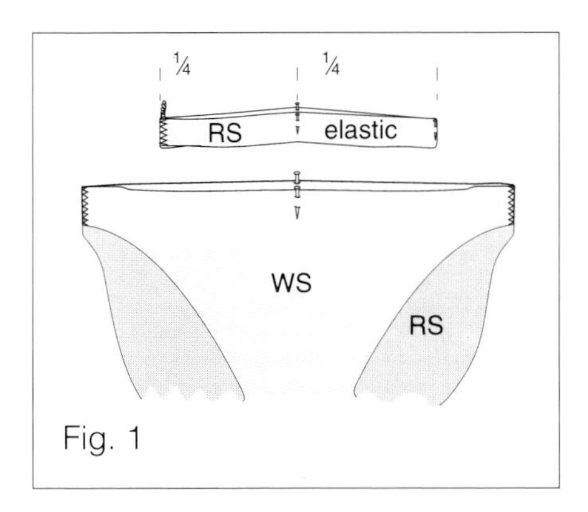

Fig. 1

SEWING IN A CIRCLE

Begin to sew in a circle by sewing diagonally from the raw edge to the stitching line. Continue sewing in a circle, keeping the fabric and elastic in a straight line. Return to the starting point and sew over the diagonal stitches and continue along the sewn edge for a further 2 cm (¾ in). Pull on the looper threads to secure stitching (Fig. 2). Cut thread and secure ends with stitch sealant (page 19).

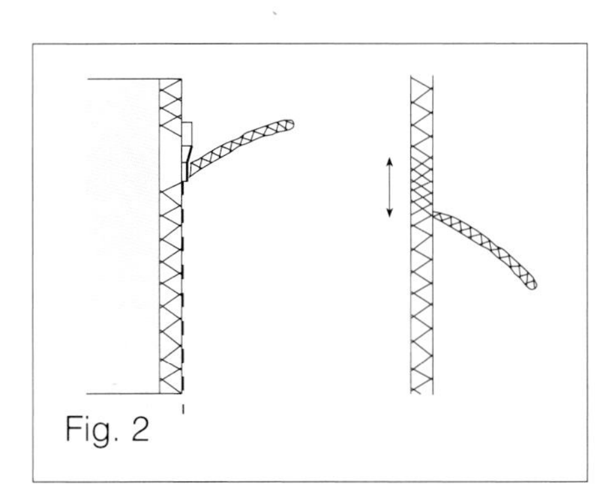
Fig. 2

SEWING ELASTIC TO FORM A CIRCLE

With RS together, sew from the bottom to the top, keeping the elastic next to the blade. Sew until the last stitch is off the elastic. Stop with the needle in the upright position. Pull on the needle thread to loosen it. Release the pressure foot, take the elastic out, and turn it over. Insert the elastic into the overlocker again, keeping it next to the blade as before. Lower the pressure foot, pull on the needle thread to tighten, and sew so that the first stitch is on the elastic. Continue sewing to the end of the elastic. Chain off. In this way, the top of the elastic will not have any end threads to secure (Fig. 3).

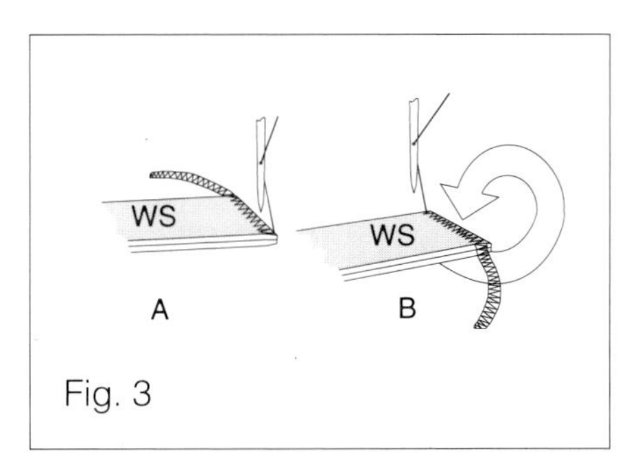

Fig. 3

SEWING CURVES

Inside curve: (Fig. 4)

Keep the fabric straight, in line with the edge of the plate. Push the fabric into the overlocker as you sew towards the pressure foot. Keep your eye on the blade, not on the needle.

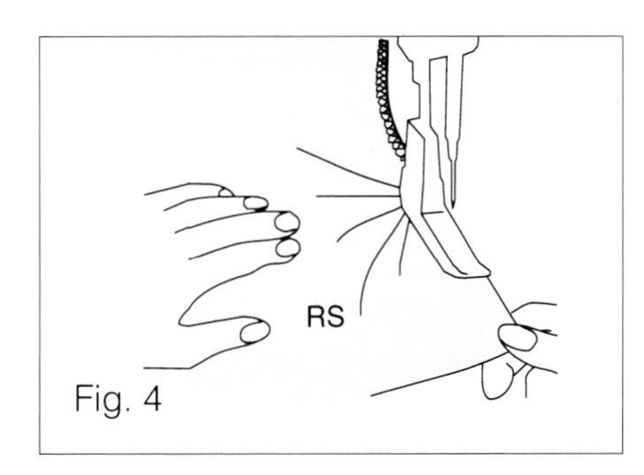

Fig. 4

Outside curve:

Keep the fabric as straight as possible, in line with the edge of the plate. Pull the fabric out from the presser foot as you sew. Keep your eye on the blade, not on the needle.

SEAMS

Seams are usually sewn together with four-thread overlocking; however, when sewing lingerie or underwear, a narrower seam is often used to prevent it scratching or causing discomfort.

When making lingerie from non-stretch or underwear fabric, use three-thread overlocking – the seams on lingerie do not take too much strain and therefore they do not need to be very wide. When sewing leisurewear from stretch fabrics, a four-thread finish is required to strengthen the seam and allow for extra stretch and wear.

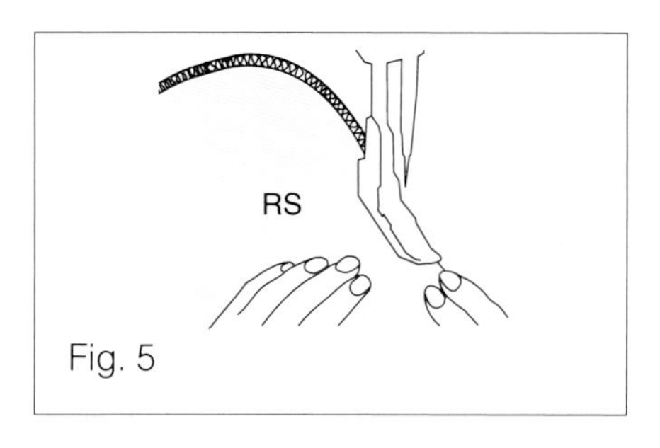

Fig. 5

TO FINISH OFF SEAMS

Finishing or chaining off using stitch sealant: (Fig. 6a)

End the stitching by leaving a chain of overlock stitches. Pull on the looper threads to secure the stitching. Cut the chain off as close to the seam or stitching as possible, and apply a drop of stitch sealant. Allow to dry for one minute.

Ending by hand: (Fig. 6b)

End the stitching by sewing a chain of overlock stitches. Undo the needle and knot with looper threads. Thread the threads through a large-eye needle and sew them back into the stitching for 3-5 cm (1¼-5 in).

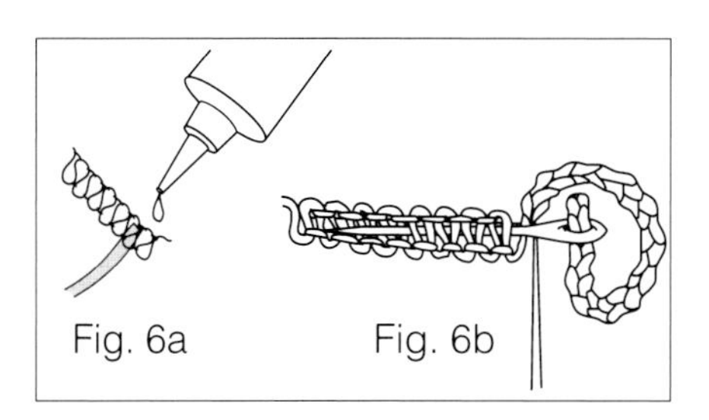
Fig. 6a Fig. 6b

DECORATIVE FINISHES USING THE OVERLOCKER

THREE-THREAD OVERLOCKING

NEEDLE	THREAD	TENSION
Right needle	polyester cotton thread	4 - 8 (balanced)
Upper looper	polyester cotton thread	1 - 5 (balanced)
	floss	0 - 2 (balanced)
	metallic thread	1 - 5 (balanced)
Lower looper	polyester cotton thread	1 - 5 (balanced)
	floss	0 - 2 (balanced)
	metallic thread	1 - 5 (balanced)

Take left needle out
Differential feed: Depends on the thickness of the fabric
• The moving blade must be in the cutting position

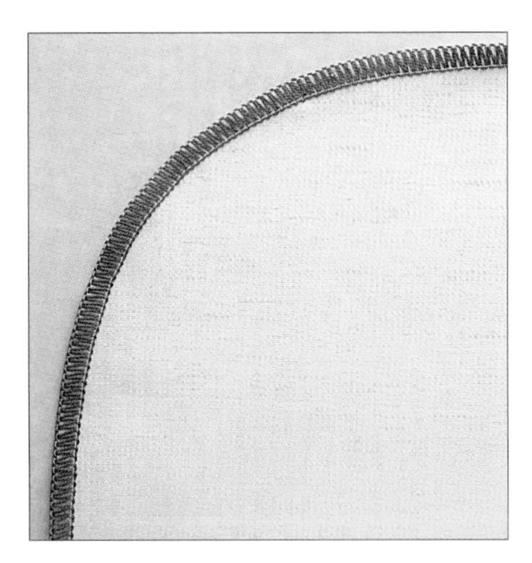

THREE-THREAD WIDE OVERLOCKING

NEEDLE	THREAD	TENSION
Left needle	polyester cotton thread	4 - 8 (balanced)
Upper looper	embroidery thread	0 - 1 (balanced)
	metallic thread	1 - 5 (balanced)
	floss	0 - 2 (balanced)
Lower looper	polyester cotton thread	4 - 8 (balanced)

Take right needle out.
Differential feed: Depends on the thickness of the fabric
• The moving blade must be in the cutting position

FLATLOCKING

Flatlocking is a variation on the basic overlock stitch. The flat stitches are made when two layers of fabric (or one layer of fabric and lace) are overlocked together using three threads and then pulled open, which causes the seam to lie flat. This decorative seam is reversible as either the ladders or the loops can be on the right side. As flatlocking eliminates bulk and seams on the wrong side, it is ideal for sewing lingerie.

• The width of flatlock depends on the width of the lace, the size of the fabric pieces to be joined, and the size of the article in relation to the decorative stitching. Depending on the width of flatlock required, use the left or right needle with both loopers.

• When sewing a flatlocked seam, the needle tension should be set lower while the tension on the lower looper is set higher.

• Flatlocking can be used to join lace onto the edge of a piece of fabric or to sew it on top of the fabric. When sewing flatlocking on fabric and lace, keep the lace at the bottom and the fabric on top.

• A flatlocked seam can be sewn onto the raw edge of the fabric, or the fabric can be folded double so that the flatlocking is in the centre.

• When joining different colours of fabric, the flatlocking is sewn on the raw edge with the moving blade in the cutting position.

• For a decorative flatlocked seam in the centre of the fabric, disengage the moving blade and while sewing keep the folded edge of the fabric in line with the edge of the plate.

• When sewing flatlocked seams, the stitching should face downwards or outwards when the seam is open.

• For a decorative flatlocked finish on the right side of the fabric, place the wrong sides of the fabric or lace together before sewing.

• For a decorative ladder stitch on the right side, place the right sides of the fabric or lace together.

NOTE: Sew slowly when using decorative thread to prevent it from snapping or hooking as this may damage the overlocker.

FLATLOCKING WITH FLOSS

Floss is a superstretch thread. made from bulked nylon. It is soft but strong and stretches with the fabric. Use good quality floss, available in two ply and four ply. Four ply is thicker and therefore better to use for decorative stitching on lingerie and underwear.

1. Place WS of fabric together.
2. Pull the seam open afterwards to lie flat.

NEEDLE	THREAD	TENSION
Right needle	polyester cotton thread	0 - 2 (loosen)
Upper looper	floss	0 - ½
	polyester cotton	5 - 7 (tighten)
Lower looper	floss	2 - 5 (tighten)

Take left needle out
Differential feed: Depends on the thickness of the fabric
- The moving blade must be in the cutting position

WIDE FLATLOCKING WITH FLOSS

See as described under **Flatlocking with Floss** (above).

NEEDLE	THREAD	TENSION
Left needle	polyester cotton thread	0 - 2 (loosen)
Upper looper	floss	0 - ½
Lower looper	polyester cotton thread	5 - 8 (tighten)
	floss	2 - 5 (tighten)

Take right needle out
Differential feed: Depends on the thickness of the fabric
- The moving blade must be in the cutting position

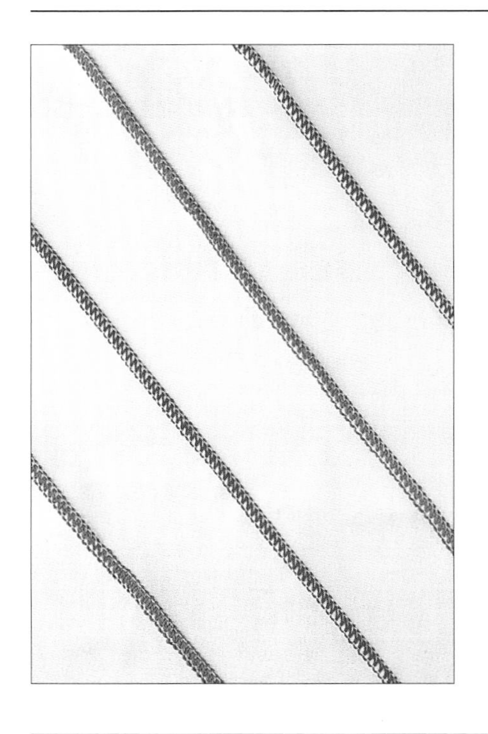

FLATLOCKING WITH EMBROIDERY THREAD

Use embroidery thread, also known as crochet or perle cotton (all no. 8/12), or ribbon thread. When sewing with embroidery thread, the upper looper tension must always be set as close to 0 as possible. If the tension has been set on 0 (as low as possible) but is still too tight, bypass a threading point on your overlocker, usually the first threading point.

1. Place WS of fabric together and sew.
2. Pull the seam open afterwards to lie flat.

NEEDLE	THREAD	TENSION
Right needle	polyester cotton thread	0 - 2 (loosen)
Upper looper	embroidery thread	0 (loosen)
Lower looper	polyester cotton thread	5 - 8 (tighten)
	or floss	2 - 5 (tighten)

Take left needle out
Differential feed: Depends on the thickness of the fabric
- The moving blade must be in the cutting position

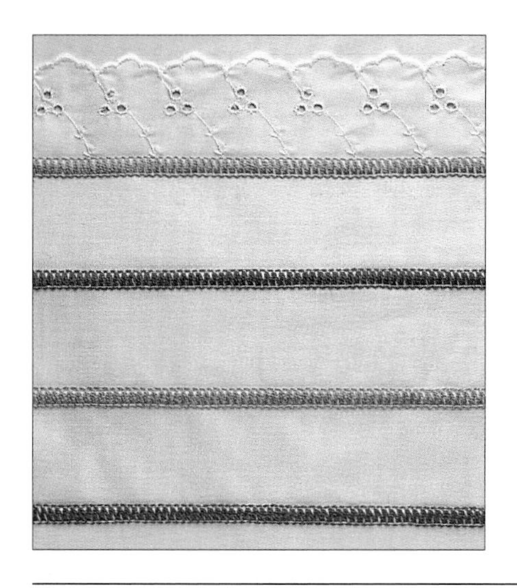

WIDE FLATLOCKING WITH EMBROIDERY THREAD

1. Place WS of fabric together and sew.
2. Pull the seam open afterwards to lie flat.

NEEDLE	THREAD	TENSION
Left needle	polyester cotton thread	0 - 2 (loosen)
Upper looper	embroidery thread	0 (loosen)
Lower looper	polyester cotton thread	5 - 8 (tighten)
	floss	2 - 5 (tighten)

Take right needle out
Differential feed: Depends on the thickness of the fabric
• The moving blade must be in the cutting position

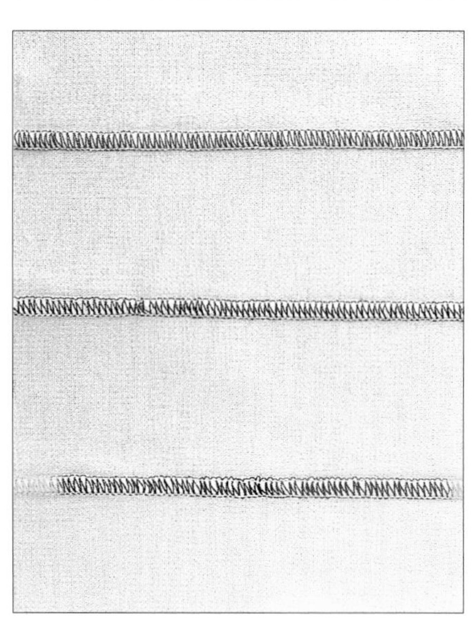

FLATLOCKING WITH METALLIC THREAD

Use good quality, strong metallic threads which are available in plain or variegated shades. These metallic threads can be used to create interesting effects when flatlocking lingerie and underwear.

1. Place WS of fabric together and sew.
2. Pull the seam open afterwards to lie flat.

NEEDLE	THREAD	TENSION
Right needle	polyester cotton thread	0 - 2 (loosen)
Upper looper	metallic thread	1 - 2 (loosen)
Lower looper	polyester cotton thread	5 - 8 (tighten)
	or floss	2 - 5 (tighten)

Differential feed: Depends on the thickness of the fabric
• The moving blade must be in the cutting position

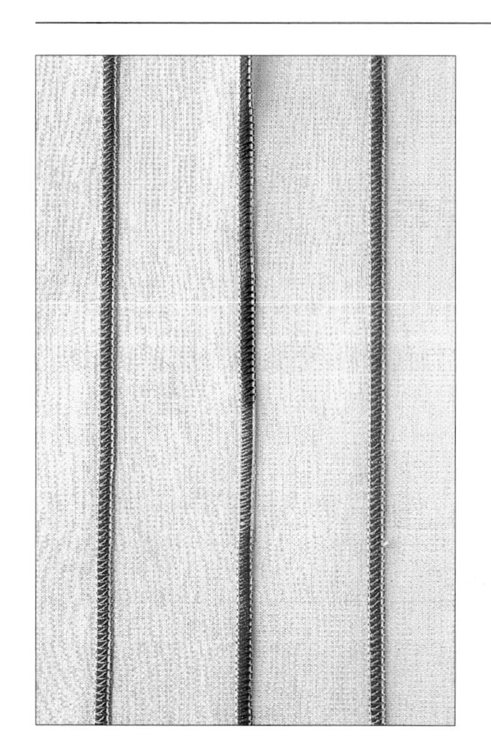

FLATLOCKING OVER RIBBON WITH METALLIC THREAD OR FLOSS

Use 3 mm-wide (about ⅛ in) satin ribbon when sewing with the right needle, and 5 mm-wide (about ¼ in) satin ribbon when sewing with the left needle.

Ensure that the ribbon is not wider than the flatlocking.

1. If the ribbon is sewn onto the edge with lace, place the lace at the bottom of the fabric fold, WS of the lace and fabric together. Place the ribbon on top, and sew. Keep the ribbon on the inside of the blade so that the fabric edges (not the ribbon) are cut.
2. Pull the seam open afterwards to lie flat.

NEEDLE	THREAD	TENSION
Left/right needle	polyester cotton thread	0 - 2 (loosen)
Upper looper	metallic thread	1 - 2 (loosen)
	or floss	0 - ½ (loosen)
Lower looper	polyester cotton thread	5 - 8 (tighten)
	or floss	2 - 5 (tighten)

Differential feed: Depends on the thickness of the fabric
• The moving blade must be in the cutting position

FLATLOCKED HEM WITH EMBROIDERY, METALLIC THREAD OR FLOSS

Flatlocking can also be used when sewing a hem. Use either the left or the right needle, ensuring that the hem is in proportion to the article's size. Disengage the moving blade before sewing.

1. Fold the fabric back to the WS to the desired hem width, then fold the fabric again so that the raw edge lies inside the fold. Sew on the RS of the fabric on the fold, sewing through all the layers, and catching the raw edge in the folded edge. Ensure that while sewing you keep the folded edge in line with the edge of the plate.

2. Pull the hem open afterwards to obtain a flat hem.

NEEDLE	THREAD	TENSION
Left/right needle	polyester cotton thread	0 - 2 (loosen)
Upper looper	floss	0 - ½ (loosen)
	metallic thread	1 - 2 (loosen)
	embroidery thread	0 (loosen)
Lower looper	polyester cotton thread	5 - 8 (tighten)
	floss	2 - 5 (tighten)

Differential feed: Depends on the thickness of the fabric

• The moving blade must be disengaged

NARROW HEM WITH METALLIC THREAD

1. To sew a narrow hem, change to the B-plate attachment, rolled hem plate attachment, or lever.

2. Always make sure that you sew on a single layer of fabric.

3. Pull the fabric gently at the back while sewing for even stitching.

NOTE: The looper stitches must lock at the edge of the fabric.

NEEDLE	THREAD	TENSION
Right needle	polyester cotton thread	4 - 8 (balanced)
Upper looper	metallic thread	1 - 3
Lower looper	polyester cotton thread	1 - 5 (balanced)
	metallic thread	5 (balanced)
	floss	0 - 2 (balanced)

Take left needle out

Differential feed: Depends on the thickness of the fabric

• The moving blade must be in the cutting position

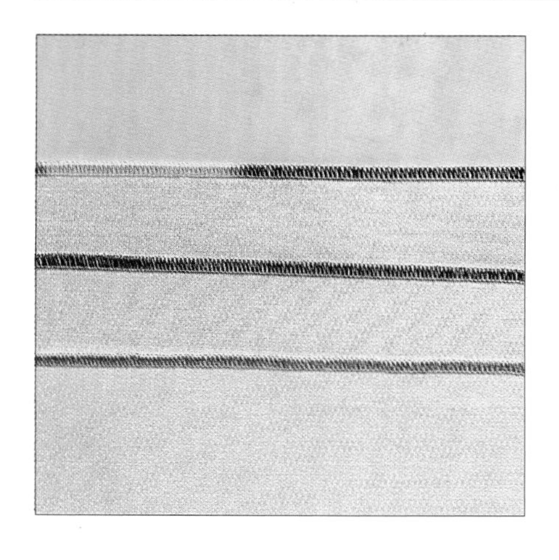

NARROW HEM WITH FLOSS

NEEDLE	THREAD	TENSION
Right needle	polyester cotton thread	4 - 8 (balanced)
Upper looper:	floss	0 - 2 (balanced)
Lower looper:	polyester cotton thread	1 - 5 (balanced)
	floss	0 - 2 (balanced)

Take left needle out

Differential feed: Depends on the thickness of the fabric

• The moving blade must be in the cutting position

PATTERNS

All the patterns used have a seam allowance included:

- a 6 mm (¼ in) seam allowance is included for sewing seams together on stretch fabrics
- a 1 cm (½ in) seam allowance is included for all non-stretch fabrics.

Patterns sizes are available in small, medium or large:

Small (10-12)
Medium (12-14)
Large (14-16)

TAKING MEASUREMENTS TO DETERMINE SIZE (Fig. 7a and 7b)

1. *High bust:* Place tape measure under arms and measure across the widest part of the back and above full bustline.

2. *Full bust:* Take measurement across the widest part of the back, under the arms and across full bust. Keep tape measure flat and straight. Exhale before measuring.

3. *Under bust:* Place the tape measure under the bust and measure. Ensure that the tape measure is flat and straight across the back and under the bust. Exhale before taking this measurement.

NOTE: It is essential to take accurate measurements to determine your size. Remove all bulky outer clothing, and take measurements while wearing only your underwear.

4. *Waist:* Measure your waist by tying a piece of string or thread around your waist and allowing it to roll to the natural waistline. Exhale before measuring.

5. *Top length:* Measure from collarbone, over bust to the waist, adding 15-20 cm (6-8 in) length.

6. *Hips:* Take your measurement around the fullest part of the buttocks, noting the distance from the waist. Keeping your fingers on the tape measure, position it so that you are able to climb in and out of the tape measure comfortably.

7. *Crotch depth:* Sit upright on a flat surface. Measure from the waist over the hip to the flat surface.

8. *Inner leg:* Measure from the crotch to the ankle.

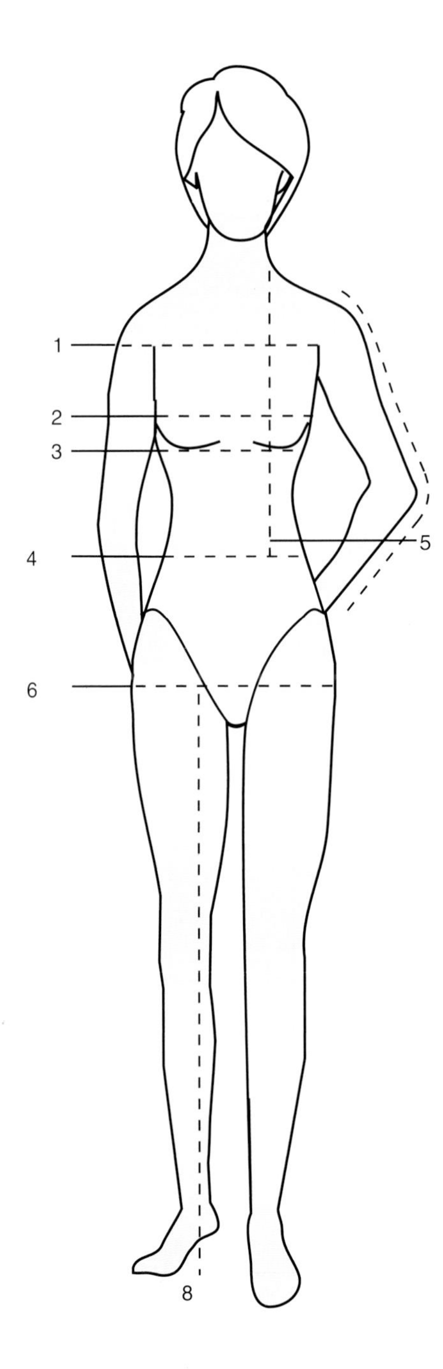

Fig. 7a

NOTE: If there is a difference of 5 cm (2 in) or more between the full bust and the high bust measurement (see points 1 and 2 on this page), select your pattern size according to the high bust measurement.

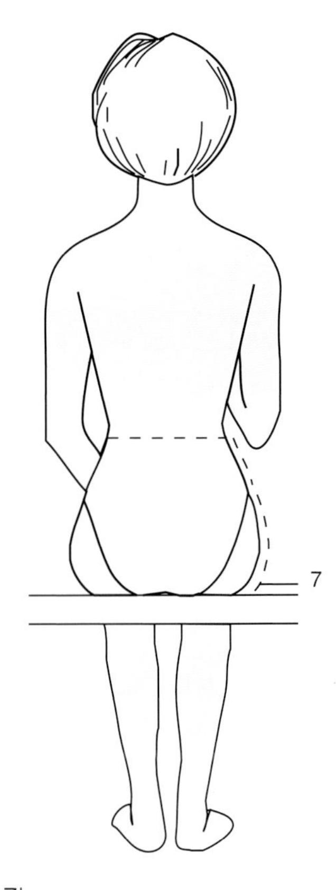

Fig. 7b

SYMBOLS USED ON PATTERNS

- Straight grain - ⟷
- Place on fold -
- Cut on bias -
- Casing for elastic - ------------
- Pattern size:

Small - — — — —

Medium - ————

Large - —·—·—·—·—

NOTE: Ensure that when scaling up a graph pattern that you take accurate measurements and make the correct calculations. This is extremely important, otherwise your garment will not fit properly.

PREPARING AND CUTTING OUT THE PATTERN

The patterns used in this book have been drawn onto graph paper and are half size (or indicated otherwise). Enlarge and draw onto dressmakers' tracing paper, or draw onto graph paper to full size. Remember that seam allowances have been included (these are indicated on each pattern).

NOTE: For bras, bra tops, cropped tops, camisoles and teddies, the size is determined by the bust measurement.
For panties, knickers and petticoats, the size is determined by the hip measurement.

HOW TO SCALE UP A GRAPH PATTERN (Fig. 8)

First check the scale that the pattern has been drawn to. The scale in this book is 1 square = 1 cm (½ in). This means that each square in the printed pattern in this book represents 1 cm (½ in) of squared paper.

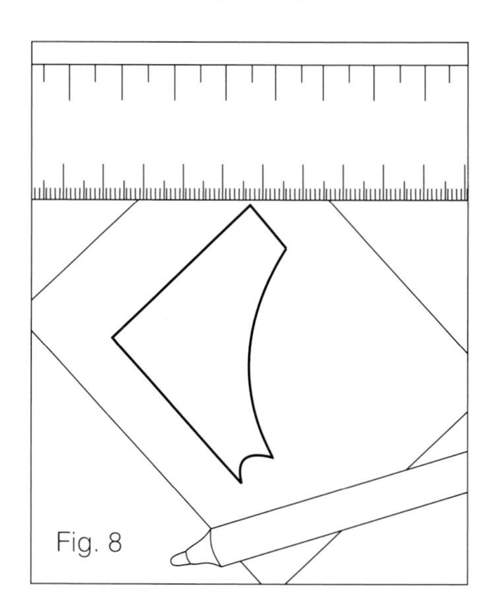
Fig. 8

1. Draw a rectangle around the graph pattern which you want to enlarge so that the pattern pieces fit into the space without extra rows at the edges. Number the lines starting from 0 (Fig. 9).

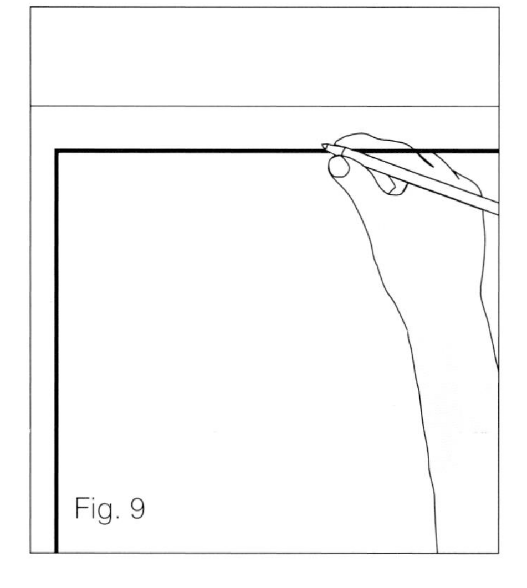
Fig. 9

2. Check the scale of the graph and mark off the same number of squares on the graph paper. In this book, 1 square = 1 cm (½ in) sq. Number lines to correspond with the numbers on the graph pattern.

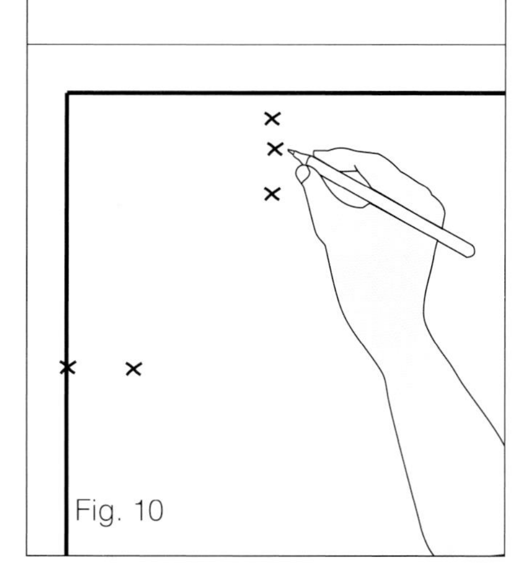
Fig. 10

3. Decide on a starting point, for example, the neckline. Using the numbers as a guide, locate its position in the rectangle both horizontally and vertically and mark the position with an X or a dot. Continue to mark all points which cross the lines, and also where lines change direction, with an X or a dot (Fig. 10).

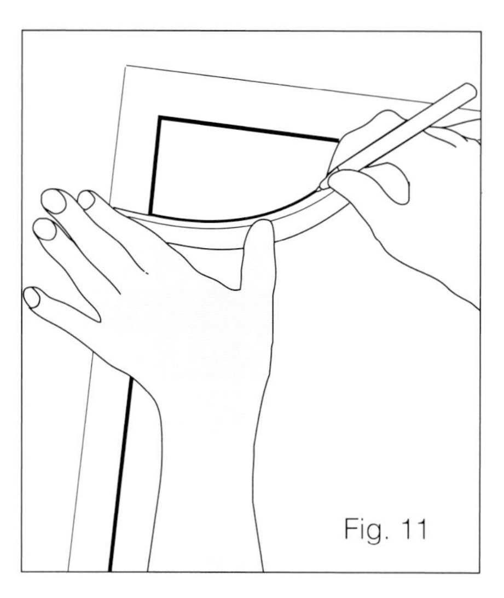
Fig. 11

4. Draw in the lines with a ruler. Transfer all pattern markings and cut out the pattern (Fig. 11).

ESTIMATING THE AMOUNT OF FABRIC REQUIRED

After drawing the patterns onto dressmaker's tracing paper or graph paper, you must determine how much fabric is needed. Place the pattern pieces on a table or sheet of white paper the same width as the fabric. Remember to take into account the pattern pieces which must be placed on a fold or on the bias.

FABRICS

There are two main groups of fabrics used in this book: stretch and non-stretch. Choose the fabric according to the type of garment you are going to make.

Stretch fabrics (Pics. 14, 15 and 16)
Single or double (interlock) knit, nylon or cotton Lycra, and stretch lace are examples of stretch fabric suitable for panties, briefs, bras, and leisurewear. There is also a large range of T-shirt fabrics available.

NOTE: Remember to pre-wash all your woven and knitted fabrics and elastics before cutting out to allow shrinkage. Wash and dry the fabric and elastic in the same way as you would treat the completed garment.

Non-stretch fabrics

Satin, silk, crêpe de Chine, rayon, crinkle polyester, organza, faille, polyester Jacquard, wrap knit and angeline are examples of non-stretch fabrics; suitable for camisoles, French knickers, tedddies, petticoats and dressing gowns.

NOTE: Lycra is crease resistant and doesn't lose its shape. It shrinks approximately 3 cm per metre (1¼ in per yard), so pre-wash first before sewing

LACE

Lace can be used very effectively to decorate lingerie and underwear, and should be chosen with care. Cotton, nylon and stretch lace are available. The type and the width of the lace you choose depends on the type of fabric, the size of the garment and the placement of the lace on the garment (where it will not scratch or chafe). The raised motif is the right side. There are various types of lace available:

EDGING OR FLOUNCE LACE (Pic. 1)

Edging or flounce lace has one scalloped edge and one straight edge. Edging lace is narrower than flounce lace and is sometimes pre-gathered. It is used as a trimming on garments or as a hem finishing. Flounce lace is suitable for frills and hem finishings. Broderie anglaise is a cotton edging lace and is textured with open embroidery.

GALLOON LACE (Pic. 2)

This is a lace with a scallop on both sides. Sometimes galloon lace can be cut and used as appliqué lace. It is also suitable for borders, hem finishes or cut-out work.

NOTE: Silk is a natural fibre, it is crease resistant and available in varying qualities. Rayon is a synthetic silk but creases more easily than real silk..

INSERTION LACE (Pic. 3)

Insertion lace has two similar edges, either straight or scalloped. Both sides of the lace are sewn onto the body of the garment, and if desired, the fabric can be cut away at the back. It is also used for band trimmings or straps, and is available in 6 mm-1.5 cm (¼-½ in) widths.

BEADING OR EYELET LACE (Pic. 4)

This is edging or insertion lace with openings for threading decorative ribbon or band trimmings through. It can also be used for straps.

APPLIQUÉ LACE (Pic. 4)

Appliqué lace consists of an individual motif, and is used as a trimming. The motifs can be single or double, and can be bought in right- and left-hand pairs. Appliqué lace is also used for cut-out work.

ALL-OVER OR STRETCH LACE (Pic. 5)

This lace has two straight edges and motifs that are repeated regularly throughout the entire fabric. It is available in widths of 90, 115 or 150 cm (36, 45 or 60 in). Stretch lace is usually used for an entire garment. The motifs can also be cut out individually and used as appliqué lace.

NOTE: If possible do not tumble dry lingerie and underwear where elastic has been used as the heat of the tumble dryer will damage and weaken it.

ELASTIC

Elastic is available in a wide variety of widths and colours, and is either knitted or woven:

- Knitted elastic consists of a rubber core covered in a nylon yarn, and provides strength and stretch. It is mainly used when sewing on T-shirt fabric (Pic. 6)
- Woven elastic (Pic. 7) is more tightly woven. More yarn is used in the manufacturing process. Lycra is knitted around a nylon yarn, and it is therefore stronger than knitted elastic and lasts longer (Pic. 6).

The elastic you choose depends on the estimated life-span of the garment you are making. It can have two straight edges, one side can be decorated or scalloped, or both edges can be decorated or scalloped.

WAIST ELASTIC (Pic. 8)

Waist elastic width varies from 1.5-5 cm (½-2 in), is woven and is used on ladies' underwear and lingerie.

PETTICOAT ELASTIC (Pic. 9)

Petticoat elastic is knitted and is 1.5 cm (½ in) wide. It is used for the waist of petticoats.

WAIST BRIEF ELASTIC (Pic. 10)

Waist brief elastic width varies from 2-4 cm (¾-1½ in), is woven and is used on boys' and men's briefs

WAIST BRIEF ELASTIC, ENCASED (Pic. 10)

This elastic is used when making boys' and men's briefs, is 2 cm (¾ in) wide and encased in the fabric. It is available only in white and black.

LEG, ARM AND NECKLINE ELASTIC (Pic. 11)

These elastic widths vary from 6 mm-1 cm (¼-½ in). It is used on ladies' panties and tops, and on girls' panties for waist and leg elastic. It can be woven or knitted.

BRIEF LEG ELASTIC (Pic. 10)

This elastic is used on boy's and men's briefs, is 1 cm (½ in) wide and is encased in the fabric. It is available only in white and black.

PLUSH, LIP OR FOLDOVER ELASTIC (Pic. 12)

This is a woven elastic with a marked fold line in the centre. The width is usually 1-1.5 cm (½ in). Foldover elastic is available in cotton, with a natural look, and in trilobal, which is shiny. It is used when making ladies' sports and cropped tops, bras and panties.

STRETCH LACE ELASTIC (Pic. 13)

The widths of this elastic vary from 6 mm-15 cm (¼-6 in). It can be used

1. EDGING AND FLOUNCE LACE
2. GALLOON LACE
3. INSERTION LACE
4. APPLIQUÉ AND BEADING LACE
5. STRETCH LACE
6. KNITTED ELASTIC
7. WOVEN ELASTIC
8. WAIST ELASTIC
9. PETTICOAT ELASTIC
10. BRIEF ELASTIC
11. LEG, ARM AND NECKLINE ELASTIC
12. PLUSH ELASTIC

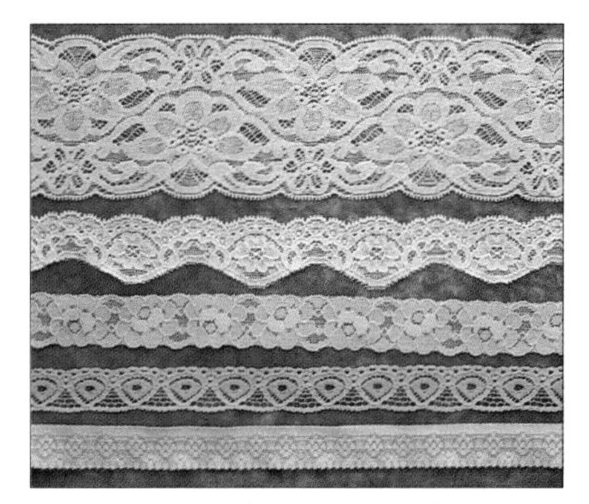

13. STRETCH LACE ELASTIC

14. SINGLE KNIT T-SHIRT FABRIC

15. COTTON AND NYLON LYCRA

16. DOUBLE KNIT T-SHIRT FABRIC

as leg or waist elastic, or decoratively on the right side of lingerie or underwear. Stretch lace elastic sometimes has a gummed back (for example, on stay-up stockings) to ensure that the elastic does not roll over.

DECORATIONS

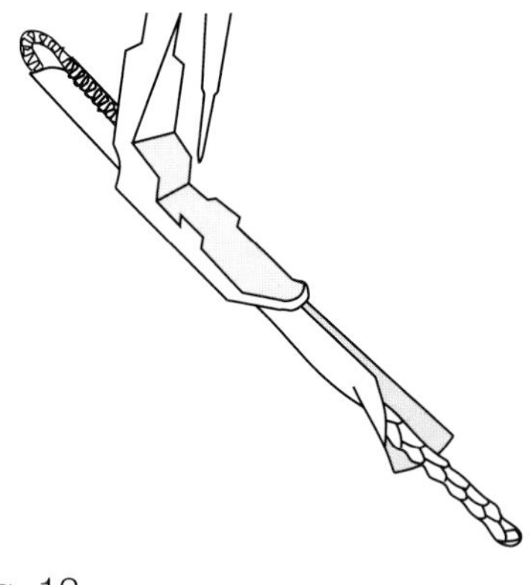

Fig. 12

STRAPS

Spaghetti straps:

These straps are ideal for using on lingerie, underwear, swimwear and evening wear.

Cut strips from fabric 4-5 cm-wide (1½-2 in) to the required length. Sew a chain of stitches on your overlocker, 10-15 cm (4-6 in) long. Insert the chain into the strap, using three-thread overlocking and stitch length 2-2½. Keep the chain as close to the folded edge as possible, and hold the chain with one hand. Remove the strap from the overlocker when you are finished sewing. Gently pull on the chain and the strap will then turn itself right side out (Fig. 13).

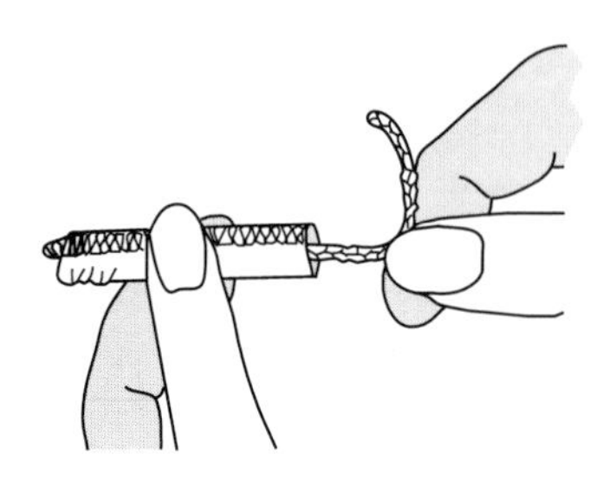

Fig. 13

Elastic:

Use 5-6 mm-wide (¼ in) elastic. Only use three threads, and use either the left or right needles, depending on the width of the elastic. Feed elastic through, over and underneath the pressure foot. Some makes of overlockers have a special attachment for sewing over elastic or cord. Thread loopers with floss or embroidery thread. Use stitch length 1-2, depending on the type of decorative thread used. Sew over elastic, holding elastic in front and at the back, and be careful not to sew on, but rather over the elastic.

Plaited ribbon: (Fig. 14)

Sew over ribbon, thread or cord using metallic thread or floss. Thread ribbon, thread or cord over and under the pressure foot. Some makes of overlockers have a special foot or attachment for sewing over cord or elastic. Sew over cord, holding it in front and at the back, and be careful not to sew on, but over the cord. Use three strings and plait – using three different colours is effective.

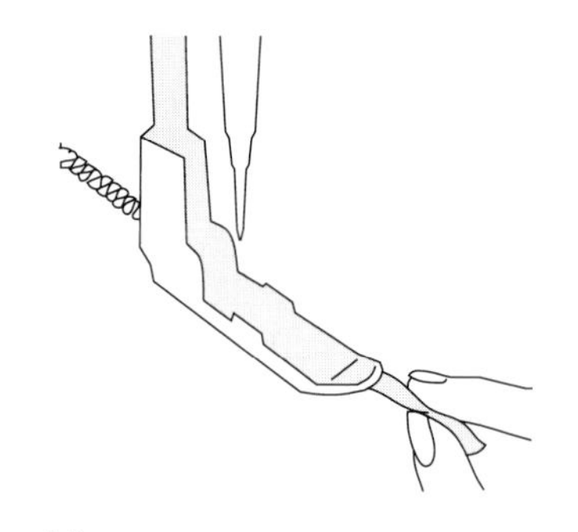

Fig. 14

BOWS

To make small, decorative bows to finish off panties, bras, camisoles and cropped tops, use 3-5 cm-wide (1¼-2 in) ribbon. Tie the ribbon into a knot. Pin it onto the garment, tie a bow and sew on by hand.

ROSES

Ribbon:

1. Cut a strip of ribbon (about 1 m [1 yd]).

2. Hold ribbon in one hand, WS facing towards you.

3. Cut a V in the end of the ribbon on right-hand side (A).

4. Fold ribbon on left-hand side (B) upwards to form a corner. Fold the ribbon behind and through to the bottom (Fig. 15).

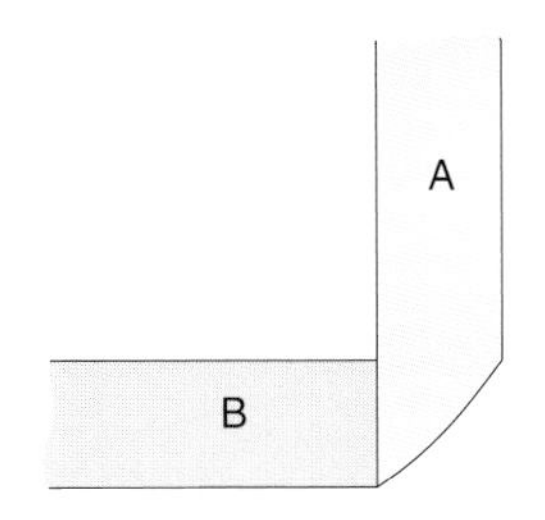

Fig. 15

5. Now take (A) and fold towards back, from right to left.

6. Take (B) and fold towards back, from the bottom to the top.

7. Take (A) and fold towards back, from left to right.

8. Take (B) and fold towards back, from top to bottom.

9. Repeat steps 5 - 8 ten to fifteen times.

10. Hold the last fold at the back with thumb and forefinger, and let go of the other.

11. Pull on (A) with V facing in until a rose is formed.

12. Secure at the back by hand.

PRODUCTS USED FOR PROJECTS

ROTARY CUTTER AND BOARD

Rotary cutters are available in two sizes, and are ideal for cutting fine, slippery and delicate fabrics. They can be used by those who are right- or left-handed. As the fabric does not lift from the surface while cutting, a rotary cutter ensures accurate, clean edges. When using a rotary cutter, always cut on a special rotary board, which is also available in different sizes and thicknesses. The board is made from a polypropylene and will therefore protect both the cutting surface and the blade.

SCISSORS

Always use a good quality pair of sewing scissors, with sharp blades for precision cutting. The size of the pair of scissors you choose depends on the project you are undertaking.

PINS

Use long, sharp, glass-headed pins which can be clearly seen. Old and rusted pins will damage or snag delicate fabrics and leave marks, so always use stainless steel pins, which do not rust.

MARKING TOOLS

Fabric marker pens are used to transfer markings onto your fabric. These are water-soluble and are available from haberdashers. The markings of the auto-fade pen will disappear within 48 hours, depending on the fabric.

The other markings, however, have to be washed out with cold water. Take care not to use the latter pens on delicate fabrics, as washing will leave water marks. All markings must be removed before pressing.

Alternatively, marking pencils and tailor's chalk are available in a variety of shapes, sizes and colours. They are sharply pointed for marking easily and directly onto the fabric. The chalk can be rubbed off afterwards.

MEASURING TOOLS

TAPE MEASURE

A tape measures is usually 150 cm (60 in) long and made from non-stretch fibre glass. It should be numbered on both sides.

To measure awkward angles and curves, lie the tape measure on its side (upright) so that you are able to bend it according to the curve to be measured.

> NOTE: Left-over bits of soap make a good substitute for tailor's chalk.

HANDY GAUGE

This metal or plastic ruler is 15 cm (6 in) long with a sliding marker for making small, quick measurements on seams, hems, darts or pleats.

QUILTERS' RULER

The quilters' ruler measures 60 cm (24 in) in length and 10 cm (4 in) in width, with these markings shown lengthwise and widthwise. The ruler also indicates various angles such as 30°, 45° and 90°. The quilters' ruler is a useful accessory to have when designing your own patterns.

GRAPH PAPER

This is paper which has two square sizes ruled on the same sheet. The smaller squares are 1 cm (½ in) square and the larger (usually darker) squares are each 5 cm (2 in) square. This paper varies in size and is used to design and draw patterns to full size.

DRESSMAKERS' TRACING PAPER

There are several types of strong tracing paper used for transferring patterns onto, for example, Vi-Trace or Easy-Trace. These are sold by the metre (yard) at haberdashers or needlework shops, and do not tear or crease easily.

STITCH OR SEAM SEALANT

This is a transparent liquid which prevents fraying and unravelling by sealing the ends of threads. It leaves no marks and remains soft when dry, and is therefore ideal to use when making clothing such as lingerie. It is also used to secure threads on buttonholes, and to control runs in stockings and tights.

FABRIC GLUE

Fabric glue is a water-based product Use fabric glue to temporarily glue on a motif or decoration before sewing it on by hand.

> NOTE: Comfort and fit are the most important factors to remember when making a braS, bra tops or cropped tops. Take accurate measurements before beginning a project.

LINGERIE

Wearing beautiful lingerie always makes us feel special; however, we also need everyday underwear which may not be as glamorous, but which is also attractive and comfortable. Whatever your preferences or needs, you'll find plenty of ideas here to suit them! Choose from French and cami-knickers, or camisoles and teddies for something more special and stylish, or make pretty panties and bras in styles and fabrics of your choice.

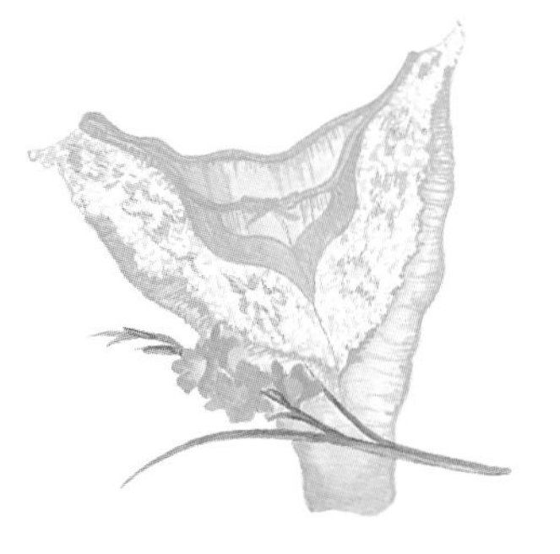

LADIES' PANTIES

This section shows you how to design panties to suit your style and figure. The instructions below are for basic full, high-cut and bikini panties.

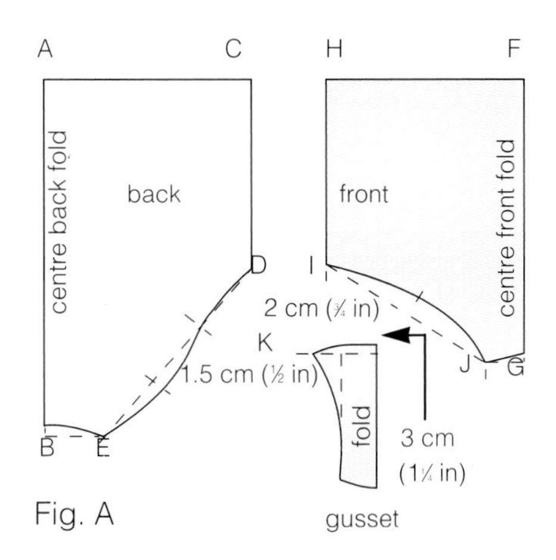

Fig. A

DESIGNING AND MEASURING FULL PANTIES (Fig. A)

REQUIREMENTS
Tape measure
Dressmakers' tracing paper or graph paper
Pencil and ruler

TO DESIGN A PATTERN FOR FULL PANTIES

BACK

1. A – B: Measure the crotch depth and add on 5 cm (2 in).

2. A – C: Take one quarter of the hip measurement. Minus 4 cm (1½ in) from this measurement.

3. C – D: The average depth of the side for full panties is 18 cm (7 in).

4. B – E: Mark 6 cm (2¼ in) for the crotch.

5. Rule from D - E, divide into 3 equal parts, and draw in curve, as shown.

FRONT

6. F – G: Measure the crotch depth.

7. F – H: Take one quarter of the hip meansurement. Minus 4 cm (1½ in) from this measurement.

8. H – I: The average depth of the side for full panties is 18 cm (7 in).

9. G – J: Mark 3 cm (1¼ in) for the crotch.

10. Rule from I - J, divide line in half, and draw in curve, as shown.

GUSSET

11. Draw a rectangle 12 cm (4¾ in) x 3 cm (1¼ in).

12. At back extend 3 cm (1¼ in) and mark K, as shown.

13. Curve outwards 1 cm (½ in) at back and front, as shown.

DESIGNING AND MEASURING HIGH-CUT PANTIES (Fig. B)

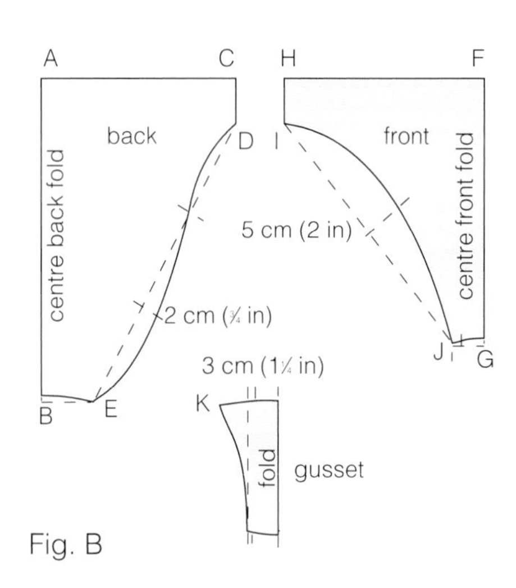

Fig. B

TO DESIGN A PATTERN FOR HIGH-CUT PANTIES

REQUIREMENTS
Tape measure
Dressmakers' tracing paper or graph paper
Pencil and ruler

BACK

1. A – B: Measure the crotch depth.

2. A – C: Take one quarter of the hip measurement. Minus 4 cm (1½ in) from this measurement.

3. C – D: The average depth of the side for high-cut panties is 4 cm (1½ in).

4. B – E: Mark 6 cm (2¼ in) for the crotch.

5. Rule from D - E, divide into 3 equal parts,.and draw in curve, as shown.

FRONT

6. F – G: Measure the crotch depth and minus 5 cm (2 in).

7. F – H: Take one quarter of the hip measurement. Minus 4 cm (1½ in) from this measurement.

8. H – I: The average depth of the side for high-cut panties is 4 cm (1½ in)

9. G – J: Mark 3 cm (1¼ in) for the crotch.

10. Rule from I - J, divide line in half, and draw in curve, as shown.

GUSSET

11. Draw a rectangle 12 cm (4¾ in) x 3 cm (1¼ in).

12. At back extend 3 cm (1¼ in) and mark K, as shown.

13. Curve 1 cm (½ in) outwards at back and front, as shown.

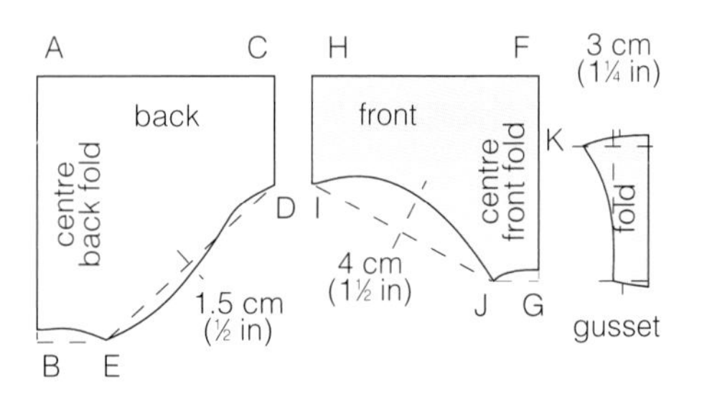

Fig. C

DESIGNING AND MEASURING BIKINI PANTIES (Fig. C)

REQUIREMENTS
Tape measure
Dressmakers' tracing paper or graph paper
Pencil and ruler

TO DESIGN A PATTERN FOR BIKINI PANTIES

BACK
1. A – B: Measure the crotch depth and minus 5 cm (2 in).

2. A – C: Take one quarter of the hip measurement. Minus 4 cm (1½ in) from this measurement.

3. C – D: The average depth of the side for bikini panties is 10 cm (4 in).

4. B – E: Mark 6 cm (2¼ in) for the crotch.

5. Rule from E - D; divide line in half, and draw in curve, as shown.

FRONT
6. F – G: Measure the crotch depth and minus 5 cm (2 in).

7. F – H: Take one quarter of the hip measurement and minus 4 cm (1½ in).

8. H – I: The average depth of the side for bikini panties is 10 cm (4 in).

9. G – J: Mark 3 cm (1¼ in) for the crotch.

10. Rule from I to J, divide the line in half, and draw in curve, as shown.

GUSSET
11. Draw a rectangle measuring 12 cm (4¾ in) by 3 cm (1¼ in).

12. At back extend 3 cm (1¼ in) and mark K, as shown.

13. Curve outwards 1 cm (½ in) at back and front, as shown.

FULL PANTIES

Full panties are often preferred by those who need extra support over the stomach and hips, or by those who want to avoid unattractive ridges showing under fitted clothes.

REQUIREMENTS
70 cm (¾ yd) single or double knit T-shirt fabric, cotton or nylon Lycra, non-stretch fabric or stretch lace
1-1.25 m x 1 cm-wide (1-1¼ yd x ½ in) leg or plush elastic for legs
70-80 cm x 2 cm-wide (¾ yd x ¾ in) waist elastic or
1.5-3 cm-wide (½-1¼ in) stretch lace elastic (leg elastic can also be used as waist elastic) for waist
Matching polyester cotton thread
Floss
Pre-made bows or roses for decoration (see page 18)
Stitch sealant (see page 19)

SEAM ALLOWANCE
6 mm (¼ in) on all seams

STITCHES
Straight stitch, length 3-4
Zig-zag stitch, width 1 and length 2 or overcasting stitch, width 4 and length 2½
Three-thread overlocking

PATTERNS
Patterns 1, 2 and 3

METHOD
1. Enlarge pattern pieces on pages 74 and 75 onto graph paper and cut out, or make your own pattern (see **Designing and Measuring Full Panties**, p. 22).

2. Pin pattern pieces onto fabric. Cut out 1 x back (on fold), 1 x front (on fold) and 2 x gusset (gusset piece and lining).

3. Pin RS of back panel to RS of gusset, and WS of front panel to RS of gusset lining, raw edges together (Fig. 1). Sew together using three-thread overlocking, stitch length 2-2½.

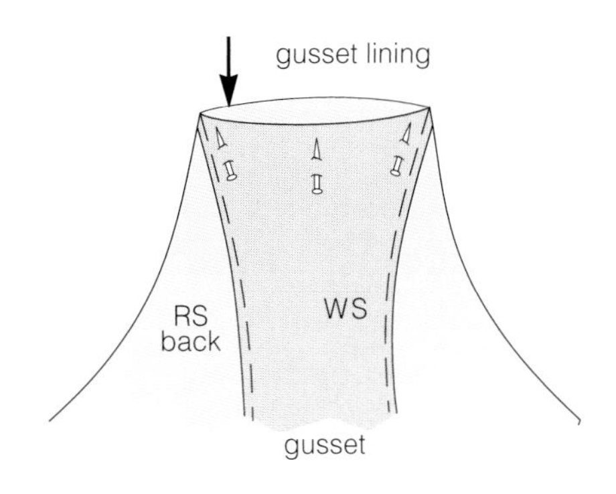

Fig. 1

4. With RS of back panel and gusset facing up, pin RS of front panel onto RS of gusset, raw edges together (Fig. 2). Sandwich gusset lining

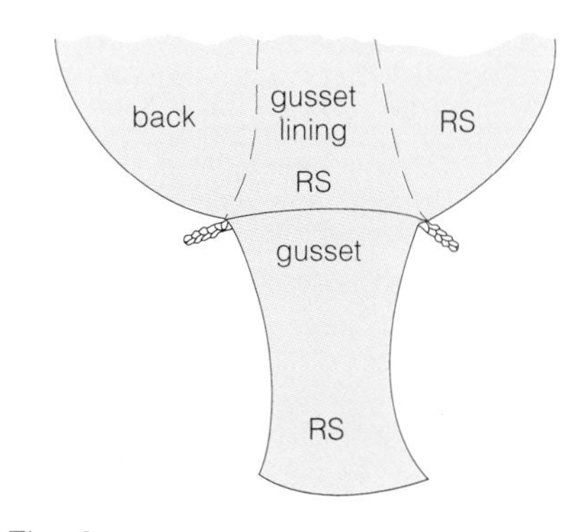

Fig. 2

around back and front panel; pin RS of gusset lining to WS of front panel, raw edges together (Fig. 3). Sew together using three-thread overlocking and stitch length 2-2½.

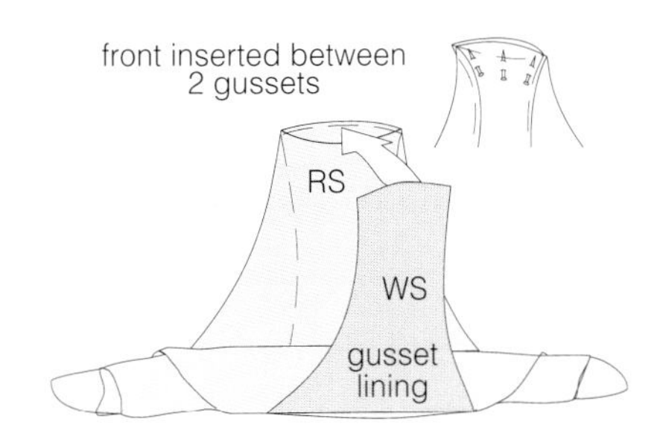

Fig. 3

5. Turn panties through gusset pieces so that both gusset seams are enclosed (Fig. 4).

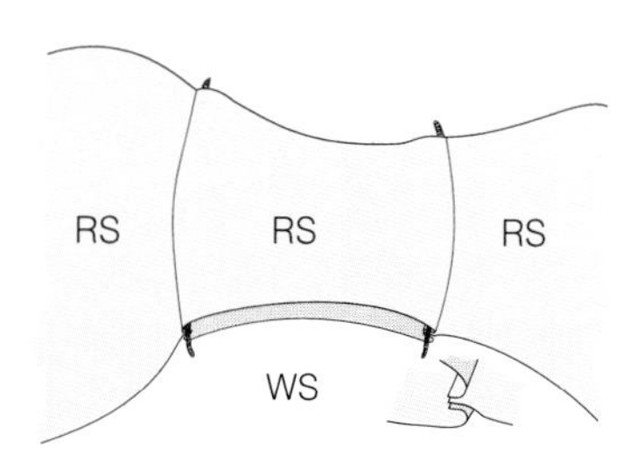

Fig. 4

6. Lay panties on a flat surface and measure leg opening (Fig. 5). Cut the elastic to three-quarters of this measurement.

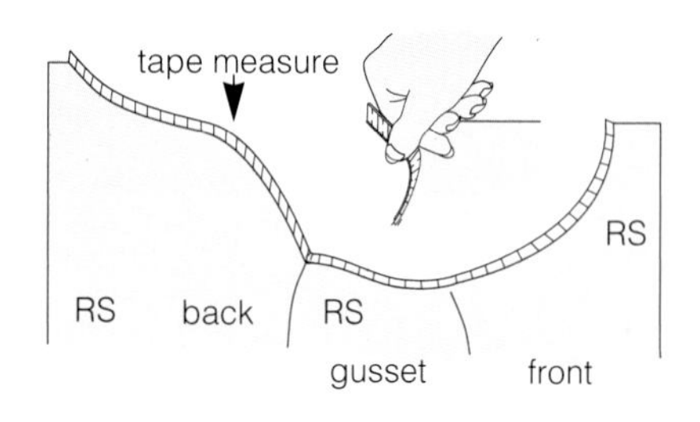

Fig. 5

7. If using leg elastic, with RS together, place elastic on top of fabric. Insert fabric and elastic into overlocker and secure the elastic by sewing a few stitches using three-thread overlocking and stitch length 3-3½. **Quarter pin mark** fabric and elastic (Fig. 6).

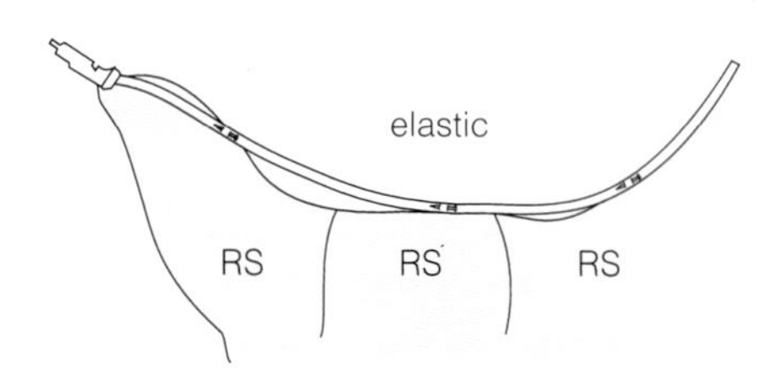

Fig. 6

8. Pin the elastic to fabric, matching up the pins.

9. Continue sewing, attaching elastic to fabric. Hold the fabric and elastic in front and at the back, and keep the elastic next to the blade, cutting 1 mm (1⁄16 in) off the fabric (Fig. 7).

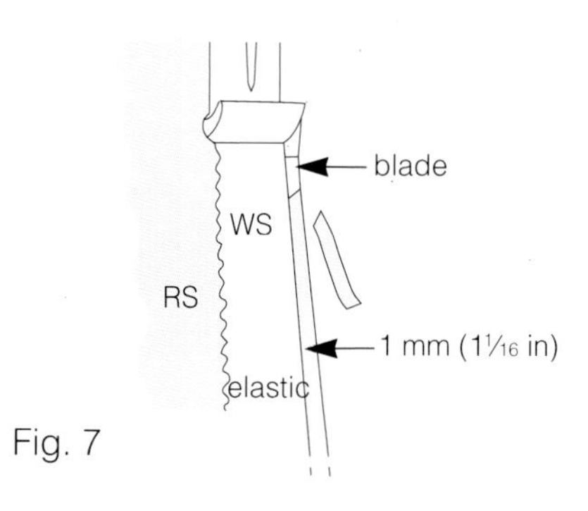

Fig. 7

10. If using plush elastic, insert raw edge of fabric into folded plush elastic and secure using sewing machine and straight stitch.

11. **Quarter pin mark** the fabric and the elastic. Sew elastic to fabric.

12. Repeat for the other leg.

13. With RS together, pin side seams, and sew using three-thread overlocking and stitch length 2-2½.

14. Lay panties on a flat surface and measure waist opening (Fig. 8). Cut elastic to three-quarters of this measurement, or take the waist measurement less 10 cm (4 in).

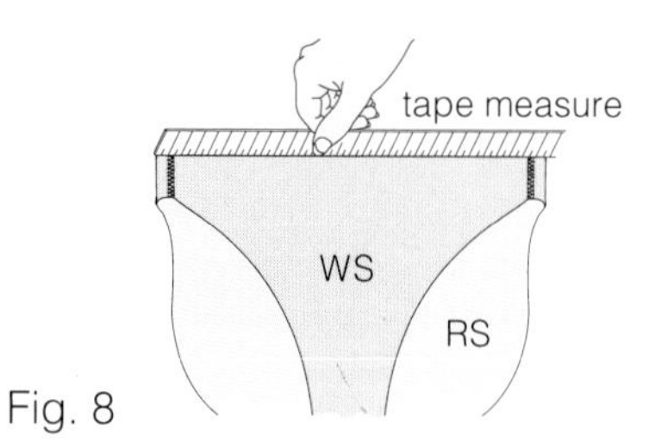

Fig. 8

15. With RS together, join ends of **elastic to form a circle** (p. 9); sew, using three-thread overlocking and stitch length 2 (Fig. 9).

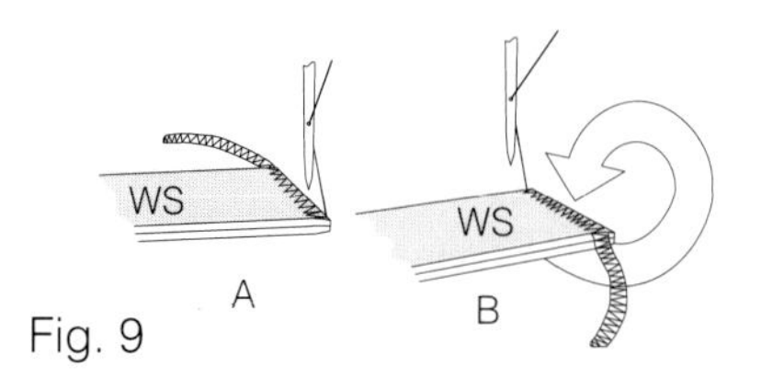

Fig. 9

16. **Quarter pin mark** the waist and waist elastic (Fig. 10).

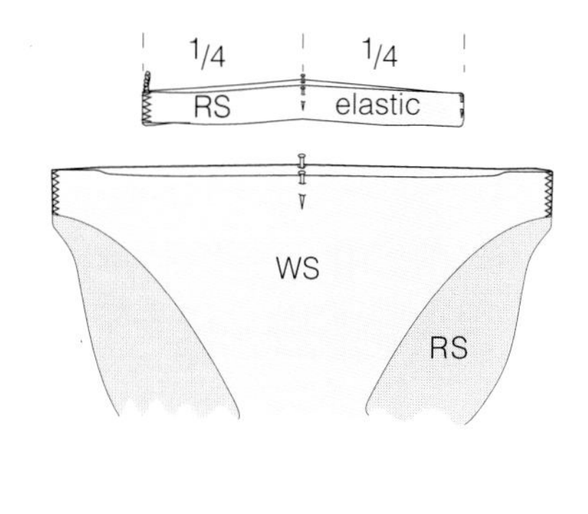

Fig. 10

17. With RS together, pin elastic to waist matching up the pins.

18. Keeping the elastic on top and with RS together, sew elastic to waist using three-thread overlocking and stitch length 3-3½ (Fig. 11). Keep the elastic next to the blade and cut 1 mm (1⁄16 in) off the fabric.

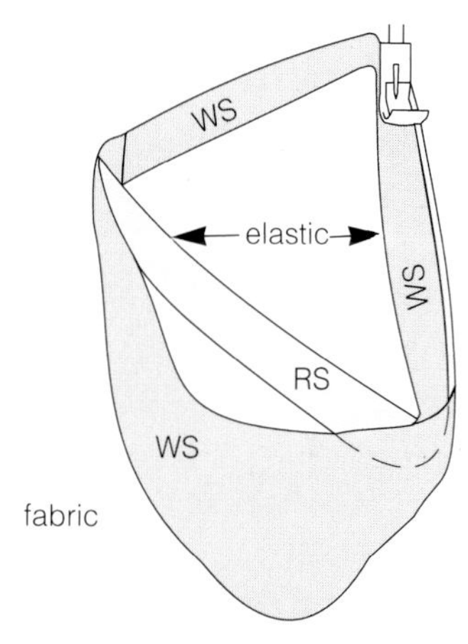

Fig. 11

19. If using stretch lace elastic with a scalloped edge, pin the WS of the stretch lace elastic onto the RS of the fabric. Using the sewing machine and zig-zag stitch, or overcasting stitch, sew along the raw edges.

20. Secure all loose ends by hand or with stitch sealant.

21. Position bows or roses on front panel and sew on by hand.

FULL PANTIES WITH FRONT LACE INSET

REQUIREMENTS
35 cm (⅜ yd) T-shirt fabric or Lycra
30 cm (12 in) stretch lace for inset
1-1.25 m x 1 cm-wide (1-1¼ yd x ½ in) leg elastic for legs
70-80 cm x 1.5-2 cm wide (¾ yd x ½-¾ in) waist elastic OR 1 cm-wide (½ in) leg elastic for waist
Embroidery thread, no. 8 or 12
Matching polyester cotton thread
Floss
Pre-made bows or roses for decoration (see page 18)
Stitch sealant (see page 19)

SEAM ALLOWANCE
6 mm (¼ in) on all seams

STITCHES
Flatlocking with embroidery thread
Three-thread overlocking

PATTERNS
Patterns 2, 3, 4 and 5

FULL PANTIES, P. 23

METHOD

1. Enlarge pattern pieces on pages 75 and 76 onto graph paper and cut out.

2. Pin the pattern pieces onto the fabric and cut out 1 x back (on fold), 1 x lace centre front (on fold), 2 x side front and 2 x gusset (gusset piece and lining).

3. Pin WS of lace centre front panel to WS of both side front panels.

4. Keeping the stretch lace at the bottom, sew together using flatlocking and stitch length 2½-3.

5. Pin RS of the back panel to RS of the gusset and WS of the back panel to RS of the gusset lining, with raw edges together (Fig. 1, p. 23). Sew using three-thread overlocking and stitch length 2-2½.

6. With RS of back panel and gusset facing up, pin RS of front panel onto RS of gusset, raw edges together (Fig. 2, p. 23). Sandwich gusset lining around back and front panel and pin RS of gusset lining to WS of front panel, raw edges together (Fig. 3, p. 23). Sew together using three-thread overlocking, stitch length 2-2½.

7. Turn panties through gusset pieces so that both gusset seams are enclosed (Fig. 4, p. 24).

8. Lay panties on a flat surface and measure leg opening (Fig. 5, p. 25). Cut the leg elastic to three-quarters of this measurement.

9. With RS together, place elastic on top of fabric. Insert fabric and elastic into overlocker and secure the elastic by sewing a few stitches using three-thread overlocking and stitch length 3-3½. **Quarter pin mark fabric** and elastic (Fig. 6, p. 24).

10. Pin elastic to fabric, matching up the pins.

11. Continue sewing, attaching the elastic to the fabric. Hold the fabric and elastic in front and at the back, and keep the elastic next to the blade, cuting 1 mm (1/16 in) off the fabric (Fig. 7, p. 24).

12. Repeat for the other leg.

13. With RS together, pin side seams, and sew using three-thread overlocking and stitch length 2-2½.

14. Lay panties on a flat surface and measure waist opening (Fig. 8, p. 24). Cut waist elastic to three-quarters of this measurement.

15. With RS together, join ends of **elastic to form a circle** (p. 9) and sew using three-thread overlocking and stitch length 2 (Fig. 9, p. 24).

16. **Quarter pin mark** waist and waist elastic (Fig. 10, p. 24).

17. With RS together, pin elastic to waist, matching up the pins.

18. Keeping the elastic on top, sew the elastic to the waist using three-thread overlocking and stitch length 3-3½ (Fig. 11, p. 24). Keeping the elastic next to the blade, cut 1 mm (1/16 in) off the fabric.

19. Secure all loose ends by hand or with stitch sealant.

20. Position bows or roses on front panel and sew on by hand.

NOTE: Wash lingerie by hand.

FULL PANTIES WITH SIDE LACE INSETS

REQUIREMENTS
- 40 cm (16 in) T-shirt fabric or Lycra
- 30 cm (12 in) stretch lace for inset
- 1 - 1.25 m x 1 cm-wide (1-1¼ yd x ½ in) leg elastic for legs
- 70-80 cm x 1.5-2 cm-wide (¾ yd x ½-¾ in) waist elastic OR 1 cm-wide (½ in) leg elastic for waist
- Matching polyester cotton thread
- Floss
- Pre-made bows or roses for decoration (see page 18)
- Stitch sealant (see page 19)

SEAM ALLOWANCE
6 mm (¼ in) on all seams

STITCHES
Flatlocking with floss
Three-thread overlocking

PATTERNS
Patterns 3, 6, 7, 8 and 9

METHOD
1. Enlarge pattern pieces on pages 75 and 77 onto graph paper and cut out.

2. Pin pattern pieces onto fabric and cut out 1 x centre back (on fold), 2 x lace side back, 1 x centre front (on fold), 2 x lace side front, 2 x gusset (gusset piece and lining).

3. Pin WS of lace front and back side panels to WS of both centre panels.

4. Keeping the stretch lace at the bottom, sew together using **flatlocking with floss,** stitch length 2½-3.

5. Pin RS of back panel to RS of gusset and WS of back panel to RS of gusset lining, raw edges together (Fig. 1, p. 23). Sew together using three-thread overlocking and stitch length 2-2½.

6. With RS of the back panel and gusset facing up, pin RS of the front panel to RS of gusset, raw edges together (Fig. 2, p. 23). Sandwich gusset lining around the back and front panels. Pin RS of gusset lining to WS of front panel, raw edges together (Fig. 3, p. 23). Sew using three-thread overlocking and stitch length 2-2½.

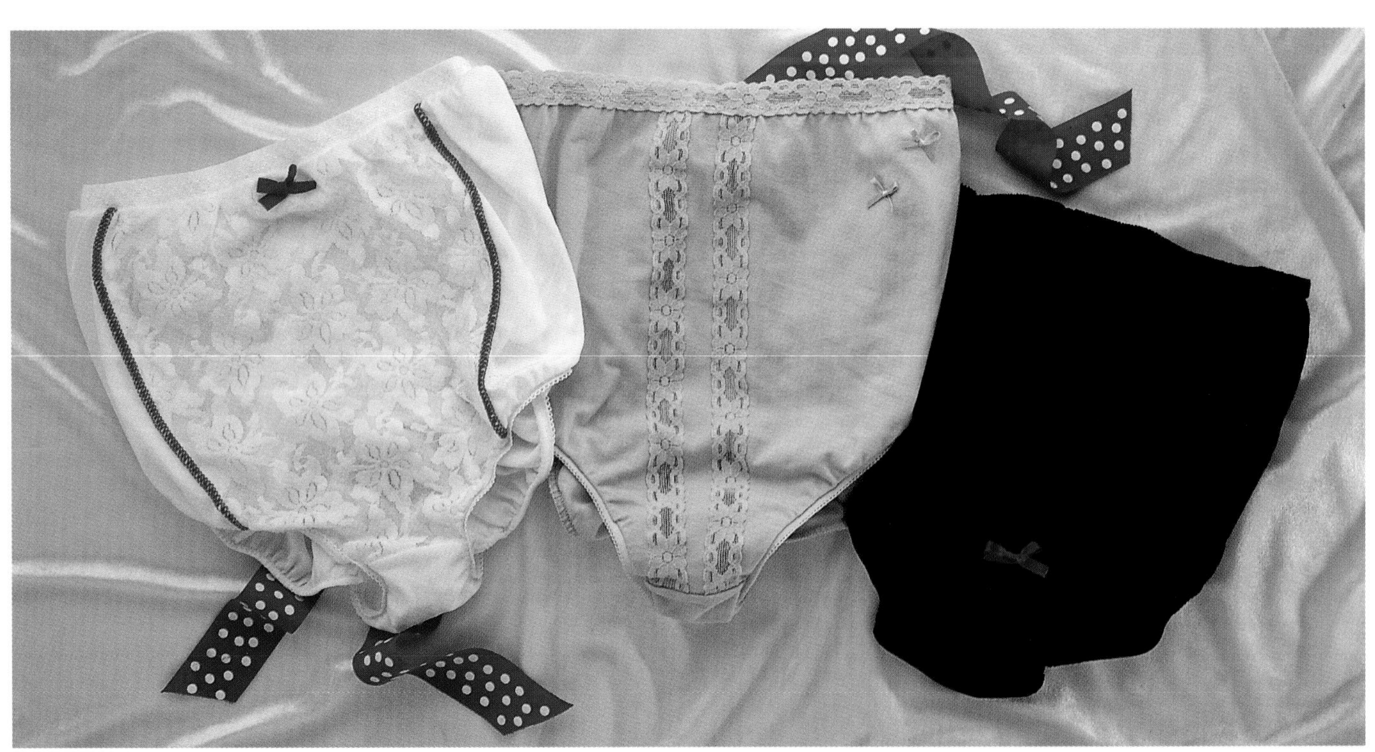

FULL PANTIES WITH FRONT LACE INSET, P 25, FULL PANTIES, P. 23 AND FULL PANTIES WITH SIDE LACE INSETS

7. Turn panties through gusset pieces so that both gusset seams are enclosed (Fig. 4, p. 24).

8. Lay panties on a flat surface. Measure leg opening (Fig. 5, p. 24). Cut leg elastic to three-quarters of this measurement.

9. With RS together, place elastic on top of fabric. Insert fabric and elastic into overlocker. Secure elastic by sewing using three-thread overlocking and stitch length 3-3½. **Quarter pin mark** fabric and elastic (Fig. 6, p. 24).

10. Pin elastic to fabric, matching up the pins.

11. Continue sewing, attaching elastic to fabric. Hold fabric and elastic in the front and at the back. Keep elastic next to the blade and cut 1 mm (1/16 in) off the fabric (Fig. 7, p. 24).

12. Repeat for the other leg.

13. With RS together, pin side seams, and sew using three-thread overlocking and stitch length 2-2½.

14. Lay panties on a flat surface and measure waist opening (Fig. 8, p. 24). Cut waist elastic to three-quarters of this measurement.

15. With RS together, join ends of **elastic to form a circle** (p. 9). Sew using three-thread overlocking and stitch length 2 (Fig. 9, p. 24).

16. **Quarter pin mark** waist and waist elastic (Fig. 10, p. 24).

17. With RS together, pin elastic to waist, matching up the pins.

18. Keeping elastic on top, sew elastic to waist using three-thread overlocking and stitch length 3-3½ (Fig. 11, p. 24). Keep elastic next to blade and cut 1 mm (1/16 in) off the fabric.

19. Secure all loose ends by hand or with stitch sealant.

20. Position bows or roses on front panel and sew on by hand.

HIGH-CUT PANTIES

These comfortable panties have a flattering high-cut leg.

REQUIREMENTS
60 cm (24 in) single or double knit T-shirt fabric, cotton or nylon Lycra, non-stretch fabric or stretch lace
1-1.25 m x 1 cm-wide (1-1¼ yd-½ in) leg or plush elastic for legs
70-80 cm x 1.5-3 cm-wide (¾ yd x ½-1¼ in) waist elastic OR stretch lace elastic (if waist elastic or stretch lace elastic is wider than 3 cm (1¼ in), cut 2 cm (¾ in) off from waist) for waist
Matching polyester cotton thread
Floss
Pre-made bows or roses for decoration (see page 18)
Stitch sealant (see page 19)

SEAM ALLOWANCE
6 mm (¼ in) on all seams

STITCHES
Straight stitch, stitch length 3-4
Zig-zag stitch, width 1 and length 2
Overcasting stitch, width 4, length 2½
Three-thread overlocking

PATTERNS
Patterns 1, 2 and 3

METHOD
1. Enlarge the pattern pieces on pages 74 and 75 onto graph paper and cut out, or make your own pattern (see **Designing and Measuring High-Cut Panties**, page 22).

2. Pin pattern pieces onto fabric. Cut out 1 x back (on fold), 1 x front (on fold) and 2 x gusset (gusset piece and lining).

3. Pin RS of back panel to RS of gusset and WS of back panel to RS of gusset lining, raw edges together (Fig. 1, p. 23). Sew together using three-thread overlocking, stitch length 2-2½.

4. With RS of back panel and gusset together, pin RS of front panel onto the RS of the gusset, raw edges together (Fig. 2, p. 23). Sandwich gusset lining around back and front panel and pin RS of gusset lining to WS of front panel, raw edges together (Fig. 3, p. 23). Sew together using three-thread overlocking and stitch length 2-2½.

5. Turn panties through gusset pieces so that both gusset seams are enclosed (Fig. 4, p. 24).

6. Lay panties on a flat surface and measure leg opening (Fig. 5, p. 24). Cut the elastic to three-quarters of this measurement.

7. If using leg elastic, with RS together, place elastic on top of fabric, insert fabric and elastic into overlocker and secure the elastic by sewing a few stitches using three-thread overlocking and stitch length 3-3½. **Quarter pin mark** the fabric and elastic (Fig. 6, p. 24).

8. Pin elastic to fabric, matching up the pins.

9. Continue sewing, attaching the elastic to the fabric. Hold the fabric and elastic in the front and at the back, and keep the elastic next to the blade, cutting 1 mm (1/16 in) off the fabric (Fig. 7, p. 24).

10. If using plush elastic, insert fabric and plush elastic into folded elastic and secure elastic by sewing a few stitches. using sewing machine and straight stitch. **Quarter pin mark** fabric and elastic (Fig. 6, p. 24).

11. Pin elastic to fabric, matching up the pins.

12. Continue sewing, attaching the elastic to the fabric. Hold the fabric and elastic in front and at the back.

13. Repeat for the other leg.

14. With RS together, pin side seams and sew using three-thread overlocking and stitch length 2-2½.

15. Lay panties on a flat surface and measure waist opening (Fig. 8, p. 24). Cut waist elastic or stretch lace elastic to three-quarters of this measurement, or take the waist measurement less 10 cm (4 in).

16. With RS together, join ends of **elastic to form a circle** (p. 9) and sew using three-thread overlocking and stitch length 2 (Fig. 9, p. 24).

17. Quarter pin mark waist and waist elastic (Fig. 10, p. 24).

18. With RS together, pin elastic to waist matching up the pins.

19. Keeping the elastic on top and with RS together, sew elastic elastic to waist using three-thread overlocking and stitch length 3-3½ (Fig. 11, p. 24). Keep elastic next to the blade and cut 1 mm (1 1/16 in) off fabric.

20. If using stretch lace elastic with a scalloped edge, pin WS of lace to RS of fabric and sew using sewing machine and zig-zag stitch, or overcasting stitch along the raw edge.

21. Secure all loose ends by hand or with stitch sealant.

22. Position bows or roses on front panel, and sew on by hand.

HIGH-CUT PANTIES WITH A LACE WAIST

REQUIREMENTS
- 35 cm (⅜ yd) T-shirt fabric, Lycra or stretch lace
- 70-80 cm x 6-8 cm-wide OR
- 1 m - 1.25 m x 1 cm-wide (1-1½ yd x ½ in) leg elastic for legs
- 12-14 cm-wide (¾ yd x 2¼-3¼ in or 4¾-5½ in) stretch lace elastic for waist
- Matching polyester cotton thread
- Floss
- Pre-made bows or roses for decoration (see page 18)
- Stitch sealant (see page 19)

SEAM ALLOWANCE
6 mm (¼ in) on all seams

STITCHES
Overcasting stitch, width 4, length 2½
Three-thread overlocking

PATTERNS
Use patterns 3, 10 and 11 for 6-8 cm lace waist, and patterns 3, 12 and 13 for 12 - 14 cm lace waist

METHOD
1. Enlarge the pattern pieces on pages 75 and 78 onto graph paper and cut out.

2. Pin pattern pieces onto fabric and cut out 1 x back (on fold), 1 x front (on fold), 2 x gusset (gusset piece and lining).

3. Pin RS of back to RS of gusset and WS of back panel to RS of gusset lining, raw edges together (Fig. 1, p. 23). Sew together using three-thread overlocking, stitch length 2-2½.

4. With RS of back panel and gusset facing up, pin RS of front panel onto RS of gusset, raw edges together (Fig. 2, p. 23). Sandwich gusset lining around back and front panel and pin RS of gusset lining to WS of front panel, raw edges together (Fig. 3, p. 23). Stitch together using three-thread overlocking, stitch length 2-2½.

5. Turn panties through gusset pieces so that both gusset seams are enclosed (Fig. 4, p. 24).

6. Lay panties on a flat surface and measure leg opening (Fig. 5, p. 24). Cut the leg elastic to three-quarters of this measurement.

7. With RS together, place elastic on top of fabric. Insert the fabric and elastic into the overlocker and secure elastic by sewing a few stitches using three-thread overlocking and stitch length 3-3½. **Quarter pin mark** fabric as well as elastic (Fig. 6, p. 24).

8. Pin elastic to fabric, matching up the pins.

9. Continue sewing, attaching elastic to fabric. Hold fabric and elastic in front and at the back and keep elastic next to blade, cutting 1 mm (1/16 in) off the fabric (Fig. 7, p. 24).

10. Repeat for the other leg.

11. Cut stretch lace elastic to waist measurement less 10 cm (4 in).

12. With RS together, join ends of stretch lace **elastic to form a circle** (p. 9) and sew using three-thread overlocking, stitch length 2 (Fig. 9, p.24).

13. Pin mark centre front and back. **Quarter pin mark** stretch lace elastic.

14. Position seam of stretch lace elastic on side seam. Pin WS of stretch lace elastic to RS of fabric. Pin front panel 3 cm (1¼ in) from both side seam pin marks of stretch lace elastic.

15. Pin back panel 2 cm (¾ in) from both side seam pin marks of stretch lace elastic.

16. Sew stretch lace elastic to raw edge of fabric using sewing machine and overcasting stitch.

17. Secure all loose ends by hand or with stitch sealant.

18. Position bows or roses on front panel and sew on by hand.

HIGH-CUT PANTIES WITH WAIST ELASTIC

REQUIREMENTS
- 25 cm (10 in) T-shirt fabric, Lycra or stretch lace
- 1 m-1.25 m x 1 cm-wide (1-1½ yd x ½ in) leg elastic for legs
- 70-80 cm x 5 cm-wide (¾ yd-2 in) waist elastic
- Matching polyester cotton thread
- Floss
- Pre-made bows or roses for decoration (see page 18)
- Stitch sealant (see page 19)

SEAM ALLOWANCE
6 mm (¼ in) on all seams

STITCHES
Straight stitch, stitch length 3-4
Three-thread overlocking

PATTERNS
Patterns 3, 14 and 15

METHOD

1. Enlarge pattern pieces on pages 75 and 79 onto graph paper and cut out.

2. Pin pattern pieces onto fabric and cut out 1 x back (on fold), 1 x front (on fold), 2 x gusset (gusset piece and lining).

3. Pin RS of back to RS of gusset and WS of back panel to RS of gusset lining, raw edges together (Fig. 1, p. 23). Sew together using three-thread overlocking, stitch length 2-2½.

4. With RS of back panel and gusset facing up, pin RS of front panel onto RS of the gusset, raw edges together (Fig. 2, p. 23). Sandwich gusset lining around back and front panel and pin RS of gusset lining to WS of front panel, raw edges together (Fig. 3, p. 23). Sew together using three-thread overlocking, stitch length 2-2½.

5. Turn panties through gusset pieces so that both gusset seams are enclosed (Fig. 4, p. 24).

6. Lay panties on a flat surface and measure leg opening (Fig. 5, p. 24). Cut the leg elastic to three-quarters of this measurement.

7. With RS together, place elastic on top of the fabric. Insert the fabric and elastic into overlocker and secure the elastic by sewing a few stitches using three-thread overlocking and stitch length 3-3½. **Quarter pin mark** fabric and elastic (Fig. 6, p. 24).

8. Pin elastic to fabric, matching up the pins.

9. Continue sewing, attaching elastic to fabric. Hold the fabric and elastic in front and at the back, and keep elastic next to the blade, cutting 1 mm (1/16 in) off fabric (Fig. 7, p. 24).

HIGH-CUT PANTIES, P. 27 AND HIGH-CUT PANTIES WITH LACE WAIST, P. 28

10. Repeat for the other leg.

11. Lay panties on a flat surface and measure waist (Fig. 8, p. 24). Cut waist elastic to this measurement,minus 10 cm (4 in).

12. **With RS together**, join ends of waist **elastic to form a circle** (p. 9) and sew using three-thread overlocking, stitch length 2 (Fig. 9, p. 24).

13. Pin mark the centre front and back. **Quarter pin mark** waist elastic.

14. Position the seam of the waist elastic on side seam.

15. Pin WS of waist elastic to RS of front panel matching up centre front pins. Pin front panel 2 cm (¾ in) from both side seam pin marks.

16. Pin WS of waist elastic to RS of back panel matching up the centre back pins. Pin back panel 2 cm (¾ in) from both side seam pin marks of waist elastic.

17. Sew waist elastic to fabric using sewing machine, twin needle and straight stitch (Fig. 12).

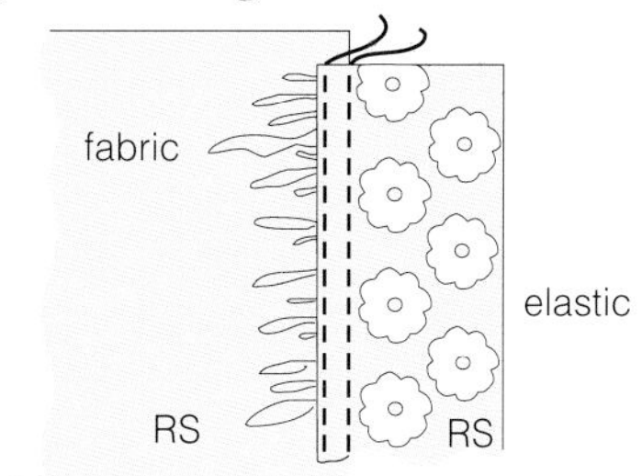

Fig. 12

18. Secure all loose ends by hand or with stitch sealant.

19. Position bows or roses on front panel and sew on by hand.

NOTE: If making panties using strech lace or non-stretch fabrics, use 20-25 cm (8-10 in) T-shirt fabric for the gusset.

HIGH-CUT PANTIES WITH STRETCH LACE AT LEGS

REQUIREMENTS
35 cm (⅜ yd) T-shirt fabric or Lycra
80 cm-90 cm x 6-8 cm-wide (⅞ yd x 2¼-3¼ in) stretch lace elastic for legs
50-60 cm x 1 cm-wide leg elastic OR 6 mm-wide (20-24 in x ½ in) nylon elastic for legs
70-80 cm x 2-3 cm-wide (¾ yd x ¾-1¼ in) waist elastic for waist
Matching polyester cotton thread
Floss
Pre-made bows or roses for decoration (see page 18)
Stitch sealant (see page 19)

BRA WITH STRETCH LACE, P. 40, BIKINI PANTIES WITH STRETCH LACE, P.36, AND HIGH-CUT PANTIES WITH BRODERIE ANGLAISE, P.31

SEAM ALLOWANCE
6 mm (¼ in) on all seams

STITCHES
Zig-zag stitch, width 1 and length 2
Three-thread overlocking

PATTERNS
Patterns 2, 3 and 16

METHOD

1. Enlarge the pattern pieces on pages 75 and 79 onto the graph paper and cut them out.

2. Pin pattern pieces onto fabric and cut out 1 x back (on fold), 1 x front (on fold), 2 x gusset (gusset piece and lining).

3. Pin WS of the stretch lace elastic to RS of fabric. The stretch lace elastic must be 2 cm (¾ in) wide at the front gusset edge, and gradually become 6 cm (2¼ in) wide in the centre, tapering back to 2 cm (¾ in) at the side seam.

4. Ensure that when you are pinning on the stretch lace elastic, that the front gusset edge and the side seam edge are not wider than the gusset and the back side seam edge (Fig. 13).

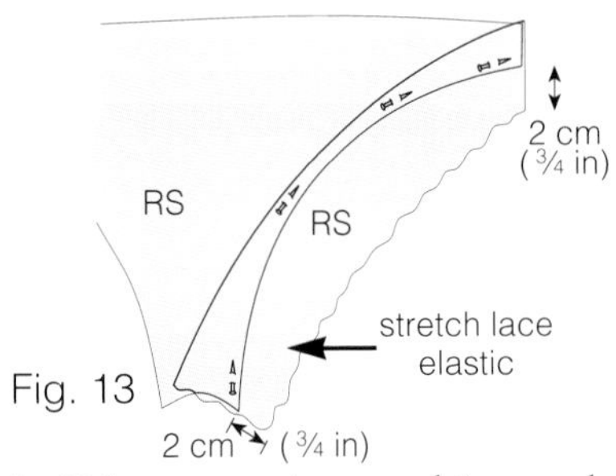

Fig. 13

5. Using a sewing machine and zig-zag stitch, sew stretch lace elastic to front panel (Fig. 14).

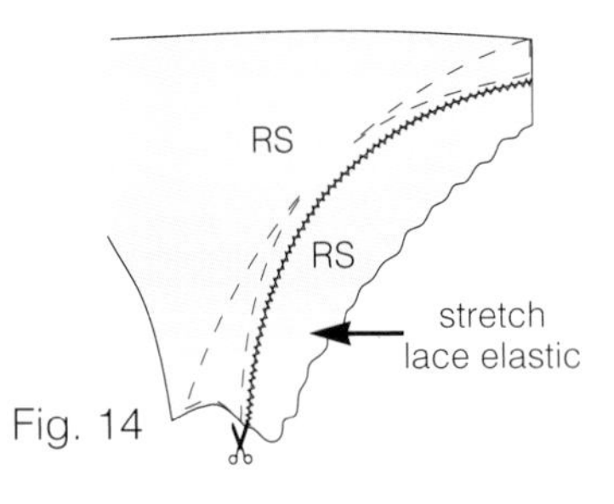

Fig. 14

6. Cut fabric and stretch lace elastic away next to stitching (Fig. 14).

7. Pin RS of the back panel to RS of the gusset and WS of the back panel to RS of the gusset lining, raw edges together (Fig. 1, p. 23).

8. Sew together using three-thread overlocking and stitch length 2-2½.

9. Lay panties on a flat surface and measure leg and crotch opening (see Fig. 15). Cut the leg elastic to three-quarters of this measurement.

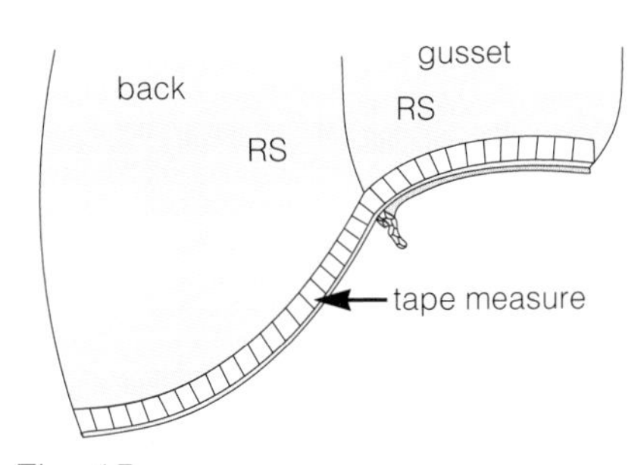

Fig. 15

10. If using leg elastic, with RS together, place the elastic on top of the fabric. Insert the fabric and elastic into the overlocker and secure the elastic by sewing a few stitches using three-thread overlocking and stitch length 3-3½.

11. If using nylon elastic, place elastic on RS of fabric. Use the elastic gatherer, or feed elastic over and under the pressure foot. Insert the fabric under foot and keep elastic on the inside of the blade. Secure elastic by sewing a few stitches using three-thread overlocking, stitch length 2-3.

12. Divide the fabric and the elastic into two equal parts (Fig. 16).

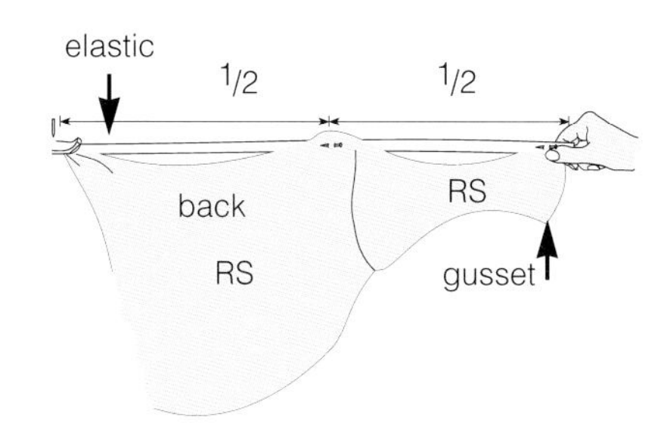

Fig. 16

13. Pin elastic to fabric, matching up the pins (Fig. 17).

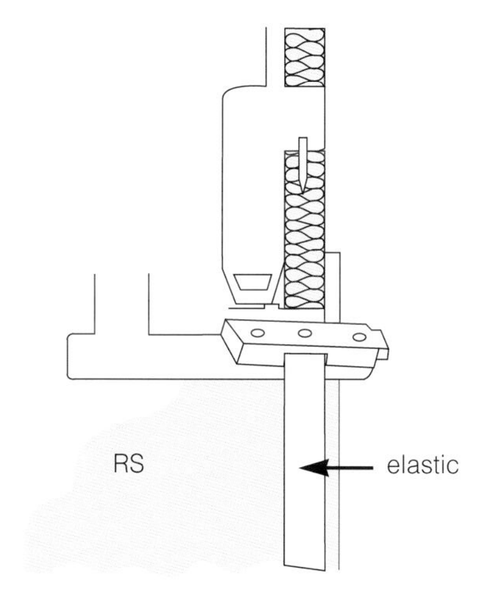

Fig. 17

14. Continue sewing, attaching the elastic to the fabric. Hold the fabric and elastic in front and at the back, and keep the elastic next to the blade, cutting 1 mm (1/16 in) off the fabric (Fig. 7, p. 24).

15. Repeat for the other leg.

16. Pin the gusset and the gusset lining together. Pin the RS of the front panel to the RS of the gusset and sew together using three-thread overlocking and stitch length 2-2½.

17. With RS together, pin side seams and sew using three-thread overlocking and stitch length 2-2½.

18. Lay panties on a flat surface and measure waist opening (Fig. 8, p. 24). Cut waist elastic to three-quarters of this measurement.

19. **With RS together** join ends of waist **elastic to form a circle** (p. 9) and sew using three-thread overlocking and stitch length 2 (Fig. 9, p. 24).

20. **Quarter pin mark** waist and waist elastic (Fig. 10, p. 24).

21. With RS together, pin elastic to waist matching up the pins.

22. Keeping elastic on top, sew elastic to waist using three-thread overlocking and stitch length 3-3½ (Fig. 11, p. 24). Keep elastic next to the blade and cut 1 mm (1/16 in) off fabric.

23. Secure all loose ends by hand or with stitch sealant.

24. Position bows or roses on front panel and sew on by hand.

HIGH-CUT PANTIES WITH BRODERIE ANGLAISE AT LEGS

REQUIREMENTS
35 cm (3/8 yd) T-shirt fabric or Lycra
90 cm-1 m x 8-10 cm-wide (1 yd x 3¼-4 in) broderie anglaise for legs
80 cm-1 m x 1 cm-wide (7/8-1 yd x ¼ in) leg elastic OR 6 mm-wide (¼ in) nylon elastic for legs
70-80 cm x 2 cm-wide (¾ yd x ¾ in) waist elastic (leg elastic can also be used for the waist) for waist
Matching polyester cotton thread
Floss
Pre-made bows or roses for decoration (see page 18)
Stitch sealant (see page 19)

SEAM ALLOWANCE
6 mm (¼ in) on all seams

STITCHES
Zig-zag stitch, width 1, length 2
Three-thread overlocking

PATTERNS
Patterns 2, 3 and 17

METHOD
1. Enlarge pattern pieces on pages 75 and 79 onto graph paper and cut out.

2. Pin pattern pieces onto fabric and cut out 1 x back (on fold), 1 x front (on fold), 2 x gusset (gusset piece and lining).

3. Pin RS of the back panel to RS of the gusset and WS of the back panel to RS of the gusset lining, raw edges together (Fig. 1, p. 23). Sew together using three-thread overlocking and stitch length 2-2½.

4. Lay panties on a flat surface and measure leg and crotch opening (Fig. 5, p. 24). Cut leg elastic to three-quarters of this measurement.

5. If using leg elastic, pin RS together, and place the elastic on top of the fabric. Insert the fabric and elastic into the overlocker and secure the elastic by sewing a few stitches using three-thread overlocking and stitch length 3-3½.

6. If using nylon elastic, place the elastic on RS of fabric. Use elastic gatherer or feed elastic over and under the pressure foot. Insert the fabric under foot, and keep the elastic on the inside of the blade. Secure the elastic by sewing a few stitches using three-thread overlocking and stitch length 2-3.

7. Divide the fabric and elastic into two equal parts.

8. Pin elastic to fabric, matching up the pins.

9. Continue sewing, attaching elastic to fabric. Hold fabric and elastic in front and at the back, and keep elastic next to the blade, cutting 1 mm (1/16 in) off the fabric (Fig. 7, p. 24).

10. Repeat for the other leg.

11. With WS of broderie anglaise to RS of fabric, pin broderie anglaise onto front panel (Fig. 13, p. 30). The lace must be 2 cm (¾ in) wide at the front gusset edge, and gradually become the full width at the centre and side seam edge. Ensure that when the broderie anglaise is pinned on, that the gusset and side seam are not wider than front of gusset and back side seam edge (Fig 13, p. 30).

12. Sew on broderie anglaise using sewing machine.

13. Cut broderie anglaise and fabric away next to stitching (Fig. 14, p. 30).

14. Pin the gusset and gusset lining together. Pin the RS of the front panel to the RS of the gusset and sew together using three-thread overlocking and stitch length 2-2½.

15. With RS together, pin side seams and sew using three-thread overlocking and stitch length 2-2½.

16. Lay panties on a flat surface and measure waist opening (Fig. 8, p. 24). Cut waist elastic to three-quarters of this measurement.

17. With RS together, join ends of waist **elastic to form a circle** (page 9) and sew using three-thread overlocking, stitch length 2 (Fig. 9, p. 24).

18. **Quarter pin mark** waist and waist elastic (Fig. 10, p. 24).

19. With RS together, pin elastic to waist matching up the pins.

20. Keeping elastic on top, sew elastic to waist using three-thread overlocking and stitch length 3-3½ (Fig. 11, p. 24). Keep elastic next to the blade and cut 1 mm (1/16 in) off fabric.

21. Secure all loose ends by hand or with stitch sealant.

22. Position bows or roses on front panel and sew on by hand.

BIKINI PANTIES

Pert and pretty, bikini panties are worn by those who are!

REQUIREMENTS
50 cm (20 in) single or double knit T-shirt fabric, cotton or nylon Lycra, non-stretch fabric or stretch lace
1-1.25 m x 1 cm-wide (1-1¼ yd x ½ in) leg or plush elastic for legs
70-80 cm x 2 cm-wide (¾ yd x ¾ in) waist elastic OR 1.5 m x 3 cm-wide (2 yd x 1¼ in) stretch lace elastic (leg elastic can also be used for the waist)
Matching polyester cotton
Floss
Pre-made bows or roses for decoration (see page 18)
Stitch sealant (see page 19)

SEAM ALLOWANCE
6 mm (¼ in) on all seams

STITCHES
Three-thread overlocking
Straight stitch, length 3-4

PATTERNS
Patterns 1, 2 and 3

METHOD
1. Enlarge pattern pieces on pages 74 and 75 on graph paper and cut out, or make your own (see **Designing and Measuring Bikini Panties**, page 23).

2. Pin pattern pieces onto fabric. Cut out 1 x back (on fold), 1 x front (on fold) and 2 x gusset (gusset piece and lining).

3. Pin RS of back panel to RS of gusset and WS of back panel to RS of gusset lining, raw edges together (Fig. 1). Sew together using three-thread overlocking, stitch length 2-2½.

4. With RS of back panel and gusset facing up, pin RS of front panel onto RS of gusset, raw edges facing up (Fig. 2, p. 23). Sandwich gusset lining around back and front panel and pin RS of gusset lining to WS of front panel, raw edges together (Fig. 3, p. 23). Sew together using three-thread overlocking, stitch length 2-2½.

5. Turn panties through gusset pieces so that both gusset seams are enclosed (Fig. 4, p. 24).

6. Lay the panties on a flat surface and measure the leg opening (Fig. 5, p. 24). Cut the elastic to three-quarters of this measurement.

7. If using leg elastic, with RS together, place elastic on top of fabric, insert fabric and elastic into overlocker. Secure elastic by sewing a few stitches using three-thread overlocking, stitch length 3-3½.

8. **Quarter pin mark** fabric and elastic (Fig. 6, p. 24). Pin elastic to fabric, matching up pins.

9. Continue sewing, attaching elastic to the fabric. Hold fabric and elastic in front and at the back, and keep the elastic next to the blade cutting 1 mm (1/16 in) off fabric (Fig. 7, p. 24).

10. If using plush elastic, insert fabric into folded elastic and secure with a few stitches using sewing machine and straight stitch.

11. **Quarter pin mark** fabric and elastic. Pin elastic to fabric, matching up pins.

12. Continue sewing, attaching elastic to fabric. Hold fabric and elastic in front and at the back.

13. Repeat for the other leg.

14. With RS together, pin side seams, and sew using three-thread overlocking and stitch length 2-2½.

15. Lay the panties on a flat surface and measure waist opening (Fig. 8, p. 24). Cut the waist elastic or stretch lace elastic to three-quarters of this measurement, or take waist measurement less 10 cm (4 in).

16. With RS together, join ends of **elastic to form a circle** (p. 9) and sew using three-thread overlocking and stitch length 2 (Fig. 9, p. 24).

17. **Quarter pin mark** waist asnd elastic (Fig. 10, p. 24). Pin elastic to waist, matching up the pins.

18. Keeping elastic on top and with RS together, sew elastic to waist using three-thread overlocking, stitch length 3-3½. Keep elastic next to the blade and cut 1 mm (1/16 in) off the fabric (Fig. 11, p. 24).

19. Secure all loose ends by hand or with stitch sealant.

20. Position bows or roses on front panel and sew on by hand.

BIKINI PANTIES WITH A LACE WAIST

REQUIREMENTS
30 cm (12 in) T-shirt fabric, Lycra or stretch lace
1-1.25 m x 1 cm-wide (1-1½yd x ½ in) leg elastic for legs
70-80 cm x 6-8 cm-wide OR 12-14 cm-wide (¾ yd x 2¼-3¼ in OR 4¾-5½ in) stretch lace elastic for waist
Matching polyester cotton thread
Floss
Pre-made bows or roses for decoration (see page 18)
Stitch sealant (see page 19)

SEAM ALLOWANCE
6 mm (¼ in) on all seams

STITCHES
Overcasting stitch, width 4, length 2½
Three-thread overlocking

PATTERNS
Use patterns 3, 18 and 20 for 6-8 cm waist, and patterns 3, 19 and 21 for 12-14 cm waist

METHOD
1. Enlarge pattern pieces on pages 75 and 80 onto graph paper and cut out.

2. Pin pattern pieces onto fabric and cut out 1 x back (on fold), 1 x front (on fold) and 2 x gusset (gusset piece and lining).

3. Pin RS of the back to RS of the gusset and WS of the back panel to RS of the gusset lining, raw edges together (Fig. 1, p. 23). Sew together using three-thread overlocking and stitch length 2-2½

4. With RS of the back panel and the gusset facing up, pin RS of front panel onto RS of gusset, raw edges together (Fig. 2, p. 23). Sandwich the gusset lining around the back and front panel and pin RS of the gusset lining to WS of the front panel, raw edges together (Fig. 3, p. 23). Sew together using three-thread overlocking and stitch length 2-2½.

5. Turn panties through gusset pieces so that both gusset seams are enclosed (Fig. 4, p. 24).

6. Lay panties on a flat surface and measure the leg opening (Fig. 5, p. 24). Cut leg elastic to three-quarters of this measurement.

7. With RS together, place elastic on top of fabric. Insert fabric and elastic into overlocker; secure elastic by sewing a few stitches using three-thread overlocking, stitch length 3-3½. **Quarter pin mark** fabric and elastic (Fig. 6, p. 24). Pin elastic to fabric, matching up the pins.

8. Continue sewing, attaching elastic to fabric. Hold fabric and elastic in front and at the back, and keep elastic next to the blade, cutting 1 mm (1/16 in) off the fabric (Fig. 7, p. 24).

9. Repeat for the other leg.

10. Cut stretch lace elastic to waist measurement less 10 cm (4 in).

11. With RS together join ends of stretch lace **elastic to form a circle** (p. 9). Sew using three-thread overlocking, stitch length 2 (Fig. 9, p. 24).

12. Pin mark the centre front and back. **Quarter pin mark** the stretch lace elastic.

13. Position the stretch lace elastic seam on centre front.

BIKINI PANTIES, P.33, AND HIGH-CUT PANTIES WITH WAIST ELASTIC, P.28

14. With WS of stretch lace elastic to RS of fabric, pin stretch lace elastic to waist, matching up pins.

15. Sew stretch lace elastic to fabric using the sewing machine and overcasting stitch.

16. Secure all loose ends by hand or with stitch sealant.

17. Position bows or roses on front panel and sew on by hand.

BIKINI PANTIES WITH FRONT STRETCH LACE WAIST

REQUIREMENTS
30 cm (12 in) T-shirt fabric, Lycra or stretch lace
1 m x 1 cm-wide (1 yd x ½ in) leg elastic OR 6 mm-wide (¼ in) nylon elastic for legs
50 cm x 12-14 cm-wide (20 in x 4¾-5½ in) stretch lace elastic for waist
30-40 cm x 1 cm-wide (12-16 in x ½ in) leg elastic for waist
Matching polyester cotton thread
Floss
Pre-made bows or roses for decoration (see page 18)
Stitch sealant (see page 19)

SEAM ALLOWANCE
6 mm (¼ in) on all seams

STITCHES
Overcasting stitch, width 4, length 2½
Three-thread overlocking

PATTERNS
Patterns 3, 22 and 23

METHOD

1. Enlarge pattern pieces on pages 75 and 80 onto graph paper and cut them out.

2. Pin pattern pieces onto fabric and cut out 1 x back (on fold), 1 x front (on fold), 1 x front lace waist (on fold) and 2 x gusset (gusset piece and lining).

3. Pin RS of back to RS of gusset and WS of back panel to RS of gusset lining, raw edges together (Fig. 1, p. 23). Sew together using three-thread over-locking, stitch length 2-2½.

4. With RS of back panel and gusset facing up, pin RS of front panel onto RS of the gusset, raw edges together (Fig. 2, p. 23). Sandwich gusset lining around back and front panel and pin RS of gusset lining to WS of front panel, raw edges together (Fig. 3, p. 23). Sew together using three-thread overlocking, stitch length 2-2½.

5. Turn panties through gusset pieces so that both gusset seams are enclosed (Fig. 4, p. 24).

6. Lay panties on a flat surface and measure leg opening (Fig. 5, p. 24). Cut elastic to three-quarters of this measurement.

7. If using leg elastic, with RS together, place elastic on top of fabric. Insert the fabric and elastic into overlocker and secure elastic by sewing a few stitches using three-thread overlocking and stitch length 3-3½.

8. If using nylon elastic, place elastic on RS of fabric. Use elastic gatherer, or feed elastic over and under the pressure foot. Insert fabric under foot, keeping elastic on inside of blade. Secure the elastic by sewing a few stitches using three-thread overlocking and stitch length 2-3.

9. Divide fabric and elastic into two equal parts. Pin elastic to fabric matching up the pins (Fig. 16, p. 31).

10. Continue sewing, attaching the elastic to fabric. Hold the fabric and the elastic in front and at the back, and keep the elastic next to the blade, cutting 1 mm (1/16 in) off the fabric (Fig. 7, p. 24).

11. Repeat for the other leg.

12. Measure the waist of the back panel and cut leg elastic to three-quarters of this measurement.

13. Sew leg elastic onto waist of back panel. With RS together, place elastic on top of fabric. Insert the fabric and elastic into overlocker and secure elastic by sewing a few stitches using three-thread overlocking and stitch length 3-3½. Divide fabric and elastic into two equal parts. Pin elastic to fabric, matching up pins.

14. Continue sewing attaching elastic to fabric. Hold fabric and elastic in front and at the back, keeping elastic next to the blade, cutting 1 mm (1/16 in) off fabric (Fig. 7, p. 24).

15. Pin WS of stretch lace elastic to RS of front panel and sew together using the sewing machine and overcasting stitch.

16. With RS together, pin side seams and sew using three-thread overlocking and stitch length 2-2½.

17. Secure all loose ends by hand or with stitch sealant.

18. Position bows or roses on front panel and sew on by hand.

BIKINI PANTIES WITH NYLON LACE OR STRETCH LACE ELASTIC IN FRONT AND SIDES

REQUIREMENTS
30 cm (12 in) T-shirt fabric or Lycra
80-90 cm x 4-5 cm-wide (⅞ yd x 1½-2 in) nylon lace or stretch lace elastic for front legs and sides (not wider than back side seam edge)
50-60 cm x 1 cm-wide leg elastic OR 6 mm-wide (22-24 in x ½ in OR ¼ in) nylon elastic for legs
70-80 cm x 2 cm-wide (¾ yd x ¾ in) waist elastic for waist
Matching polyester cotton thread
Floss
Pre-made bows or roses for decoration (see page 18)
Stitch sealant (see page 19)

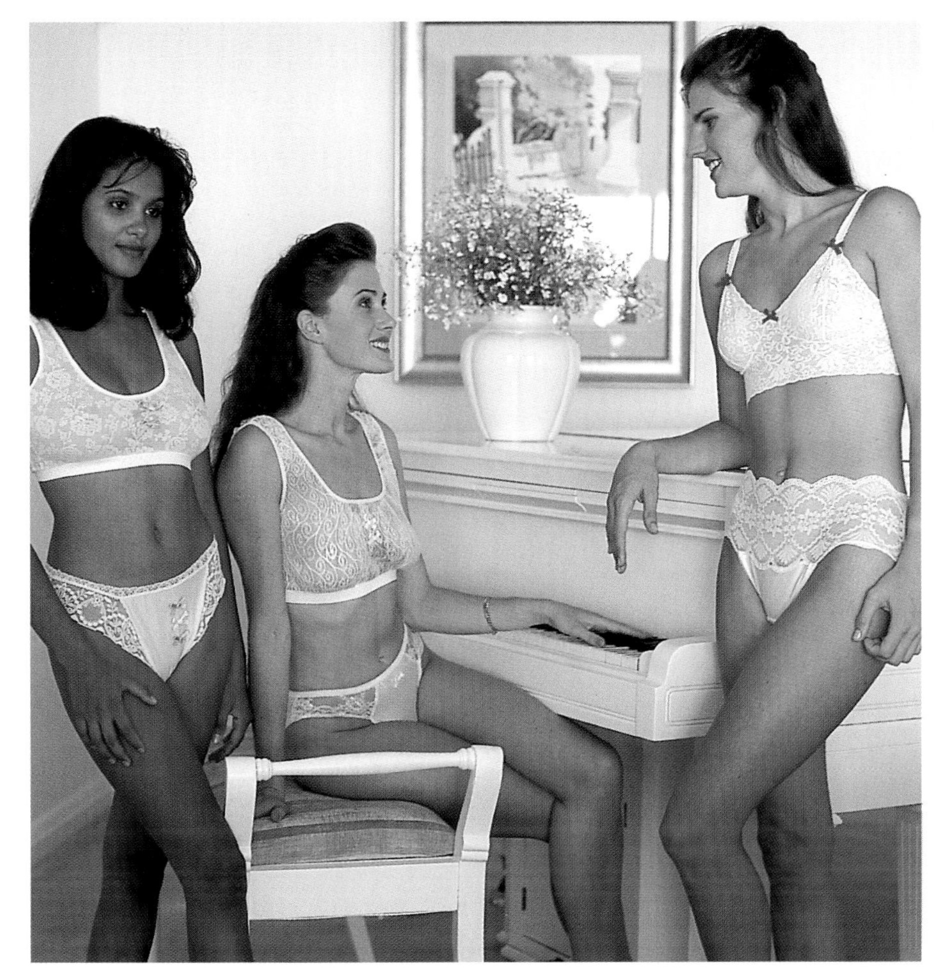

BIKINI WITH LACE AT FRONT AND SIDES, P. 34, TOPS, P. 43, BIKINI PANTIES, P.36, HIGH-CUT PANTIES WITH LACE WAIST, P. 28, BRA WITH LACE, P. 40

SEAM ALLOWANCE
6 mm (¼ in) on all seams

STITCHES
Zig-zag stitch, width 1 and length 2
Three-thread overlocking

PATTERNS
Patterns 2, 3 and 24

METHOD

1. Enlarge pattern pieces on pages 75 and 81 onto graph paper and cut out.

2. Pin pattern pieces onto fabric and cut out 1 x back (on fold), 1 x front (on fold) and 2 x gusset (gusset piece and lining).

3. Pin RS of back panel to RS of gusset and WS of back panel to RS of gusset lining, raw edges together (Fig. 1, p. 23). Sew together using three-thread overlocking, stitch length 2-2½.

4. Lay panties on a flat surface and measure leg and crotch opening (Fig. 5, p. 24). Cut leg elastic to three-quarters of this measurement.

5. If using leg elastic, pin RS together, place the elastic on top of the fabric. Insert the fabric and elastic into the overlocker and secure the elastic by sewing a few stitches using three-thread overlocking and stitch length 3-3½.

6. If using nylon elastic, place the elastic on RS of fabric. Use the elastic gatherer, or feed elastic over and under pressure, foot. Insert fabric under foot, keep elastic on inside of blade and secure by sewing a few stitches using three-thread overlocking, stitch length 2-3.

7. Divide fabric and elastic into two equal parts.

8. Pin elastic to fabric matching up the pins (Fig. 16, p. 31).

9. Continue sewing, attaching elastic to fabric. Hold fabric and elastic in front and at the back, and keep elastic next to the blade, cutting 1 mm (1/16 in) off fabric (Fig. 7, p. 24).

10. Repeat for the other leg.

11. Pin WS of lace to RS of fabric. The lace must be 2 cm (¾ in) wide at the gusset, and gradually become the full width at the centre and side seam edge. Ensure that when the lace is pinned on, the gusset seam edge is not be wider than the edge (Fig. 18). At side seam, extend lace by 10 cm (4 in) and cut edge of the lace straight.

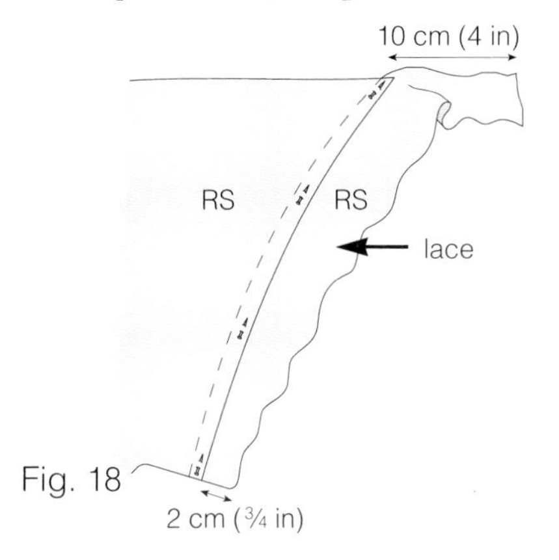

Fig. 18

12. Using the sewing machine and zig-zag stitch, sew lace to front panel (Fig. 19).

13. Cut fabric and lace away next to stitching (Fig. 19).

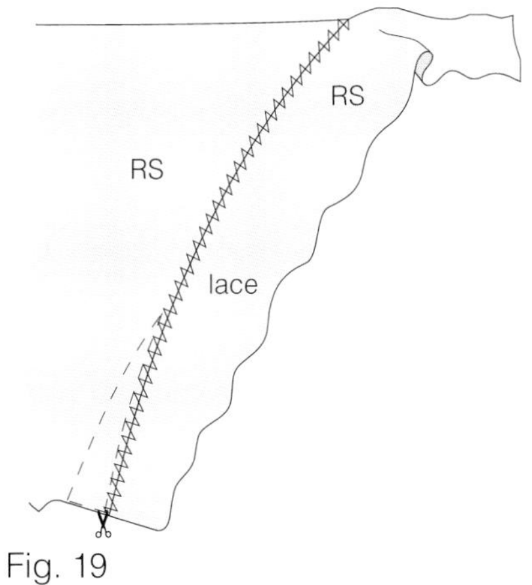

Fig. 19

14. Pin gusset and gusset lining together. Pin RS of front panel to RS of gusset and sew together using three-thread overlocking and stitch length 2-2½.

15. With RS together, pin the lace on the front panel to the back at the side seams, and sew together using three-thread overlocking and stitch length 2-2½.

16. Lay panties on a flat surface and measure waist opening (Fig. 8, p. 24). Cut waist elastic to three-quarters of this measurement.

17. With the RS together, join the ends of the waist elastic to form a circle (p. 9) and sew using three-thread overlocking and stitch length 2 (Fig. 9, p. 24).

18. **Quarter pin mark** waist and waist elastic (Fig. 10, p. 24).

19. With RS together, pin elastic to waist matching up the pins.

20. Keeping the elastic on top, sew the elastic to the waist using three-thread overlocking and stitch length 3-3½ (Fig. 11, p. 24). Keep the elastic next to the blade and cut 1 mm (1/16 in) off the fabric.

21. Secure all loose ends by hand or with stitch sealant.

22. Position bows or roses on front panel and sew on by hand.

NOTE: If you find that the polyester cotton thread keeps snapping even though the tension is set correctly, it is probably because the cotton is dry due to exposure to the sunlight. Place the reels in an empty container and leave them in the refrigerator for a day or two. The cotton will absorb the moisture and regain its elasticity. This procedure can be repeated approximately every six months.

BIKINI PANTIES WITH STRETCH LACE AT SIDES

REQUIREMENTS
30 cm (12 in) T-shirt fabric or Lycra
30 cm x 5-6 cm-wide stretch lace elastic (12 in x 2-2¼ in) for front sides (stretch lace elastic must not be wider than back side seam)
1 m x 1 cm-wide leg elastic OR 6 mm-wide (1 yd x ½ OR ¼ in) nylon leg elastic for legs
70-80 cm x 1 cm (¾ yd x ½ in) leg elastic for waist
Matching polyester cotton thread
Floss
Pre-made bows or roses for decoration (see page 18)
Stitch sealant (see page 19)

SEAM ALLOWANCE
6 mm (¼ in) on all seams

STITCHES
Flatlocking with floss
Three-thread overlocking

PATTERNS
Patterns 2, 3, 25 and 26

METHOD
1. Enlarge pattern pieces on pages 75 and 81 onto graph paper and cut out.

2. Pin pattern pieces onto fabric and cut out 1 x back (on fold), 1 x centre front (on fold), 2 x side lace insets, 2 x gusset (gusset piece and lining).

3. Pin RS of the back panel to RS of the gusset and WS of the back panel to RS of the gusset lining, raw edges together (Fig. 1, p. 23). Sew together using three-thread overlocking and stitch length 2-2½.

4. Lay panties on a flat surface and measure leg and crotch opening (Fig. 5, p. 24). Cut leg elastic to three-quarters of this measurement.

5. If using leg elastic, pin RS together, and place elastic on top. Insert fabric and elastic into overlocker and secure the elastic by sewing a few stitches using three-thread overlocking and stitch length 3-3½.

6. If using nylon elastic, place the elastic on RS of the fabric and use the elastic gatherer, or feed elastic over and under the presser foot. Insert fabric under the foot, keep the elastic on inside of the blade, and secure the elastic by sewing a few stitches using three-thread overlocking and stitch length 2-3.

7. **Quarter pin mark** fabric and elastic (Fig. 6, p. 24).

8. With RS together, pin elastic to fabric, matching up the pins.

9. Continue sewing, attaching the elastic to fabric. Hold the fabric and elastic in front and at the back, and keep the elastic next to the blade, cuting 1 mm (1/16 in) off the fabric (Fig. 7, p. 24).

10. Repeat for the other leg.

11. With WS together, pin and sew stretch lace elastic to front panel using **flatlocking with floss** and stitch length 2-3.

12. Pin the gusset and the gusset lining together. Pin RS of the front to RS of the gusset and sew together using three-thread overlocking and stitch length 2-2½.

13. With RS together, pin side seams, and sew using three-thread overlocking and stitch length 2-2½.

14. Lay panties on a flat surface and measure waist opening (Fig. 8, p. 24). Cut waist elastic to three-quarters of this measurement.

15. With RS together, join ends of the **elastic to form a circle** (p. 9) and sew using three-thread over locking, stitch length 2 (Fig. 9, p. 24).

16. **Quarter pin mark** waist and waist elastic (Fig. 10, p. 24).

17. With RS together, pin elastic to waist, matching up the pins.

18. Keeping the elastic on top, sew the elastic to the waist using three-thread overlocking and stitch length 3-3½ (Fig. 11, p. 24). Keep the elastic next to the blade and cut 1 mm (1/16 in) off the fabric.

19. Secure all loose ends by hand or with stitch sealant.

20. Position bows or roses on front panel and sew on by hand.

HIGH-CUT PANTIES WITH STRETCH LACE, P. 30, AND G-STRING

G-STRING

A G-string is completely invisible under your clothes, being only a little bigger than the stitching!

REQUIREMENTS
40 cm (16 in) T-shirt fabric, Lycra or stretch lace
2 m (2¼ yd) plush elastic for legs and waist
Matching polyester cotton thread
Floss
Pre-made bows for decoration (see page 18)
Stitch sealant (see page 19)

SEAM ALLOWANCE
6 mm (¼ in) on all seams

STITCHES
Straight stitch, length 3-4
Three-thread overlocking

PATTERNS
Patterns 27 and 28

METHOD

1. Enlarge the pattern pieces on page 81 onto graph paper and cut out.

2. Pin pattern pieces onto fabric and cut out 1 x back (on fold), 1 x front (on fold) and 1 x gusset (on fold).

3. With RS together, pin the front and the back together at crotch seam. Pin WS of gusset lining to WS of back. Sew using three-thread overlocking and stitch length 2-2½.

4. Fold the gusset piece over so that the gusset seam is encased and pin to front panel.

5. Lay G-string on a flat surface and measure the leg opening. Cut the plush elastic to three-quarters of this measurement.

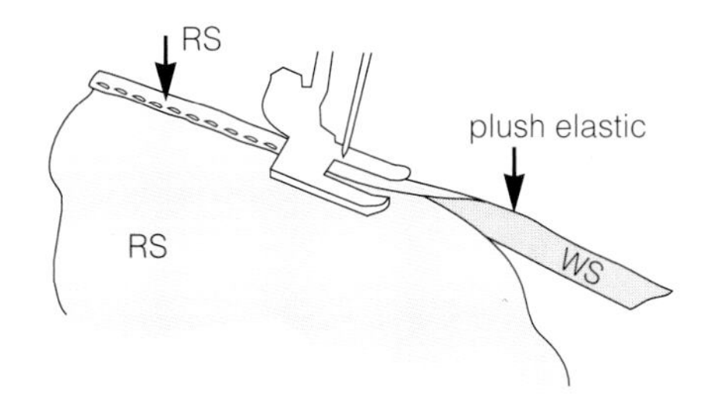

Fig. 20

6. Sew plush elastic in leg opening. Insert the fabric into plush elastic (Fig. 20) and secure elastic by sewing a few stitches using sewing machine and straight stitch.

7. **Quarter pin mark** fabric and elastic (Fig. 6, p. 24).

8 Pin elastic to fabric, matching up the pins.

9. Continue sewing, attaching the plush elastic to the fabric. Hold the fabric and the elastic in front and at the back.

10. Repeat for the other leg.

11. Lay G-string on a flat surface and measure front and back waist. Cut plush elastic to three-quarters of these measurements.

12. Sew plush elastic to front and back waist. Insert fabric into folded plush elastic and secure with a few stitches using sewing machine and straight stitch..

13. Divide the fabric and elastic into two equal parts and pin elastic to fabric.

14. Continue sewing, attaching plush elastic to fabric. Hold the fabric and elastic in front and at the back.

15. With RS together, pin and sew side seams using three-thread overlocking and stitch length 2-2½.

16. Secure all loose ends by hand or with stitch sealant.

17. Position bows on front panel and sew on by hand.

GIRLS' FULL AND HIGH-CUT PANTIES

The instructions given below are for both full and high-cut panties.

REQUIREMENTS
40-50 cm (16-20 in) T-shirt fabric
50 cm - 1 m x 1 cm-wide (20 in - 1 yd x ½ in) leg elastic for legs
40-60 cm x 1-2 cm-wide (16-24 in x ½-¾ in) waist elastic (leg elastic can also be used for the waist)
Matching polyester cotton thread
Floss
Pre-made bows or roses for decoration (see page 18)
Stitch sealant (see page 19)

SEAM ALLOWANCE
6 mm (¼ in) on all seams

STITCHES
Zig-zag stitch, width 1 and length 2
Three-thread overlocking

PATTERNS
Use patterns 29, 30 and 31 for full panties and patterns 32, 33 and 34 for high-cut panties

METHOD
1. Enlarge pattern pieces on pages 82 and 83 onto graph paper and cut out.

2. Pin pattern pieces onto fabric and cut out 1 x back (on fold), 1 x front (on fold), 2 x gusset (crotch piece and lining) (see page 00 for layout).

3. Pin RS of the back panel to RS of the gusset and WS of the back panel to RS of the gusset lining, raw edges together (Fig. 1, p. 23). Sew together using three-thread overlocking and stitch length 2-2½.

4. With RS of back panel and gusset facing up, pin RS of front panel onto

GIRLS' FULL AND HIGH-CUT PANTIES

RS of the gusset, raw edges together (Fig. 2, p. 23). Sandwich gusset lining around back and front panel and pin RS of gusset lining to WS of front panel, raw edges together (Fig. 3, p. 23). Sew together using three-thread overlocking, stitch length 2-2½.

5. Turn panties through gusset pieces so that both gusset seams are enclosed (Fig. 4, p. 24).

6. Lay panties on a flat surface and measure leg opening (Fig. 5, p. 24). Cut the leg elastic to three-quarters of this measurement.

7. With RS together, place the elastic on top of the fabric. Insert fabric and elastic in overlocker and secure elastic by sewing a few stitches using three-thread overlocking and stitch length 3-3½. **Quarter pin mark** fabric and elastic (Fig. 6, p. 24).

8. Pin elastic to fabric, matching up the pins.

9. Continue sewing, attaching the elastic to fabric. Hold fabric and elastic in front and at the back, and keep elastic next to blade, cutting 1 mm (1/16 in) off the fabric (Fig. 7, p. 24).

10. Repeat for the other leg.

11. With RS together, pin the side seams and sew together using three-thread overlocking and stitch length 2-2½.

12. Lay panties on a flat surface and measure waist opening (Fig. 8, p. 24). Cut waist elastic to three-quarters of this measurement.

13. With RS together, join ends of waist **elastic to form a circle** (p. 9) and sew using three-thread overlocking, stitch length 2 (Fig. 9, p. 24).

14. **Quarter pin mark** waist, and waist elastic (Fig. 10, p. 24). Pin elastic to waist, RS together, matching up pins.

15. Keeping the elastic on top, sew the elastic to the waist using three-thread overlocking and stitch length 3-3½ (Fig. 11, p. 24). Keep the elastic next to the blade and cut 1 mm (1/16 in) off the fabric.

16. Secure all loose ends by hand or with stitch sealant.

17. Position bows or roses on front panel and sew on by hand.

BRAS, BRA TOPS AND CROPPED TOPS

Soft brassieres have become very popular – not only are they attractive and feminine, but they are also very comfortable to wear.

BRA WITH NYLON OR STRETCH LACE ELASTIC, AND BIKINI PANTIES, P. 33

BRA WITH NYLON LACE OR STRETCH LACE ELASTIC

REQUIREMENTS
20 cm (8 in) T-shirt fabric, Lycra or stretch lace
50 cm x 4-6 cm-wide (20 in x 1½-2¼ in) stretch lace elastic or nylon lace for bra cups
1.3-1.5 m x 1 cm-wide (1½-1⅞ yd x ½ in) leg elastic for underarms
70-80 cm x 2 cm-wide (¾ yd x ¾ in) waist elastic OR 14 cm-wide (5½ in) stretch lace elastic for under bust
Matching polyester cotton thread
Metallic thread or floss
Pre-made bows or roses for decoration (see page 18)
Stitch sealant (see page 19)

SEAM ALLOWANCE
6 mm (¼ in) on all seams

STITCHES
Zig-zag stitch, width 1 and length 2
Flatlocking with metallic thread or floss
Three-thread overlocking

PATTERNS
Pattern 36

METHOD
1. Enlarge the pattern piece on page 83 onto graph paper and cut out.

2. Pin pattern piece onto fabric and cut out 2 x front.

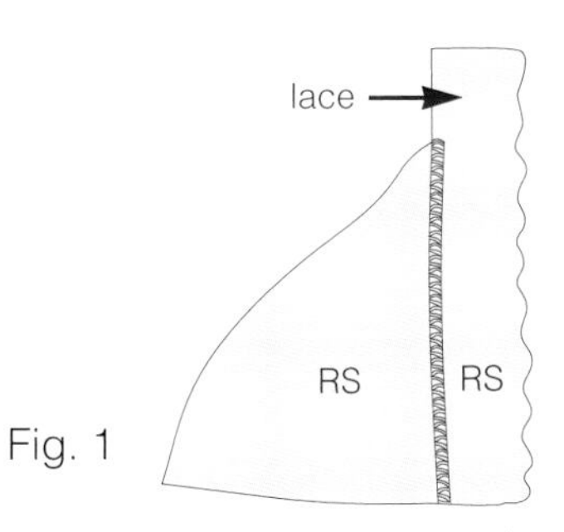

Fig. 1

3. With WS together, pin lace to the inner edge of the bra cup. Sew using **flatlocking with metallic thread or floss** and stitch length 2, keeping lace at the bottom. (Fig. 1).

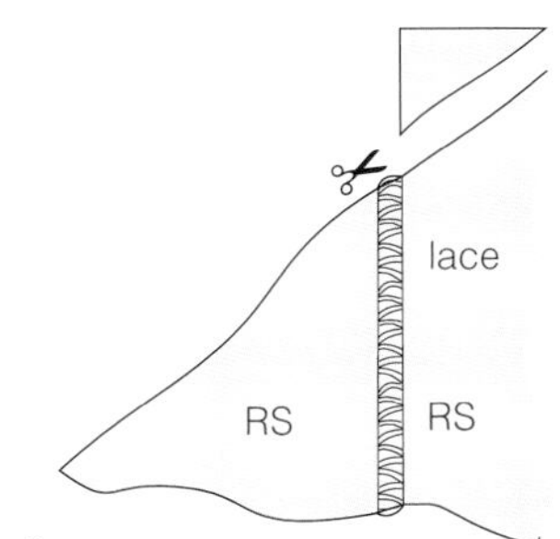

Fig. 2

4. Lay bra cup flat and cut excess lace from the top, following the bra cup underarm line (Fig. 2).

5. Repeat for the other cup.

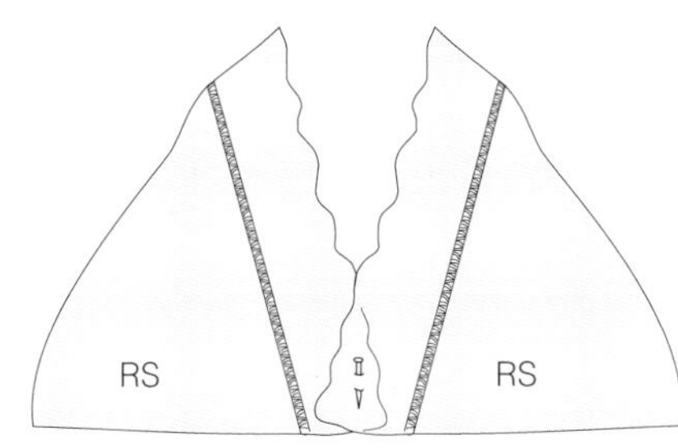

Fig. 3

6. Overlap lace front and pin to secure (Fig. 3).

7. Cut leg elastic for underarms in half, approximately 70-75 cm (28-30 in) long.

8. Measure underarm of the bra cup and insert a pin into elastic at three-quarters of this measurement. The rest of the elastic will be used for the straps and is measured later when the bra is fitted on (Fig. 4).

9. With RS together, start sewing from bottom of bra to shoulder.

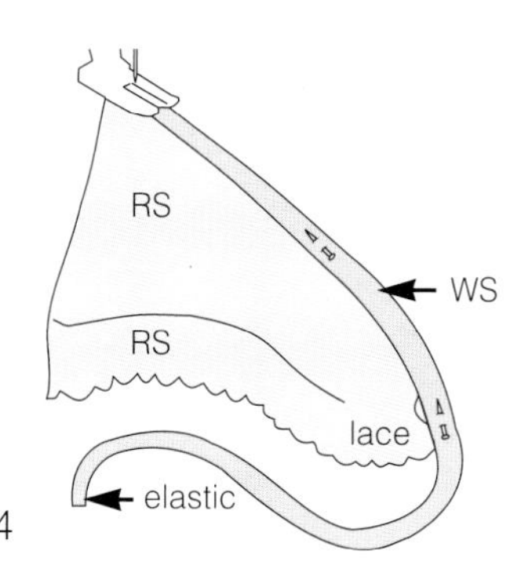

Fig. 4

Place elastic on top of fabric. Insert fabric and elastic into overlocker; secure the elastic by sewing a few stitches using three-thread overlocking and stitch length 3-3½. Divide elastic into two equal parts from pin marking on elastic (Fig. 4).

10. **Pin elastic to fabric, matching up the pins.**

11. Continue sewing, attaching elastic to fabric. Hold fabric and elastic in front and at the back; keep elastic next to blade, cutting 1 mm (1/16 in) off the fabric (Fig. 7, p. 24).

12. Measure under bust and cut waist elastic to three-quarters of under bust measurement.

13. With RS together, join ends of **elastic together to form a circle** (p. 9). Sew using three-thread overlocking; stitch length 2 (Fig. 9, p. 24).

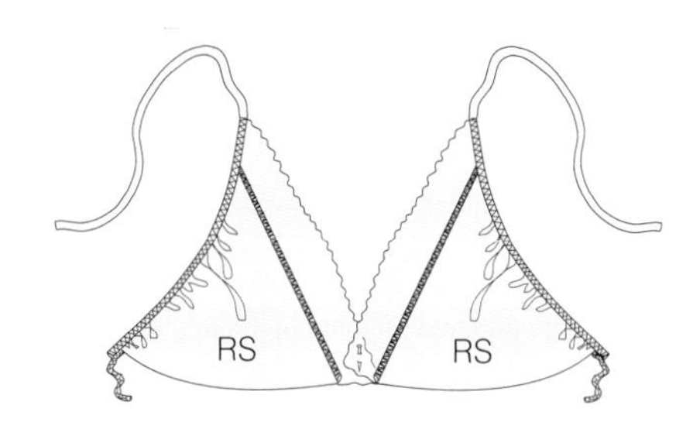

Fig. 5

14. **Quarter pin mark** elastic. Fold bra in half and mark centre front. With RS together, pin bra to waist elastic, matching the side pins with underarm the elastic of bra, and bra centre front mark with quarter pin marks of elastic (Fig. 5).

15. Sew the bra to the elastic. Keeping the bra on top, sew the elastic to the bra in front only, using three-thread overlocking and stitch length 3-3½.

16. Determine length of bra straps; cut excess leg elastic off

17. Position leg elastic for straps on WS of the back elastic between the side and quarter pins.

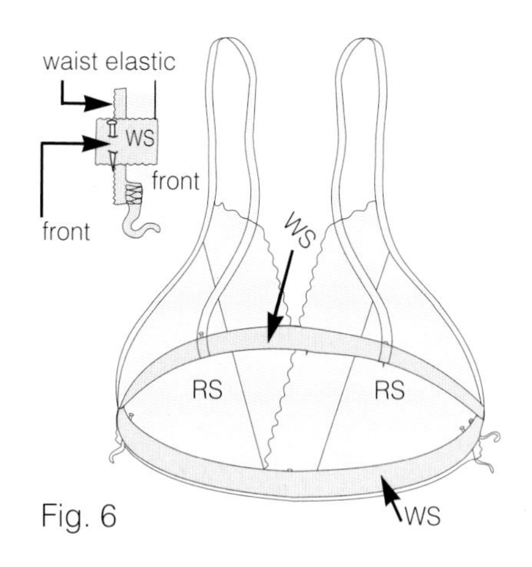

Fig. 6

18. Sew leg elastic to elastic using the sewing machine and zig-zag stitch (Fig. 6).

19. Secure all loose ends by hand or with stitch sealant.

20. Position bows or roses on front and sew on by hand.

BRA WITH 14 CM WIDE STRETCH LACE

REQUIREMENTS
1.5-1.6 m x 14 cm-wide (⅝ yd x 5½ in) stretch lace for bra cups and under bust
1-1.2 m x 1 cm-wide (1 yd x ½ in) leg elastic for straps
Matching polyester cotton thread
Floss
Pre-made bows or roses for decoration (see page 18)
Stitch sealant (see page 19)

SEAM ALLOWANCE
6 mm (¼ in) on all seams

STITCHES
Zig-zag stitch, width 1 and length 2
Three-thread overlocking

PATTERNS
Patterns 38, 39, 40 and 41

METHOD
1. Enlarge the pattern pieces on page 84 onto graph paper and cut out.

2. Pin pattern piece onto stretch lace elastic and cut out 1 x back band (on fold), 1 x front band (on fold), 2 x centre cup and 2 x side cup.

3. With RS together, pin centre and side cup together, and sew using three-thread overlocking and stitch length 2-2½(Fig. 7).

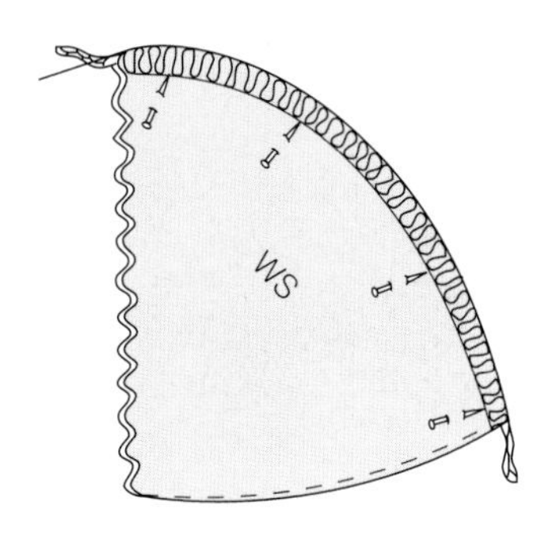

Fig. 7

4. Repeat for the other cup.

5. With RS together, pin cup to front band together and sew side seams using three-thread overlocking and stitch length 2-2½ (Fig. 8).

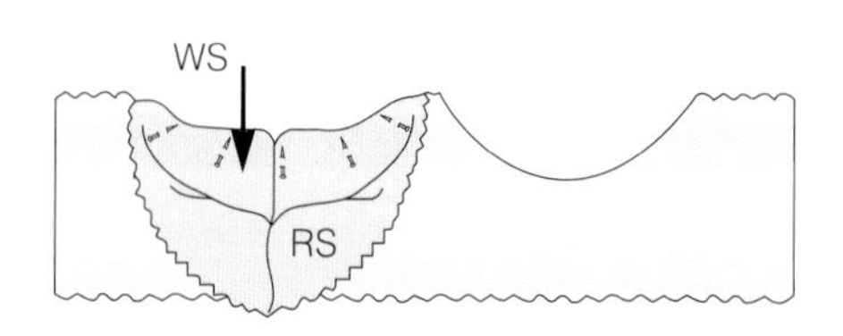

Fig. 8

6. Repeat for the other side.

7. With RS together, pin front and back band together and sew side

BRA, P.40, BRA, P. 42, HIGH-CUT PANTIES, P. 30, AND BRA TOP, P. 41

seams using three-thread overlocking and stitch length 2-2½.

8. Determine length of bra straps. Cut leg elastic to this measurement. Cut two straps.

9. Pin mark centre back and sides.

10. Pin front straps to WS of top of both bra cups, and back sraps to WS of stretch lace elastic between centre and side marks.

11. Sew back straps on using sewing machine and zig-zag stitch. Sew front straps on by hand.

12. Secure all loose ends by hand or with stitch sealant.

13. Position bows or roses on the front and sew on by hand.

BRA TOP WITH NYLON LACE OR STRETCH LACE ELASTIC

REQUIREMENTS
40 cm (16 in) T-shirt fabric, Lycra or stretch lace
70-75 cm x 4 cm-wide (¾ yd x 1½ in) stretch lace elastic or nylon lace for cups
.2 m x 1 cm-wide (2¼ yd x ½ in) leg elastic for underarms and back neckline
70-80 cm x 2 cm-wide (¾ yd x ¾ in) waist elastic for under bust
Matching polyeser cotton thread
Metallic thread or floss
Pre-made bows or roses for decoration (see page 18)
Stitch sealant (see page 19)

SEAM ALLOWANCE
6 mm (¼ in) on all seams

STITCHES
Flatlocking with metallic thread or floss

Three-thread overlocking

PATTERNS
Patterns 35 and 37

METHOD
1. Enlarge the pattern pieces on page 83 onto the graph paper and cut them out.

2. Pin pattern pieces onto the fabric and cut out 1 x back (on fold) and 2 x front.

3. With WS together, pin lace to the inner edge of bra cup.

4. Sew the lace to the bra cup using **flatlocking with metallic thread or floss** and stitch length 2, keeping the lace at the bottom (Fig. 9).

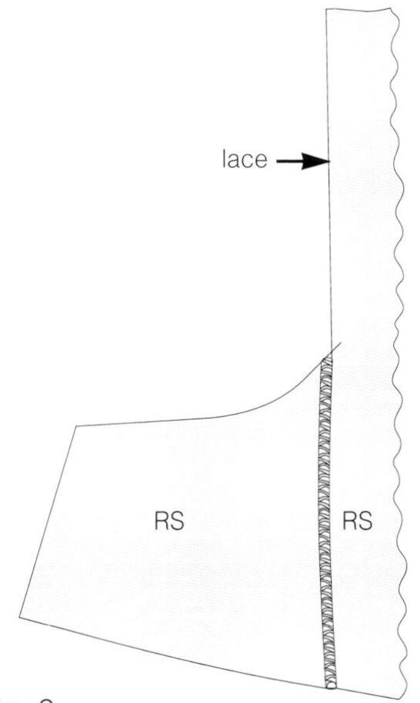

Fig. 9

5. Repeat for the other cup.

6. Overlap the lace and pin to secure (Fig. 3, p. 39).

7. Measure back neckline and cut the leg elastic to three-quarters of this measurement.

8. With RS of elastic and fabric together, sew leg elastic to back neckline. Place elastic on top of fabric, insert fabric and elastic into overlocker and secure elastic by sewing a few stitches using three-thread overlocking and stitch length 3-3½.

9. **Quarter pin mark** back neckline and elastic (Fig. 6, p. 24). Pin elastic to fabric, matching up the pins.

10. Continue sewing, attaching elastic to fabric. Hold the elastic next to the blade, cutting 1 mm (1/16 in) off the fabric (Fig. 7, p. 24).

11. With RS together, pin and sew shoulder seams using three-thread overlocking and stitch length 2-2½.

12. Measure front and back underarm opening and cut leg elastic to three-quarters of this measurement.

13. With RS together, place leg elastic on top of fabric, insert fabric and elastic into overlocker, and secure the elastic by sewing a few stitches using three-thread overlocking and stitch length 3-3½.

14. **Quarter pin mark** underarm and elastic. Pin elastic to fabric, matching up the pins (Fig. 4, p. 40).

15. With RS together, pin and sew the side seams together, using three-thread overlocking and stitch length 2-2½.

16. Measure under bust, and cut waist elastic to three-quarters of this measurement.

17. With RS together, join ends of waist **elastic to form a circle** (p. 9); sew using three-thread overlocking, stitch length 2 (Fig. 9, p. 24).

18. **Quarter pin mark** bra top and waist elastic (Fig. 10, p. 24). With RS to-gether, pin elastic to bra top, matching up the pins.

19. Keeping elastic on top, sew waist elastic to bra top using three-thread overlocking and stitch length 3-3½ (Fig. 6, p. 40).

20. Secure all loose ends by hand or with stitch sealant.

21. Position bows or roses on front and sew on by hand.

BRA IN T-SHIRT FABRIC WITH 14 CM WIDE STRETCH LACE ELASTIC

REQUIREMENTS
15 cm (6 in) T-shirt fabric
80 cm x 14 cm-wide (7/8 yd x 5½ in) stretch lace elastic
1.3-1.5 m x 1 cm-wide (3/8 yd x ½ in) leg elastic for bra cup and straps
Matching polyester cotton thread
Floss
Pre-made bows or roses for decoration (see page 18)
Stitch sealant (see page 19)

SEAM ALLOWANCE
6 mm (¼ in) on all seams

STITCHES
Zig-zag stitch, width 1 and length 2
Three-thread overlocking

PATTERNS
Patterns 38, 39, 40 and 41

METHOD
1. Enlarge the pattern pieces on page 84 onto graph paper and cut out.

2. Pin pattern pieces onto fabric: cut out 2 x centre cups, 2 x side cups. Pin pattern pieces onto stretch lace elastic: cut out 1 x back band (on fold), 1 x front band (on fold).

3. With RS together, pin centre cup and side cup together. Sew using three-thread overlocking, stitch length 2 - 2½ Repeat for other cup.

4. Measure inner edge of centre cup and cut leg elastic to three-quarters of this measurement.

5. With RS together, place leg elastic on top of fabric, insert fabric and elastic into overlocker, and secure elastic by sewing a few stitches using three-thread overlocking and stitch length 3-3½. Divide the bra cup and elastic into two equal parts. Pin elastic to fabric, matching up the pins.

6. Continue sewing, attaching elastic to fabric. Hold elastic next to blade, cutting 1 mm (1/16 in) off fabric (Fig. 7, p. 24). Repeat for the other side.

7. Measure side cup edge. Mark leg elastic for the underarms and straps with a pin at three-quarters of this measurement. Cut leg elastic about 75 cm (30 in) long. Cut two straps.

8. With RS together, place leg elastic on top, insert fabric and elastic into overlocker. Starting at bottom of bra, secure elastic by sewing a few stitches using three-thread overlocking, stitch length 3-3½. Divide bra cup and elastic into two equal parts; pin elastic to fabric to marked pin.

9. Continue sewing, attaching elastic to fabric. Hold elastic next to the blade, cutting 1 mm (1/16 in) off fabric (Fig. 7, p. 24). Repeat for other side.

10. With RS together, pin cup to front band; sew using three-thread overlocking and stitch length 2-2½. Repeat for the other side.

11. With RS together, pin front and back band together and sew side seams using three-thread overlocking and stitch length 2-2½.

12. Determine length of straps. Cut leg elastic this length. Cut two straps.

13. Quarter pin mark band.

14. Pin front straps to WS of both bra cups, and back straps to WS of stretch lace elastic between centre and side quarter pin marks.

15. Sew back straps on using sewing machine and zig-zag stitch. Sew front straps on by hand.

16. Secure all loose ends by hand or with stitch sealant.

17. Position bows or roses on the front and sew on by hand.

CROPPED TOP WITH LEG ELASTIC

REQUIREMENTS
- 40 cm (16 in) T-shirt fabric, Lycra or stretch lace
- 2 m x 1 cm-wide (2¼ yds x ½ in) leg elastic for underarms and neckline
- 70 80 cm x 2-5 cm-wide (¾ yd x ¾-2 in) waist elastic or stretch lace elastic for under bust
- Matching polyester cotton thread
- Floss
- Pre-made bows or roses for decoration (see page 18)
- Stitch sealant (see page 19)

SEAM ALLOWANCE
6 mm (¼ in) on all seams

STITCHES
Three-thread overlocking

PATTERNS
Patterns 42 and 43

METHOD
1. Enlarge the pattern pieces on page 85 onto graph paper and cut out.

2. Pin pattern pieces onto fabric and cut out 1 x back (on fold) and 1 x front (on fold).

3. With RS together, sew front to back at one shoulder seam using three-thread overlocking and stitch length 2-2½.

4. Measure back and front neckline and cut elastic to three-quarters of this measurement.

5. With RS together, sew the leg elastic to the back neckline. Place the elastic on top of the fabric, insert fabric and elastic into overlocker and secure elastic by sewing a few stitches using three-thread overlocking and stitch length 3-3½.

6. **Quarter pin mark** back neckline and elastic (Fig. 6, p. 24). Pin elastic to fabric, matching up the pins.

7. Continue sewing, attaching elastic to fabric. Hold the elastic next to the blade, cutting 1 mm (1/16 in) off the fabric (Fig. 7, p. 24).

8. With RS together, pin and sew other shoulder seam using three-thread overlocking and stitch length 2-2½.

9. Measure the underarm openings and cut leg elastic to three-quarters of this measurement.

10. With RS together, place leg elastic on top of fabric, insert fabric and elastic into overlocker, and secure elastic by sewing a few stitches using three-thread overlocking and stitch length 3-3½.

11. **Quarter pin mark** armholes and elastic (Fig. 6, p. 24). Pin elastic to fabric, matching up the pins.

12. Continue sewing, attaching elastic to fabric. Hold the elastic next to the blade, cutting 1 mm (1/16 in) off the fabric (Fig. 7, p. 24).

13. With RS together, pin and then sew the side seams together, using three-thread overlocking and stitch length 2 - 2½.

14. Measure under bust; cut elastic to three-quarters of this measurement.

15. With RS together, sew ends of **elastic together to form a circle** (p. 9) using three-thread overlocking and stitch length 2 (Fig. 9, p. 24).

16. **Quarter pin mark** top and elastic (Fig. 10, p. 24). With RS together, pin elastic to fabric, matching up pins.

17. Keeping the elastic on top, sew the elastic to top using three-thread overlocking and stitch length 3-3½ (Fig. 11, p. 24).

18. Secure all loose ends by hand or with stitch sealant.

19. Position bows or roses on the front and sew on by hand.

CROPPED TOPS WITH PLUSH AND LEG ELASTIC

CAMISOLES

Silky and feminine, a camisole can be worn as lingerie, or is the perfect garment for wearing under see-through tops. Or show a hint of camisole under a low-cut jacket. Although a camisole is usually worn at waist length, it can also be lengthened to the hip – the choice is up to you! If you prefer the longer option, use your top length measurement (see **Taking Measurements to Determine Size**, page 14).

DESIGNING AND MEASURING A CAMISOLE (Fig. 1)

It is very easy to design your own camisole. Draw a rectangle to the desired length. The width is determined by your bust measurement, plus 10 cm (4 in) to allow for extra movement. Include a seam allowance of 4 cm (1½ in), which gives 1 cm (½ in) seam allowance on either side. Fold pattern and cut in half for front and back.

Remember to allow extra if you use decorative stitching. The top and bottom edges can be finished off with lace or a decorative edging.

bust measurement + 10 cm (4 in) + 1 cm (½ in) + seam allowance

Fig. 1

CAMISOLE, P.44 AND CAMISOLE, P.45

CAMISOLE USING FLATLOCKING WITH RIBBON AND EMBROIDERY THREAD

REQUIREMENTS
- Non-stretch underwear fabric
- Length as measured
- Width as measured, adding 2-3 cm (¾-1¼ in) extra for flatlocking
- 80 cm-1 m x 4 cm-wide (⅞-1 yd x 1½ in) nylon edging lace for front decoration
- 1.3-1.5 m x 4-6 cm-wide (1½-1⅝ yd x 1½-2¼ in) nylon edging lace for lower edge
- 1 m x 1 cm-wide (1 yd x ½ in) leg elastic for straps OR pre-made straps (see page 18)
- 2½-3 m x 3-5 mm-wide (3-3¼ yd x ¼ in) satin ribbon
- Matching polyester cotton thread
- Embroidery thread
- Metallic thread
- Pre-made bows or roses for decoration (see page 18)
- Stitch sealant (see page 19)
- Marking pen

SEAM ALLOWANCE

1 cm (½ in) seam allowance on all seams

STITCHES

Zig-zag stitch, width 1 and length 2
Flatlocking with embroidery thread
Flatlocking over ribbon with metallic thread
Three-thread overlocking

METHOD

1. Design your own camisole (see **Designing and Measuring a Camisole**, page 44). Pin pattern pieces onto fabric and cut out 1 x back and 1 x front.

2. Draw lines with a marking pen on front (Fig. 2).

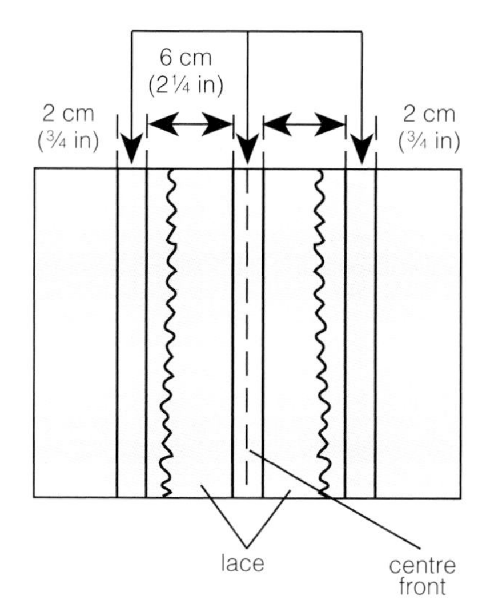

Fig. 2

3. Fold the fabric on lines marked ribbon with metallic thread, and pin the WS of the lace to RS of the camisole. Using the overlocker sew using **flatlocking over ribbon with metallic thread**, keeping the lace at the bottom and the fabric on top.

4. Sew using overlocker and **flatlocking embroidery thread** on remaining lines marked with embroidery thread.

5. With RS together, sew one side seam together using three-thread overlocking, stitch length 2-2½.

6. With WS together, pin lace to camisole along bottom edge of camisole. Sew using overlocker and **flatlocking over ribbon with metallic thread**, keeping lace at bottom.

7. Sew along top edge using overlocker and three-thread overlocking, stitch length 1-1½.

8. With RS together, pin and sew other side seam together using three-thread overlocking, stitch length 2-2½.

9. Position straps on the front and back top edges and sew using sewing machine and zig-zag stitch.

10. Secure loose ends by hand or with stitch sealant.

11. Position bows or roses on the front and sew on by hand.

CAMISOLE WITH EMBROIDERY THREAD

REQUIREMENTS
Non-stretch underwear fabric
Length as measured
Width as measured, adding 5 cm (2 in) extra for flatlocking
2.7-3 m x 4-6 cm-wide (3-3¼ yd x 1½-2¼ in) nylon edging lace for top and lower edges of camisole
1 m x 1 cm-wide(1 yd x ½ in) leg elastic for straps or pre-made straps (see page 18)
Matching polyester cotton thread
Floss
Embroidery thread
Metallic thread
Pre-made bows or roses for decoration (see page 18)
Marking pen
9 x pearl shape beads
Stitch sealant (see page 19)

SEAM ALLOWANCE
1 cm (½ in) seam allowance on all seams

STITCHES
Zig-zag stitch, width 1 and length 2
Flatlocking with embroidery thread
Three-thread overlocking

METHOD

1. Design your own camisole (see **Designing and Measuring a Camisole**, page 44).

2. Pin pattern pieces to fabric and cut out 1 x back and 1 x front.

3. Draw in lines with a marking pen on front (Fig.3). Sew using overlocker and **flatlocking with embroidery thread**, along the marked lines.

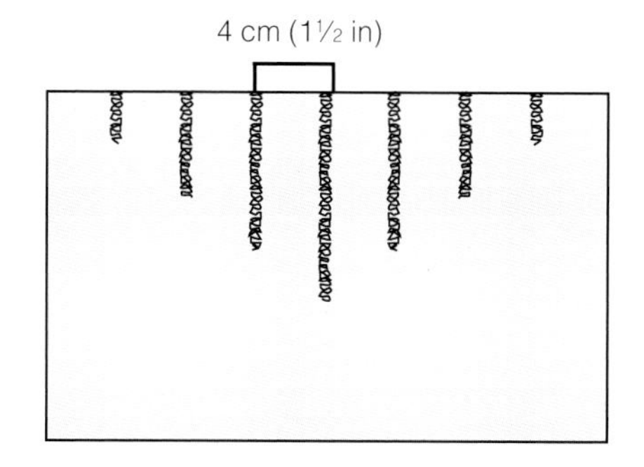

Fig. 3

4. Chain off with a chain of 10-15 cm (4-6 in) long.

5. Sew pearl beads on by hand to the end of each chain of stitches.

6. With RS together, sew one side seam together using three-thread overlocking, stitch length 2-2½.

7. Pin WS of lace to WS of top and bottom edges of camisole.

8. Sew using overlocker and **flatlocking with embroidery thread**, keeping the lace at the bottom.

9. With the RS together, pin and sew the other side seam together using three-thread overlocking and stitch length 2-2½.

10. Position straps on the front and back top edges and sew using sewing machine and zig-zag stitch.

11. Secure all loose ends by hand or with stitch sealant.

12. Position bows or roses on the front and sew on by hand.

CAMISOLE WITH PIN TUCKS

REQUIREMENTS
Non-stretch underwear fabric
Length as measured
Width as measured
40 cm (16 in) x desired length for inset for pin tucks
1.3-1.5 m x 4 cm-wide (1½-1⅝ yd x 1½ in) nylon edging lace for top edge
1.3-1.5 m x 6 cm-wide (1½-1⅝ yd x 2¼ in) nylon edging lace for lower edge
1 m x 1 cm-wide (1 yd x ½ in) leg elastic for straps or pre-made straps (see page 18)
Matching polyester cotton thread
Floss
Metallic thread
Pre-made bows or roses for decoration (see page 19)
Stitch sealant (see page 18)
Marking pen
4 mm (¼ in) round beads

SEAM ALLOWANCE
1 cm (½ in) seam allowance on all seams

STITCHES
Zig-zag stitch, width 1 and length 2
Flatlocking with floss
Three-thread overlocking with metallic thread
Three-thread overlocking

METHOD
1. Design your own camisole (see **Designing and Measuring a Camisole**, page 44). Pin pattern pieces to fabric.

2. Cut out 1 x back and 1 x front. Cut out a piece of fabric 40 cm (16 in) x desired length for pin tucks.

3. Draw lines with a marking pen 3 cm (1¼ in) apart on inset piece of fabric (Fig.4).

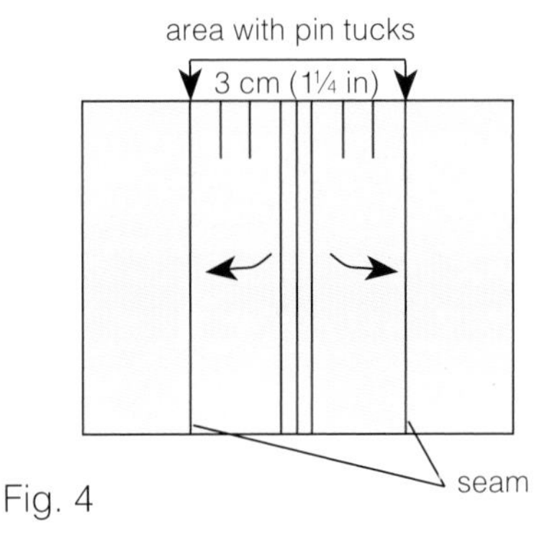

Fig. 4

4. Fold along marked lines and sew pin tucks using **three-thread overlocking with metallic thread**.

5. Mark centre front on front. Place inset piece on centre front of camisole. Using a marking pen, draw a line on either side of inset piece. Remove inset piece from camisole (Fig. 5).

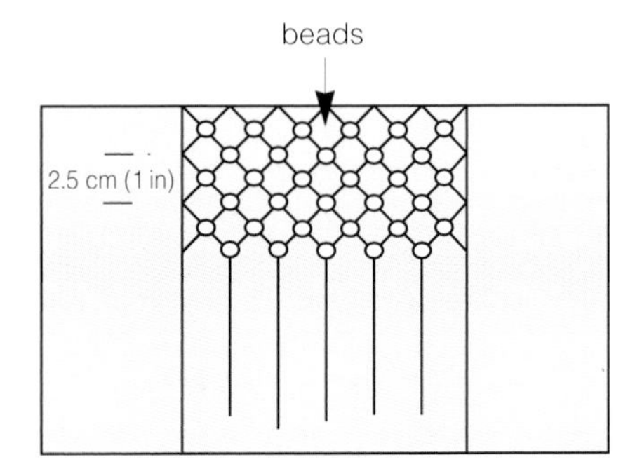

Fig. 5

6. Measure 1 cm (½ in) inwards on either side and mark. Cut front on these lines.

7. Pin inset piece to cut edges of front and sew with RS together using three-thread overlocking and stitch length 2-2½.

8. With RS together, pin and sew one side seam together using three-thread overlocking and stitch length 2-2½.

9. With WS together, pin the edging lace to the top and bottom edges of the camisole, and sew using **flatlocking with floss**, keeping the lace at the bottom.

10. Sew beads on inset piece sewing two stitchings together 2.5 cm (1 in) apart in length, pulling the alternate stitching together with a bead.

NOTE: Always use spool caps when sewing with polyester cotton thread. These will ensure that the reel unwinds evenly which, in turn, will ensure a more even tension.

CAMISOLE WITH PIN TUCKS

11. Position straps on the front and the back top edges and sew using sewing machine and zig-zag stitch.

12. Secure all loose ends by hand or with stitch sealant.

13. Position bows or roses on the front and sew on by hand.

CAMISOLE WITH LACE TRIM

REQUIREMENTS
Non-stretch underwear fabric
Length as measured
Width as measured
4 m x 4-5 cm-wide (4⅜ yd x 1½-2 in) nylon edging lace for top and bottom edges, and front decoration
1 m x 1 cm-wide (1 yd x ½ in) nylon elastic for straps or pre-made straps (see page 18)
Floss
Embroidery thread
Matching polyester cotton thread
Stitch sealant (see page 19)
Marking pen

SEAM ALLOWANCE
1 cm (½ in) seam allowance on all seams

STITCHES
Zig-zag stitch, width 1 and length 2
Flatlocking with embroidery thread
Wide flatlocking with embroidery thread
Three-thread overlocking

METHOD
1. Design your own camisole (see **Designing and Measuring a Camisole**, page 44). Pin pattern pieces onto fabric and cut out 1 x back and 1 x front.

2. With WS together, join lace for front decoration at straight edges, using overlocker and **wide flatlocking with embroidery thread**.

3. Using a marking pen, divide front panel into quarters (Fig. 6).

FRENCH KNICKERS WITH NARROW HEM, P. 50, CAMISOLES, P. 48, BIKINI, P. 33 AND CAMISOLE WITH LACE TRIM

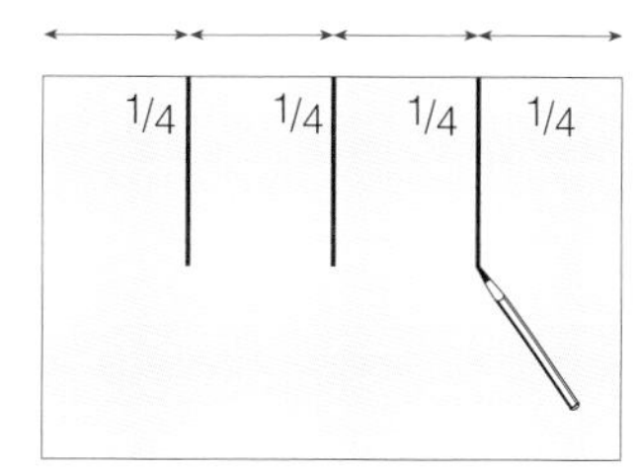

Fig. 6

4. With WS of lace on RS of fabric, pin lace on top edge, scalloped edge at the top. Start 5 cm (2 in) down the side seam, and pin lace to the top edge at the quarter mark (Fig. 7).

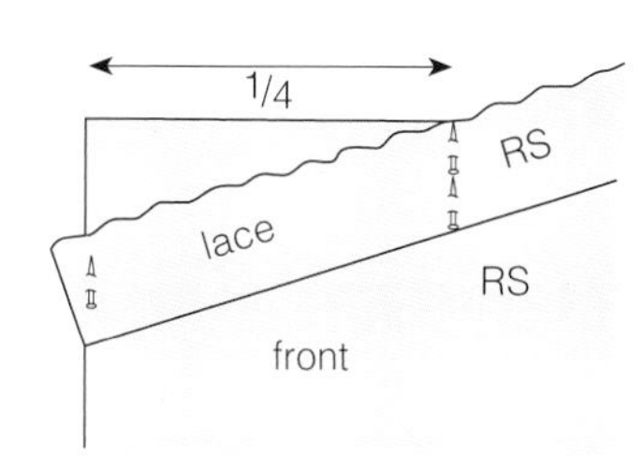

Fig. 7

5. Fold lace back on starting lace, folding the lace on the quarter mark (Fig. 8). Pin.

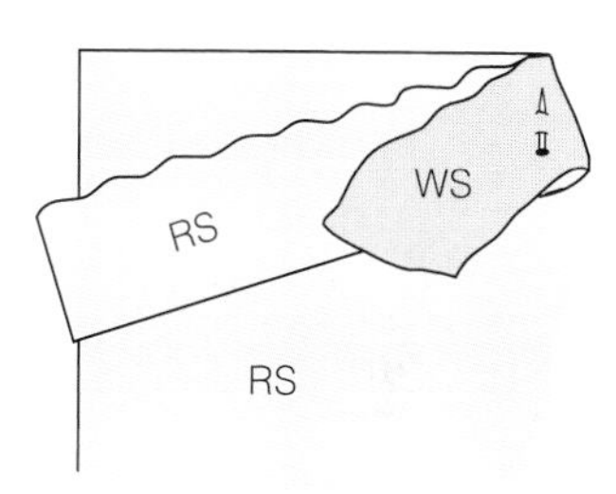

Fig. 8

6. Fold lace back and continue to pin lace along the top edge, pinning lace to halfway mark (Fig. 9).

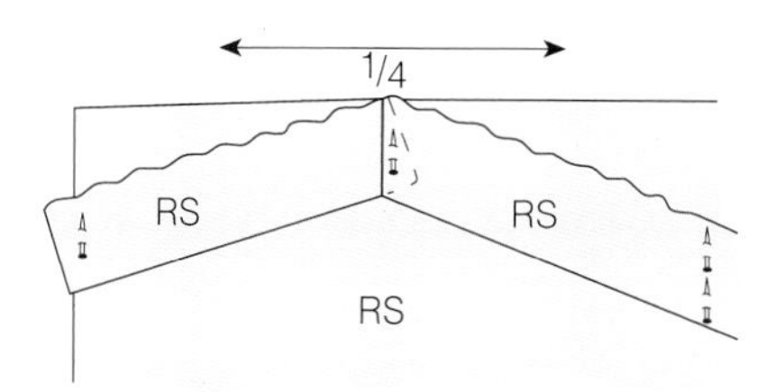

Fig. 9

7. Continue to pin lace, repeating steps 5 and 6.

8. Using sewing machine and zig-zag stitch, sew lace to front along bottom edge of lace and on quarter marks, securing the folds (Fig. 10).

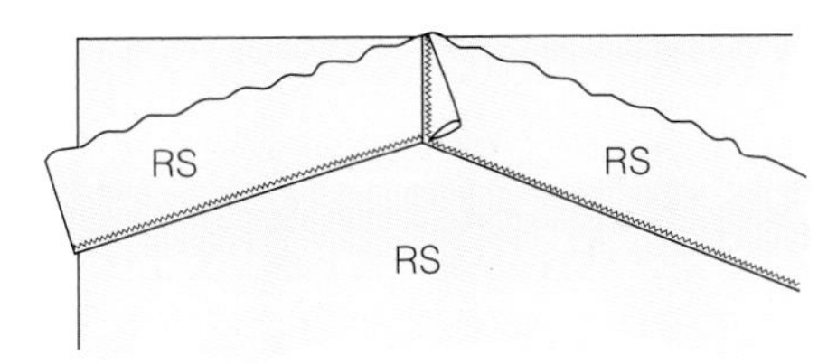

Fig. 10

9. Using a small pair of scissors, cut the fabric away behind the lace next to the zig-zag stitch. Also cut the lace triangle away at each of the quarter marks (Fig. 11).

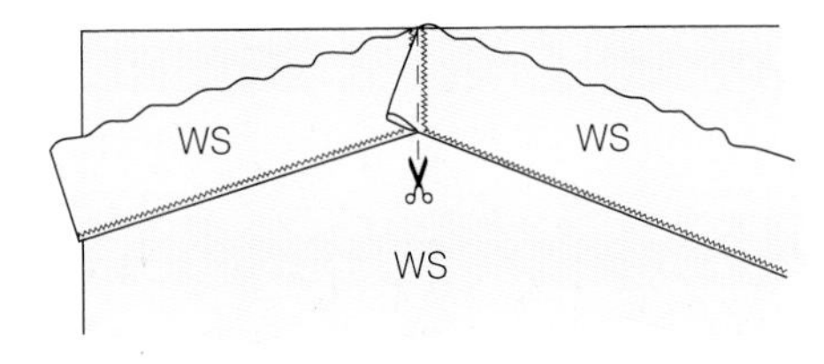

Fig. 11

10. Start 5 cm (2 in) down on back panel. Pin WS of lace to RS of fabric.

11. Using the sewing machine and zig-zag stitch, sew lace to back along bottom edge of lace.

12. Using a small pair of scissors, cut fabric away behind lace.

13. With RS together, pin the front and the back together at one side seam and sew together using overlocker and three-thread overlocking and stitch length 2-2½.

14. With WS together, pin lace to bottom edge of camisole and sew together using overlocker and **flatlocking with embroidery thread**.

15. With RS together, pin other side seam together, and sew using overlocker and three-thread overlocking and stitch length 2-2½.

16. Position the straps on the front and back top edges and sew on by hand or with sewing machine and zig-zag stitch.

17. Secure all loose ends by hand or with stitch sealant.

18. Position bows or roses on the front and sew on by hand.

CAMISOLE WITH NARROW HEM

REQUIREMENTS
Non-stretch underwear fabric
Length as measured
Width as measured, adding 2-3 cm (¾-1¼ in) for pin tucks
4 m x 5 cm-wide (4¼ yd x 2 in) nylon edging lace for bottom edge, and front decoration
1 m x 1 cm-wide (1 yd x ½ in) leg elastic for straps or pre-made straps (see page 18)
Matching polyester cotton thread
Floss
Embroidery thread
Stitch sealant (see page 19)
Marking pen

SEAM ALLOWANCE
1 cm (½ in) seam allowance on all seams

STITCHES
Zig-zag stitch, width 1 and length 2
Flatlocking with floss
Narrow hem with floss
Three-thread overlocking

METHOD
1. Design your own camisole (see **Designing and Measuring a Camisole**, page 44). Pin pattern pieces onto fabric and cut out 1 x back and 1 x front.

2. Using a marking pen, draw lines on front panel (Fig. 12).

3. On lines on either side of centre front, pin WS of lace to RS of front.

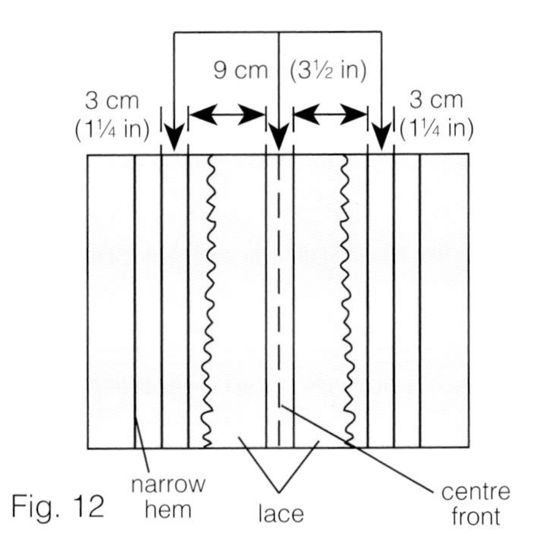

Fig. 12

4. Sew lace to front panel using overlocker and **flatlocking with floss,** keeping the lace at the bottom.

5. On remaining lines, fold remaining fabric on lines and using overlocker, sew **narrow hem with floss**.

6. With RS together, pin and sew one side seam together using overlocker and three-thread overlocking and stitch length 2-2½.

7. With WS together, pin the lace to the bottom edge of camisole and sew using overlocker and **flatlocking with floss**, keeping lace at bottom.

8. Using overlocker and **narrow hem with floss**, sew along top edge of camisole.

9. With RS together, pin and sew the other side seam together using overlocker and three-thread overlocking, stitch length 2-2½.

10. Position the straps on front and back top edges and sew on by hand or with a sewing machine and zig-zag stitch.

11. Secure all loose ends by hand or with stitch sealant.

12. Position bows or roses on the front and sew on by hand.

CAMI-KNICKERS

Cami-knickers are loose-cut and silky, an all-in-one garment combining a camisole and French knickers.

REQUIREMENTS
Cut on bias
115 cm (45 in): 1.8-2 m (2-2¼ yd) non-stretch underwear fabric
150 cm (60 in): 1.1-1.3 m (1⅕-1½ yd) non-stretch underwear fabric
3.2-3.3 m x 4-6 cm-wide (3½-3¾ yds x 1½-2¼ in) nylon lace
70-80 cm x 6 mm-wide (¾ yd x ¼ in) nylon elastic
Matching polyester cotton thread
Floss
Pre-made bows for decoration (see page 18)
Stitch sealant (see page 19)
Marking pen

SEAM ALLOWANCE
1 cm (½ in) on all seams

STITCHES
Zig-zag stitch, width 1 and length 2
Overcasting stitch, width 4 and length 2½
Three-thread overlocking

PATTERNS
Combine French knickers patterns 44 and 45 with camisole pattern, page 44

METHOD
1. Englarge pattern pieces on page 86 and 87 and cut out. For camisole: length = waist measurement, width = bust measurement + 10 cm (4 in).

2. Pin pattern pieces onto fabric and cut out 2 x back and 2 x front for French knickers, and 1 x back and 1 x front for camisole.

3. With RS together, pin and sew centre front and back seams together, using three-thread overlocking, stitch length 2-2½.

4. On top edge of front and back panels, pin WS of lace onto RS of fabric (Figs. 8 and 9, p. 47).

5. Sew lace to top edge of fabric using sewing machine and zig-zag stitch (Fig. 10, p. 47).

6. Cut the fabric away behind lace and trim corners of lace on quarter pin marks (Fig. 11, p. 47).

7. With RS together, pin and sew the side seams together using three-thread overlocking and stitch length 2-2½.

8. Pin WS of lace to RS of fabric at lower edge of front and back panels.

9. Sew lace to lower edge, using sewing machine and zig-zag stitch.

10. With RS together, sew front panel to back panel at crotch seam, using three-thread overlocking and stitch length 2-2½.

11. Mark the waistline of the cami-knickers with a marking pen.

12. Measure waist and take a firm waist measurement. Cut nylon elastic to this measurement.

13. **Quarter pin mark** the waist and elastic. Pin the elastic to WS of fabric, matching up the pins.

14. Sew elastic to waist, using the sewing machine and overcasting stitch, overlapping the ends of elastic at the side seam.

15. Secure all loose ends by hand or with stitch sealant.

16. Position bows on front panel and secure by hand.

FRENCH KNICKERS WITH LACE, P. 50

FRENCH KNICKERS

Loose-cut and sensual, French knickers are perfect for wearing under skirts or dresses. It's also a good idea to wear them over suspenders, as they hide any bumps that may show.

FRENCH KNICKERS WITH LACE

REQUIREMENTS
115 cm or 150 cm (45 or 60 in):
80-90 cm (⅞-1 yd) non-stetch underwear fabric
2 m x 2 - 4 cm-wide (2¼ yds x ¾ -1½ in) nylon lace
70-80 cm x 2-3 cm-wide (¾ yd x ¾-1¼ in) waist elastic
Matching polyester cotton thread
Floss
Pre-made bows for decoration (see page 18)
Stitch sealant (see page 19)

SEAM ALLOWANCE
1 cm seam (½ in) on all seams

STITCHES
Flatlocking using floss
Three-thread overlocking

PATTERNS
Patterns 44 and 45

METHOD
1. Enlarge pattern pieces on pages 86 and 87 onto graph paper and cut out.

2. Pin pattern pieces onto fabric and cut out 2 x back and 2 x front.

3. With RS together, pin front panel to back panel and sew inner leg seam using three-thread overlocking and stitch length 2-2½.

4. Repeat for the other leg.

5. With WS of lace and fabric together, sew lace to side edges of front and back panels, using **flatlocking with floss**, keeping lace at bottom.

6. With WS of the lace and the fabric together, sew the lace to the bottom edges of the front and the back panels, using **flatlocking with floss**, and keeping the lace at the bottom.

7. With RS together, pin crotch seam together and sew using three-thread overlocking and stitch length 2-2½.

8. Overlap the front side edges 3 cm (1¼ in) over the back side edges and pin together.

9. Measure waist and take a firm waist measurement. Cut waist elastic to this measurement.

10. **Quarter pin mark** the fabric and the waist elastic. With RS together, pin elastic to the waist, matching up the pins.

11. Keeping the elastic on top of the fabric, sew them together, using three-thread overlocking and stitch length 3-3½.

12. Secure all loose ends by hand or with stitch sealant.

13. Position bows on front and sew on by hand.

FRENCH KNICKERS WITH A NARROW HEM

REQUIREMENTS
115 cm or 150 cm (45 or 60 in):
80-90 cm (⅞-1 yd) non-stretch underwear fabric
70-80 cm x 2-3 cm-wide (¾ yd x ¾-1¼ in) waist elastic
Matching polyester cotton thread
Floss
Pre-made bows for decoration (see page 18)
Stitch sealant (see page 19)

SEAM ALLOWANCE
1 cm seam (½ in) on all seams

STITCHES
Narrow hem with floss
Three-thread overlocking

PATTERNS
Patterns 44 and 45

METHOD
1. Enlarge pattern pieces on pages 86 and 87 onto graph paper and cut out.

2. Pin pattern pieces onto fabric and cut out 2 x back and 2 x front.

3. With RS together, pin front panels and sew inner leg seam using three-thread overlocking, stitch length 2-2½.

4. Repeat for the other leg.

5. Using overlocker and **narrow hem with floss**, finish side edges of front and back panel.

6. Using overlocker and **narrow hem with floss**, finish hem edges of front and back panels.

7. With RS together, pin crotch seam together and sew using three-thread overlocking and stitch length 2-2½.

8. Overlap the front side seam 3 cm (1¼ in) over the back side seam and pin. Repeat for other side.

9. Take a firm waist measurement and cut the waist elastic to this measurement.

10. **Quarter pin mark** fabric and waist elastic (Fig. 10, p. 24). With RS to-gether, pin elastic to waist, matching up the pins.

11. Keeping the elastic on top, sew together, using three-thread overlocking and stitch length 3-3½.

12. Secure all loose ends by hand or with stitch sealant.

13. Position bows on front and sew on by hand.

NOTE: Always sew slowly when using decorative thread to prevent it from snapping as this could damage the overlocker.

TEDDY

A teddy has high-cut legs, is fitted and is ideal for wearing under contoured clothing. The projects below are for styled and designer teddies.

STYLED TEDDY

REQUIREMENTS
- Stretch fabrics – stretch lace or Lycra
- 115 cm and 150 cm (45 and 60 in): 70-80 cm (¾ yd)
- 1.2-1.3 m x 4-6 cm-wide (1¼-1½ yd x 1½-2¼ in) stretch lace elastic for front neckline and front legs
- 1.7-1.8 m x 1.5-2 cm-wide (1½-2 yd x ½ - ¾ in) stretch lace elastic for back, armholes and straps
- 70 80 cm x 1 cm-wide (¾ yd x ½ in) leg elastic for legs
- 25 cm x 15 mm-wide (10 in x ½ in) satin or nylon ribbon
- Matching polyester cotton thread
- Floss
- Stitch sealant (see page 19)
- 2-3 poppers or snap fasteners

SEAM ALLOWANCE
6 mm (¼ in) on all seams

STITCHES
Zig-zag stitch, width 1 and length 2
Three-thread overlocking

PATTERNS
Patterns 46, 47, 48 and 49

METHOD

1. Enlarge pattern pieces on pages 88 and 89 onto graph paper and cut out.

2. Pin pattern pieces onto fabric and cut out 2 x back, 1 x centre front (on fold) and 2 x side front.

3. With RS together, pin and sew centre back seam together, using three-thread overlocking and stitch length 2-2½.

4. With RS together, pin side front panel to centre front panel and sew seam together using three-thread overlocking and stitch length 2-2½. Repeat for the other side.

5. On front neckline and front legs, pin WS of stretch lace elastic to RS of fabric. Sew elastic to fabric using sewing machine and zig-zag stitch.

6. Using a small pair of scissors, cut fabric away behind lace.

7. Lay teddy on a flat surface and measure back leg opening. Cut leg elastic to three-quarters of this measurement.

8. With RS together, and elastic on top of fabric, insert into overlocker and secure elastic by sewing a few stitches using three-thread overlocking, stitch length 3-3½. Divide leg and elastic in two equal parts. Pin elastic to fabric, matching up pins.

9. Continue sewing, attaching elastic to fabric, holding the front and back. Keep elastic next to blade, cutting 1 mm (1/16 in) off fabric (Fig. 7, p. 24).

10. With RS together, pin and sew side seams together, using three-thread overlocking, stitch length 2-2½.

11. Lay teddy on a flat surface; measure armholes and back neckline. Cut leg elastic to three-quarters of this measurement, allowing extra for straps. The length of the straps can be determined when fitting on teddy.

12. Insert a pin into elastic where the three-quarter measurement is.

DESIGNER TEDDY, P. 52

13. With RS together, place elastic on top of the fabric. Insert into overlocker and secure elastic by sewing a few stitches using three-thread overlocking and stitch length 3-3½.

14. **Quarter pin mark** armholes, back neckline, and elastic (Fig. 6, p. 24). Pin elastic to fabric, matching up pins.

15. Continue sewing, attaching elastic to fabric. Hold the fabric and elastic in front and at the back. Keep the elastic next to the blade, cutting 1 mm (1/16 in) off fabric (Fig. 7, p. 24).

16. Determine length of straps and sew ends of elastic to back neckline edge using sewing machine, zig-zag stitch.

17. Fold raw edges of both crotch edges 1 cm (½ in) to WS and press. Pin ribbon on WS of both crotch edges, folding raw edges of ribbon in. Sew around edges of ribbon using sewing machine and zig-zag stitch.

18. Insert poppers or snap fasteners.

19. Secure all loose ends by hand or with stitch sealant.

DESIGNER TEDDY

REQUIREMENTS
Cut on bias
115 cm (45 in): 1-1.2 m (1-1¼ yd) non-stretch fabric
150 cm (60 in): 70 cm-1 m (¾-1 yd) non-stretch fabric
3.5-4 m x 4-6 cm-wide (3⅞-4¼ yd x 1½-2¼ in) galloon lace for front, front and back neckline, and straps
25 cm x 15 mm-wide (10 x ½ in) satin or nylon ribbon
Matching polyester cotton thread
Metallic thread or floss
Pre-made straps (see page 18)
Stitch sealant (see page 19)
3 poppers or snap fasteners
Pre-made bows for decorations (see page 18)
OPTIONAL: 1.5 m x 2 cm-wide (1 yd x ¾ in) nylon lace

SEAM ALLOWANCE
1 cm (½ in) on all seams

STITCHES
Straight stitch, length 2½
Zig-zag stitch, width 1 and length 2
Overcasting stitch, width 4 and length 1
Narrow hem with metallic thread or floss
Three-thread overlocking

OPTIONAL
Flatlocking with metallic thread or floss

PATTERNS
Patterns 50, 51 and 52

METHOD
1. Enlarge pattern pieces on pages 90 and 91 onto graph paper and cut out.

2. Pin pattern pieces onto fabric and cut out 2 x back, 1 x front (on fold) and 2 x flounce.

3. With RS together, pin and sew centre back seam together, using three-thread overlocking and stitch length 2-2½.

4. Join the galloon lace for front decoration using the sewing machine and overcasting stitch.

5. Pin WS of lace to RS of fabric on centre front.

6. Sew the lace to the front on either side using sewing machine and zig-zag stitch.

7. Using a small pair of scissors, cut fabric away behind lace.

8. Pin the WS of the lace to the RS of the fabric on the front and back of the neckline.

9. Sew the lace to the front and back neckline, sewing along the bottom edge of the lace using the sewing machine and zig-zag stitch.

10. Using a small pair of scissors, cut fabric away behind lace.

11. With RS together, pin and sew side seams together, using three-thread overlocking, stitch length 2-2½.

12. Using overlocker and **narrow hem with metallic thread or floss**, sew along edge of each flounce.

OPTIONAL
Pin WS of lace to RS of flounce edge and sew using **flatlocking with metallic thread or floss.**

13. With RS together, pin flounces to both leg openings, matching marks.

14. Sew flounces to leg openings using three-thread overlocking and stitch length 2-2½.

15. Fold the remaining raw edges of leg openings 5 mm (¼ in) to WS and sew using sewing machine and straight stitch.

16. Determine the length of the straps and sew onto the back neckline edge using the sewing machine and zig-zag stitch.

17. Fold raw edges of both crotch edges 1 cm (½ in) to WS and press. Pin the ribbon on WS of both crotch edges, folding the raw edges of the ribbon in.

18. Sew around edges of ribbon using sewing machine and zig-zag stitch.

19. Insert poppers or snap fasteners.

20. Secure all loose ends by hand or with stitch sealant

21. Position bows on front and sew on by hand.

NOTE: Never abuse your overlocker, as it can only respond when operated correctly. Do not let anyone else use your overlocker unless you or the dealer from whom you purchased your machine has shown that person how to use it correctly.

SLIPS

A full of half slip gives body and shape to your clothes.

FULL SLIP

REQUIREMENTS
Underwear fabric
When cut on bias:
115 cm (45 in): 1.5-1.8 m (1⅝-2 yd)
150 cm (60 in): 1.2-1.4 m (1¼-1½ yd)
3 m x 2-8 cm (3¼ yd x ¾-3¼ in) nylon lace
Matching polyster cotton thread
Floss
Pre-made straps or 70-80 cm x 1 cm wide (¾ yd x ½ in) leg elastic (see page 18)
Pre-made bows or roses for decoration (see page 18)
Stitch sealant (see page 19)

HALF SLIP AND HALF SLIP WITH SLIT, P. 54

SEAM ALLOWANCE
1 cm (½ in) on all seams

STITCHES
Zig-zag stitch, width 1 and length 2
Flatlocking with floss
Three-thread overlocking

PATTERNS
Patterns 53, 54 and 55

METHOD
1. Enlarge patterns pieces on pages 92 and 93 onto graph paper and cut out.

2. Pin pattern pieces to fabric and cut out 1 x back (on fold), 1 x front (on fold) and 2 x side front.

3. With RS together, pin and sew side fronts to either side of centre front, and pin and sew centre back seam together using three-thread overlocking and stitch length 2-2½.

4. Pin WS of lace onto RS of fabric on top edge of front and back panel, (Figs. 8 and 9, p. 47).

5. Sew along bottom edge of lace using sewing machine and zig-zag stitch (Fig. 10, p. 47).

6. Cut fabric away behind lace and trim corners of lace (Fig. 11, p. 47).

7. With RS together, pin and sew one side seam together using three-thread overlocking and stitch length 2-2½.

8. Pin WS of fabric and lace together at lower edge of slip .

9. Sew the lace to lower edge, using **flatlocking with floss**, keeping the lace at the bottom.

10. With RS together, pin and sew other side seam together, using three-thread overlocking and stitch length 2-2½.

11. Secure all loose ends by hand or with stitch sealant and sew roses and bows on by hand.

HALF SLIP

It is very easy to design your own half slip. The length of the slip will depend on the length of the garment you will be wearing it with.

1. Draw a rectangle.

2. Determine the required length of the slip.

3. The width of the slip is your hip measurement plus 10-15 cm (4-6 in) plus 1 cm (½ in) seam allowance on either side (Fig. 1).

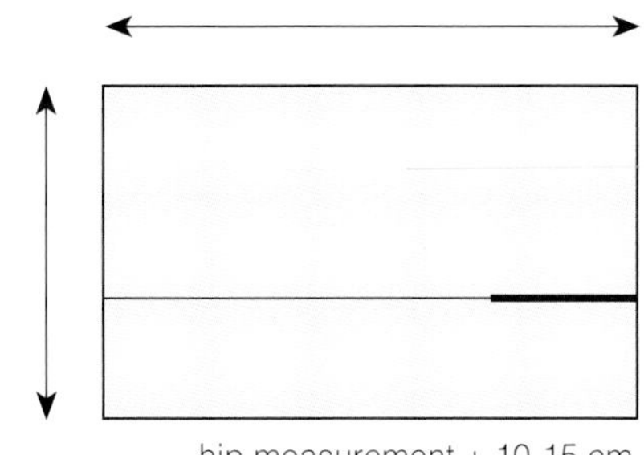

Fig. 1 hip measurement + 10-15 cm (4-6 in) + seam allowance

BASIC HALF SLIP

REQUIREMENTS
Underwear fabric
Length of slip as measured
70-80 cm x 1.5 cm-wide (¾ yd x ½ in) petticoat elastic
1.5 m x 4-6 cm (1⅝ yd x 1½-2¼ in) nylon lace
Matching polyester cotton thread
Floss
Stitch sealant (see page 19)

SEAM ALLOWANCE
1 cm (½ in) on all seams

STITCHES
Overcasting stitch, width 4 and length 2½
Flatlocking with floss
Three-thread overlocking

PATTERNS
Design your own pattern

METHOD
1. Design your own pattern (see page 53), transfer onto tracing paper and cut out.

2. Pin tracing paper pattern piece onto fabric and cut out.

3. Pin WS of lace and fabric together at lower edge of slip.

4. Sew lace to lower edge, using **flatlocking with floss**, keeping the lace at the bottom.

5. With RS together, pin and sew the side seam together, using three-thread overlocking and stitch length 2-2½.

6. Take a firm waist measurement and cut elastic to this measurement.

7. Sew ends of elastic together to form a circle using sewing machine and overcasting stitch.

8. **Quarter pin mark** the waist and the elastic (Fig. 10, p. 24). Pin WS of the elastic to RS of the fabric, matching up the pins.

9. Sew elastic to fabric using sewing machine and overcasting stitch, keeping the elastic on top.

10. Secure all loose ends by hand or with stitch sealant.

HALF SLIP WITH SLIT

This half slip can be made with the slit at the back or side.

REQUIREMENTS
Underwear fabric
Length of slip as measured
70-80 cm x 1.5 cm-wide (¾ yd x ½ in) petticoat elastic
2 m x 4-8 cm-wide (2¼ yd x 1½ - 3¼ in) nylon lace
Matching polyester cotton thread
Floss
Stitch sealant (see page 19)

SEAM ALLOWANCE
1 cm (½ in) on all seams

STITCHES
Zig-zag stitch, width 1 and length 2
Overcasting stitch, width 4 and length 2½
Three-thread overlocking

PATTERNS
Design your own pattern

METHOD
1. Design your own pattern (see page 53), transfer onto tracing paper and cut out.

2. Pin tracing paper pattern piece onto fabric and cut out.

3. Mark the length of the slit. With RS together, pin and sew the seam together to the marked point, using three-thread overlocking and stitch length 2-2½.

4. Pin the WS of the lace to the RS of the fabric at lower edge starting at the slip top edge (Fig. 2). Continue to pin the lace to the fabric, mitre corners (Fig. 2), and end at the slit again (Fig. 3).

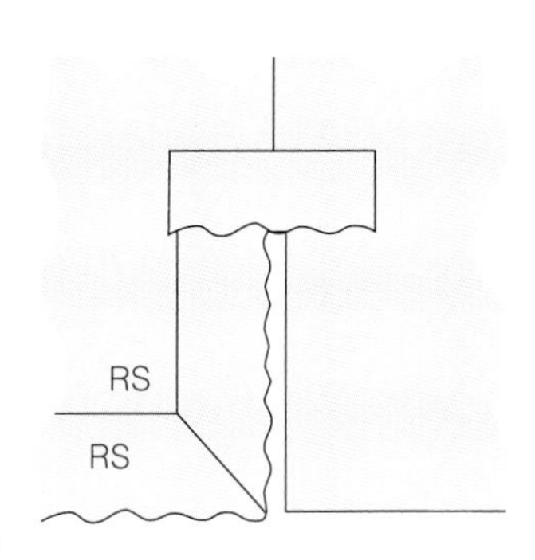

Fig. 2

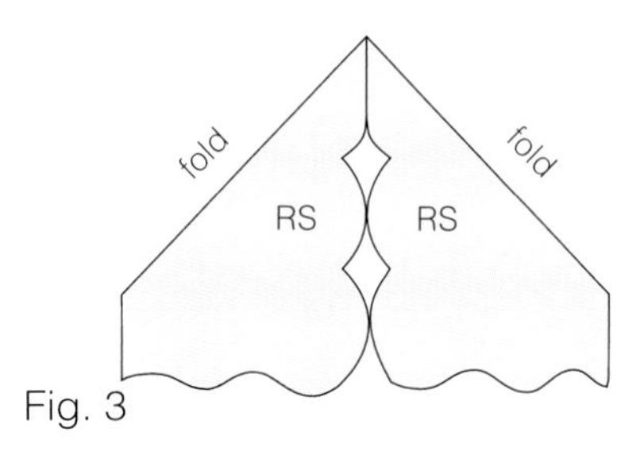

Fig. 3

5. Sew top edge of lace to the fabric using sewing machine and zig-zag stitch (Fig. 4).

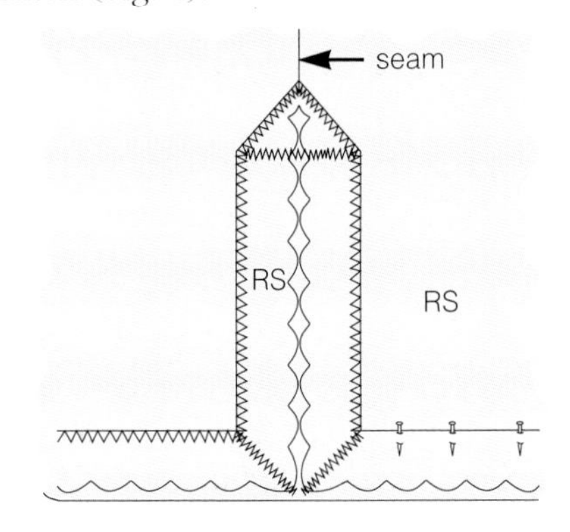

Fig. 4

6. Cut fabric and lace corners away.

7. Take a firm waist measurement and cut elastic to this measurement.

8. Sew ends of elastic together to form a circle using sewing machine and overcasting stitch.

9. **Quarter pin mark** waist and elastic (Fig. 10, p. 24). Pin WS of elastic to RS of fabric, matching up the pins.

10. Sew elastic to fabric using sewing machine and overcasting stitch, keeping the elastic on top.

11. Secure all loose ends by hand or with stitch sealant.

BODYSUITS

Fashionable yet practical, wear figure-hugging bodysuits under a transparent top, on their own with jeans, or instead of a spencer.

BODYSUIT WITH LACE INSETS

REQUIREMENTS
115 cm and 150 cm (45 and 60 in): 80 cm-1 m (⅞-1 yd) Lycra
40 cm (16 in) stretch lace
2.75-3 m x 1 cm-wide (3-3¼ yd x ½ in) brief leg elastic for neck, armholes and legs
25 cm x 15 mm-wide (10 x ½ in) satin or nylon ribbon
Matching polyester cotton thread
Floss
Stitch sealant (see page 19)
2-3 poppers or snap fasteners
4,0 mm stretch twin needle

SEAM ALLOWANCE
6 mm (¼ in) on all seams

STITCHES
Straight stitch, length 4
Zig-zag stitch, width 1 and length 2
Three-thread overlocking

PATTERNS
Patterns 56, 57, 58 and 59

METHOD
1. Enlarge pattern pieces on pages 94 and 95 onto graph paper and cut out.

2. Pin pattern pieces onto fabric and cut out 1 x back (on fold), 1 x front (on fold), 1 x front inset (on fold), 2 x side inset.

3. Pin WS of the front inset to RS of the front panel.

4. Using sewing machine and zig-zag stitch, sew inset to front panel. Cut fabric and stretch lace away next to the stitching.

5. With RS together, pin and sew one shoulder seam together, using three-thread overlocking, stitch length 2-2½.

6. Lay the bodysuit on a flat surface and measure neck opening. Cut the brief elastic to three-quarters of this measurement.

7. Place elastic on WS of fabric. Insert fabric and elastic into the overlocker and secure elastic by sewing a few stitches using three-thread overlocking and stitch length 3-3½.

8. **Quarter pin mark** neck opening and elastic (Fig. 6, p. 24). Pin elastic to fabric, matching up the pins.

9. Continue sewing, attaching elastic to fabric. Hold fabric and elastic in front and back. Keep elastic next to blade, cutting elastic 1 mm (1/16 in) off the fabric (Fig. 7, p. 24).

BODYSUIT WITH LACE INSETS, AND LACE BODYSUIT, P. 56

10. Fold elastic to the WS so that elastic is encased and sew using sewing machine and twin needle and straight stitch, keeping the fold in line with edge of the pressure foot.

11. With RS together, pin and sew other shoulder seam using three-thread overlocking, stitch length 2-2½.

12. Lay bodysuit on a flat surface and measure armhole opening. Cut the brief elastic to three-quarters of this measurement.

13. Place elastic on WS of fabric. Insert fabric and elastic into the overlocker and secure elastic by sewing a few stitches using three-thread overlocking and stitch length 3-3½.

14. **Quarter pin mark** armhole opening and elastic (Fig. 6, p. 24). Pin elastic to fabric, matching up the pins.

15. Continue sewing, attaching the elastic to the fabric. Hold the fabric and elastic in front and at the back, and keep the elastic next to the blade, cutting the elastic 1 mm (1/16 in) off the fabric (Fig. 7, p. 24).

16. Fold elastic to WS so that elastic is encased. Sew using sewing machine, twin needle and straight stitch, keeping fold in line with edge of pressure foot. Repeat for other armhole opening.

17. With RS together, pin and sew side seams using three-thread overlocking and stitch length 2-2½, up to marks. Secure ends by hand or with stitch sealant.

18. Pin WS of side insets to RS of both side seams. Using sewing machine and zig-zag stitch, sew side insets to fabric. Cut the fabric and stretch lace away next to stitching.

19. Lay bodysuit on a flat surface and measure leg opening. Cut brief elastic to three-quarters of this measurement.

20. Place elastic on WS of the fabric. Insert fabric and elastic into the overlocker and secure elastic by sewing a few stitches using three-thread overlocking and stitch length 3-3½.

21. **Quarter pin mark** leg opening and elastic (Fig. 6, p. 24). Pin elastic to fabric, matching up the pins.

22. Continue sewing, attaching the elastic to the fabric. Hold the fabric and elastic in front and at the back, and keep the elastic next to the blade, cutting the elastic 1 mm (1/16 in) off the fabric (Fig. 7, p. 24).

23. Fold elastic to the WS so that elastic is encased and sew using sewing machine and twin needle and straight stitch, keeping the fold in line with edge of the pressure foot. Repeat for the other leg opening.

24. Fold raw edges of both crotch edges 1 cm (½ in) to WS and press. Pin ribbon on WS of both crotch edges, folding raw edges of ribbon in.

25. Sew around the edges of the ribbon using sewing machine and zig-zag stitch.

26. Insert poppers or snap fasteners. Secure all loose ends by hand or with stitch sealant.

LACE BODYSUIT

REQUIREMENTS
65-75 cm (26-30 in) stretch lace
3 m x 1 cm-wide (3¼ yd x ½ in) leg elastic
25 cm x 15 mm-wide (10 in x ½ in) nylon or satin ribbon
Matching polyester cotton thread
Floss
Stitch sealant (see page 19)
2-3 poppers or snap fasteners

SEAM ALLOWANCE
6 mm (¼ in) on all seams

STITCHES
Zig-zag stitch, width 1 and length 2
Three-thread overlocking

PATTERNS
Patterns 60 and 61

METHOD
1. Enlarge pattern pieces on pages 95 and 96 onto graph paper and cut out.

2. Pin pattern pieces onto fabric and cut out 1 x back (on fold), 1 x front (on fold).

3. With RS together, pin and sew the side seams together using overlocker and three-thread overlocking, stitch length 2-2½.

4. Lay bodysuit on a flat surface and measure armholes and back neckline. Cut leg elastic to three-quarters of this measurement.

5. With WS together, place the elastic on top of fabric. Insert the fabric and elastic into the overlocker and secure the elastic by sewing a few stitches using three-thread overlocking and stitch length 3-3½.

6. **Quarter pin mark** armholes, back neckline and elastic (Fig. 6, p. 24). Pin elastic to fabric, matching up pins.

7. Continue sewing, attaching the elastic to the fabric. Hold the fabric and elastic in front and at the back, and keep the elastic next to the blade, cutting the elastic 1 mm (1/16 in) off the fabric (Fig. 7, p. 24).

8. Lay bodysuit on a flat surface and measure front neckline opening. Cut leg elastic to three-quarters of this measurement, allowing extra elastic for straps. Mark the three-quarter measurement with a pin.

9. With WS together, place the elastic on top of the fabric. Insert the fabric and elastic into the overlocker and secure the elastic by sewing a few stitches using three-thread overlocking and stitch length 3-3½.

10. **Quarter pin mark** the neckline opening and elastic (Fig. 6, p. 24). Pin the elastic to the fabric, matching up the pins.

11. Continue sewing, attaching the elastic to the fabric. Hold the fabric and the elastic in front and at the back, and keep the elastic next to the blade, cutting the elastic 1 mm (1/16 in) off the fabric (Fig. 7, p. 24).

12. Measure the length of the straps, position the straps on the back neckline, and sew both of the straps on using the sewing machine and zig-zag stitch.

13. Lay the bodysuit on a flat surface and measure the leg opening. Cut the elastic to three-quarters of this measurement.

14. With WS together, place the elastic on top of the fabric. Insert the fabric and elastic into the overlocker and secure the elastic by sewing a few stitches using three-thread overlocking and stitch length 3-3½.

15. **Quarter pin mark** leg opening and elastic (Fig. 6, p. 24). Pin elastic to fabric, matching up pins.

16. Continue sewing, attaching the elastic to the fabric. Hold the fabric and elastic in front and at the back, and keeping the elastic next to the blade, cutting the elastic 1 mm (1/16 in) off the fabric (Fig. 7, p. 24).

17. Repeat for the other leg opening.

18. Fold raw edges of both the crotch edges 1 cm (½ in) to WS and press. Pin the ribbon on WS of both crotch edges, folding raw edges of ribbon in.

19. Sew around edges of ribbon using sewing machine and zig-zag stitch.

20. Insert poppers or snap fasteners.

21. Secure all loose ends by hand or with stitch sealant.

22. Position bows on front and sew on by hand.

SPENCER, P. 58

SPENCER

This pattern is for a snug, all-in-one spencer. Alternatively, it can be worn as a top with jeans. You can also adapt this pattern to makea waist-length spencer.

REQUIREMENTS
1.3-1.4 m (1½-1¼ yd) stretch lace
1.3-1.5 m x 1 cm-wide (1½-1⅔ yd x ½ in) brief leg elastic
25 cm x 15 mm-wide (10 in x ½ in) nylon or satin ribbon
Matching polyester cotton thread
Floss
Stitch sealant (see page 19)
2-3 poppers or snap fasteners
4,0 mm stretch twin needle

SEAM ALLOWANCE
6 mm (¼ in) on all seams

STITCHES
Straight stitch, stitch length 4
Zig-zag stitch, width 1 and length 2
Three-thread overlocking

PATTERNS
Patterns 62, 63 and 64

METHOD

1. Enlarge pattern pieces on pages 96 and 97 onto graph paper and cut out.

2. Pin pattern pieces onto fabric and cut out 1 x back (on fold), 1 x front (on fold) and 2 x sleeve (on fold).

3. With RS together, pin and sew one of the shoulder seams together using three-thread overlocking and stitch length 2-2½.

4. Lay the spencer on a flat surface and measure the neck opening. Cut the elastic to three-quarters of this measurement.

5. Place the elastic on the WS of the fabric. Insert the fabric and the elastic into the overlocker and secure the elastic by sewing a few stitches using three-thread overlocking and stitch length 3-3½

6. **Quarter pin mark** neck opening and elastic (Fig. 6, p. 24). Pin elastic to fabric, matching up the pins.

7. Continue sewing, attaching the elastic to the fabric. Hold the fabric and the elastic in front and at the back, and keep the elastic next to the blade, cutting elastic 1 mm (1/16 in) off the fabric (Fig. 7, p. 24).

8. Fold the elastic to the WS so that the elastic is encased and sew using the sewing machine, twin needle and straight stitch, keeping the fold in line with the edge of the pressure foot (Fig. 1).

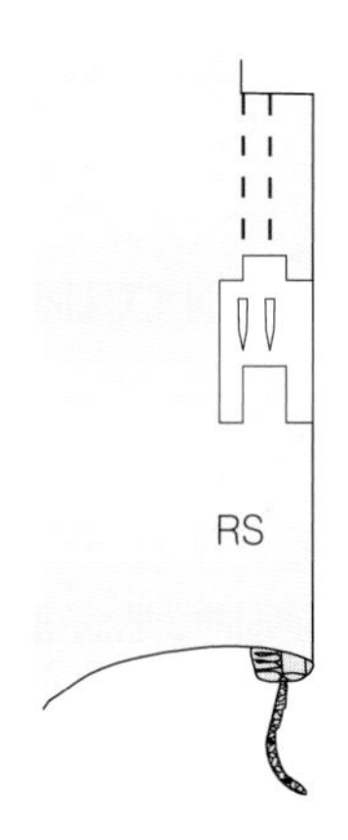

Fig.1

9. With RS together, pin and sew the other shoulder seam together using three-thread overlocking and stitch length 2-2½.

10. Fold each sleeve in half and pin mark centre on sleeve.

11. With RS together and pin marks on should seams, pin and sew sleeves into sleeve openings using three-thread overlocking and stitch length 2-2½.

12. With RS together, pin and sew sleeve and side seams together using three-thread overlocking, stitch length 2-2½.

13. Fold the hem of the sleeves under 1 cm (½ in) and sew using the sewing machine, twin needle and straight stitch. Sew 1 cm (½ in) from the folded edge.

14. Lay the spencer on a flat surface and measure the leg opening. Cut the elastic to three-quarters of this measurement.

15. Place the elastic on the WS of fabric. Insert the fabric and elastic into the overlocker and secure the elastic by sewing a few stitches using three-thread overlocking and stitch length 3-3½.

16. **Quarter pin mark** leg opening and elastic (Fig. 6, p. 24). Pin elastic to fabric, matching up the pins.

17. Continue sewing, attaching the elastic to the fabric. Hold the fabric and elastic in front and at the back, and keep the elastic next to the blade, cutting the elastic 1 mm (1/16 in) off the fabric (Fig. 7, p. 24).

18. Fold elastic to WS so that elastic is encased and sew using sewing machine, twin needle and straight stitch, keeping the fold in line with the edge of the pressure foot.

19. Repeat for the other leg opening.

20. Fold raw edges of both crotch edges 1 cm (½ in) to WS and press. Pin ribbon on WS of both crotch edges, folding raw edges of ribbon in.

21. Sew around the edges of the ribbon using sewing machine and zig-zag stitch.

22. Insert poppers or snap fasteners.

23. Secure all loose ends by hand or with stitch sealant.

NOTE: On some makes of overlocker, a special sewing table can be attached which enables you to sew a straight stitch in the centre of the fabric. This is used mainly for decorative stitching. Sew on a single layer of fabric, with the wrong side facing. Sew circles and corners on the front of the article.

KIMONO WRAP WITH DECORATIVE EDGING, P. 61, AND DRESSING GOWN WITH SHAWL COLLAR, P. 62

T-SHAPED NIGHTIE FOR LADIES AND GIRLS

Loose-fitting and easy to wear, this T-shaped nightie can be made to suit all ages and sizes! Take your top length measurements as described in the Introduction, page 14.

REQUIREMENTS
T-shirt fabric
Top length or measure length to hip if a longer nightie is desired
Matching polyester cotton thread
Floss
Metallic thread
Stitch sealant (see page 19)

SEAM ALLOWANCE
1 cm (½ in) seam alllowance on all seams

STITCHES
Three-thread wide overlocking with metallic thread or floss
Four-thread overlocking

PATTERNS
Use any basic T-shape top or drop shoulder T-shirt pattern

METHOD

1. Pin pattern pieces onto fabric and cut out 1 x back (on fold), 1 x front (on fold).

2. With RS together, pin and sew one shoulder seam using overlocker and four-thread overlocking and stitch length 2-2½.

3. Sew neckline using overlocker and three-thread overlocking with metallic thread or floss, stitch length 1-2.

4. With RS together, pin and sew the other shoulder seam using the overlocker and four-thread overlocking and stitch length 2-2½.

5. Sew both sleeve edges using overlocker and three-thread overlocking with metallic thread or floss and stitch length 1-2.

6. With RS together, pin and sew one underarm seam together using overlocker and four-thread overlocking and stitch length 2½.

7. Sew along the bottom edge of the nightie using the overlocker and three-thread wide overlocking with metallic thread or floss.

8. With RS together, pin and sew the other underarm seam together using overlocker and four-thread overlocking and stitch length 2½.

9. Secure all loose ends by hand or with stitch sealant.

T-SHAPED NIGHTIE, AND KIMONO WRAP WITH GALLOON LACE, P. 62

DRESSING GOWNS

Whether you choose to make a kimono wrap or a traditional dressing gown, either style can be worn long or short, by ladies and gents!

DESIGNING AND MEASURING A KIMONO WRAP

1. Design a kimono wrap according to Fig. 1. Mark centre front and cut in half. Design on half the front only.

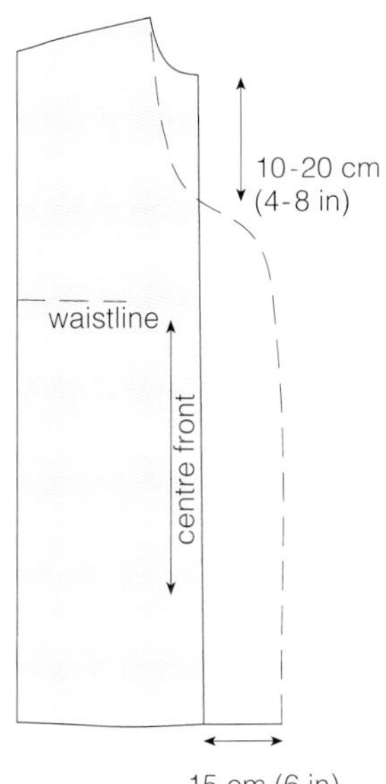

Fig. 1

2. Use a pen or a pencil and mark 10-20 cm (4-8 in) from neckline on centre front.

3. Mark the waistline on the basic front pattern.

4. Mark 15 cm (6 in) away from the centre front on waistline.

5. With a pencil, draw on the wrap from the shoulder at the neckline to the mark at the waistline (Fig. 1).

The kimono wrap can be made with a decorative edging (usually 10 - 12 cm [4 - 5 in] wide), or it can be finished off with galloon lace.

The belt will be the same width as the edging, and must be long enough to wrap around the waist and tie in a bow or knot.

KIMONO WRAP WITH DECORATIVE EDGING

REQUIREMENTS
Summer gown: Fabrics such as non-stretch underwear fabric
Winter gown: Fabrics such as towelling
Twice the length of the dressing gown
Matching polyester cotton thread
Floss
Embroidery thread
Stitch sealant (see page 19)

SEAM ALLOWANCE
1 cm (½ in) seam allowance on all seams

STITCHES
Straight stitch, length 2½
Flatlocking with embroidery thread or floss
Flatlocked hem with floss or embroidery thread
Three-thread wide overlocking with floss or embroidery thread
Narrow hem with floss
Four-thread overlocking

PATTERNS
Design your own pattern from a basic T-shirt pattern or use any kimono wrap pattern

METHOD
1. Design your own kimono wrap (see **Designing and Measuring a Kimono Wrap**, this page).

2. Pin pattern pieces onto fabric and cut out 1 x back (on fold), 2 x front, 2 x sleeves, 2 x band, 1 x belt and 2 x pockets.

3. With RS together, pin and sew the front and back shoulder seams together using the overlocker and four-thread overlocking and stitch length 2 - 2½.

4. Measure the back neckline and both the front edges to determine the length of the edging.

5. If neccessary join the edging at centre back using the overlocker and four-thread overlocking and stitch length 2-2½.

6. Fold edging in half lengthwise, WS together, and press.

7. With WS together, pin and sew sleeves into armholes using overlocker and **flatlocking with floss** or **flatlocking with embroidery thread**, stitch length 2-3.

8. Fold over the hem of sleeves 3 cm (1¼ in) to the WS and press. Fold over sleeve hem 3 cm (1¼ in) again to the WS so that the raw edge is encased.

9. Sew on the RS using the overlocker and **flatlocked hem with floss or embroidery thread** and stitch length 2-3.

10. Sew a chain using the overlocker and **narrow hem with floss**, stitch length 1-1½ for the belt loops.

11. Position and pin the belt loops to both side seams.

12. With RS together, pin and sew underarm seams together using overlocker and four-thread overlocking and stitch length 2-2½.

13. Pin the edging to WS of the neck opening, pinning the seam on the centre back.

14. Sew edging into neck opening using overlocker and **flatlocking with floss** or **flatlocking with embroidery thread** and stitch length 2-3.

15. Fold the hem of dressing gown 3-5 cm (1¼-2 in) over to the WS and press. Fold hem of dressing gown 3-5 cm (1¼-2 in) again to the WS so that the raw edge is encased.

16. Sew on the RS using overlocker and **flatlocked hem with floss or embroidery thread** and stitch length 2-3.

17. Fold belt in half lengthwise, WS together, and press.

18. Sew around all four edges of belt using overlocker and **three-thread wide overlocking with floss or embroidery thread**, stitch length 2-3, starting anew at each corner.

19. Using overlocker and **three-thread wide overlocking** and stitch length 2-3, sew on the RS around the pocket edges, starting anew at each corner.

20. Position WS of pockets on RS of dressing gown and sew on using sewing machine and straight stitch.

21. Secure all loose ends by hand or with stitch sealant.

22. Thread belt through belt loops.

KIMONO WRAP WITH GALLOON LACE

REQUIREMENTS
Summer gown: Fabrics such as non-stretch underwear fabric
Winter gown: Fabrics such as towelling
Twice the length of the dressing gown
Approximately 5 m (5½ yd) galloon lace (the length of the back neck and front opening, twice the width of the bottom sleeve, and the total width of the dressing gown at the bottom)
Matching polyester cotton thread
Metallic thread or floss
Stitch sealant (see page 19)

SEAM ALLOWANCE
1 cm (½ in) seam allowance on all seams

STITCHES
Zig-zag stitch, width 1 and length 2
Narrow hem with metallic thread or floss
Three-thread overlocking
Four-thread overlocking

PATTERNS
Design your own pattern or use any basic top or kimono wrap pattern

METHOD
1. Design your own kimono wrap (see **Designing and Measuring a Kimono Wrap**, page 61).

2. Pin pattern pieces onto fabric and cut out 1 x back (on fold), 2 x front, 2 x sleeves, 1 belt.

3. With RS together, pin and sew shoulder seams together using overlocker and four-thread overlocking and stitch length 2-2½.

4. Pin WS of lace to RS of the fabric.

5. Using sewing machine and zig-zag stitch, sew galloon lace to back and front opening along curved edges. Cut fabric away behind lace.

6. Fold each sleeve in half and pin mark centre on sleeve.

7. With RS together, pin and sew sleeves to armholes using overlocker and four-thread overlocking and stitch length 2-2½.

8. Pin WS of lace to RS of fabric at edge of both sleeves.

9. Using sewing machine and zig-zag stitch, sew lace to sleeve edges along curved edges.

10. Cut fabric away behind lace.

11. Using the overlocker and **narrow hem with metallic thread or floss**, stitch length 1-1½, sew a chain for the belt loops.

12. Position and pin the belt loops to both side seams.

13. With RS together, pin and sew underarm seams together using overlocker and four-thread overlocking and stitch length 2-2½.

14. Pin WS of lace to RS of bottom edge of dressing gown.

15. Using sewing machine and zig-zag stitch, sew lace to lower edge of dressing gown.

16. Cut fabric away behind lace.

17. Fold the belt in half lengthwise, RS together, and sew using overlocker and four-thread overlocking and stitch length 2-2½. Start off by sewing a chain. Insert the chain into the folded edge of belt and sew. Use the chain to turn belt inside out (p. 18).

18. Secure all loose ends by hand or with stitch sealant.

19. Thread the belt through the belt loops.

DRESSING GOWN WITH SHAWL COLLAR

REQUIREMENTS
Summer gown: Fabrics such as non-stretch underwear fabric
Winter gown: Fabrics such as towelling
Twice the length of the dressing gown
2.5-3 m x 5-6 cm-wide (2¾-3¼ yd x 2-2¼ in) insertion lace with motifs (twice the width of the bottom sleeve and the total width of the dressing gown at the bottom)
Matching polyester cotton thread
Embroidery thread
Metallic thread
Floss
Stitch sealant (see page 19)

SEAM ALLOWANCE
1 cm (½ in) seam allowance on all seams

STITCHES
Straight stitch, length 2½
Flatlocking with embroidery thread
Narrow hem with metallic thread or floss
Blind hem
Four-thread overlocking

PATTERNS
Use any jacket pattern with a shawl collar

METHOD
1. Pin pattern pieces onto fabric and cut out 1 x back (on fold), 2 x front, 2 x sleeves, 2 x front facing and collar, 1 x belt.

2. With RS together, pin and sew centre back seam of undercollar (part of front) together using overlocker and four-thread overlocking, stitch length 2-2½. Press seam to lie flat.

3. With RS together, pin centre back seam of undercollar onto centre back of back panel. Pin back neck and shoulders onto the front collar and shoulders.

4. Sew neck and shoulders using sewing machine and straight stitch. Clip the corners.

5. Fold each sleeve in half and pin mark centre on sleeve.

6. With RS together, pin and sew the sleeves into the armholes using overlocker and four-thread overocking, stitch length 2-2½.

7. On sleeve, measure 10 cm (4 in) from the sleeve edge and cut along this marking.

8. Fold fabric of 10 cm (4 in) piece in half lengthwise and pin WS of insertion lace with motifs to raw edges.

9. Pin the WS of the insertion lace with motifs to the WS of the sleeve.

10. Using overlocker and **flatlocking with embroidery thread**, stitch length 3-3½, sew insertion lace with motifs to both sleeves.

11. Using overlocker and **narrow hem with metallic thread or floss**, stitch length 1-1½, sew a chain for the belt loops.

12. Position and pin the belt loops to both side seams.

KIMONO WRAP WITH DECORATIVE EDGING, P. 61

13. With RS together, pin and sew underarm seams together using overlocker and four-thread overlocking and stitch length 2-2½.

14. Measure 30-35 cm (12-13¾ in) from bottom edge of dressing gown. Cut.

15. Pin WS of insertion lace with motifs to WS of dressing gown on both cut edges.

16. Using overlocker and **flatlocking with embroidery thread**, stitch length 3-3½ sew insertion lace with motifs to dressing gown.

17. With RS together, pin and sew front facing and collar together at centre back seam using overlocker and four-thread overlocking, stitch length 2-2½.

18. With RS together, pin and sew front facing and collar to front and undercollar using overlocker and four-thread overlocking, stitch length 2-2½.

19. Finish edges of facing using four-thread overlocking, stitch length 2-2½.

20. Fold facing over to WS. Press edges.

21. Fold lower edge over 5 cm (2 in). Sew blind hem along lower edge, using overlocker and **blind hem foot**. and stitch length 3-3½

22. To finish collar, fold raw edge of collar facing in 1 cm (½ in) and finish off by hand to undercollar on inside.

23. Secure all loose end by hand or with stitch sealant.

GM

LEISUREWEAR

The projects in this section include leotards, gym tops, and gym pants and leggings. Most of these attractive leisurewear garments are versatile enough to be worn either to work out in at the gym, or as casual gear – the leotard could be teamed up with jeans or shorts, and the leggings would look equally good worn while exercising or casually with a T-shirt – choose the fabric according to your needs and the occasion!

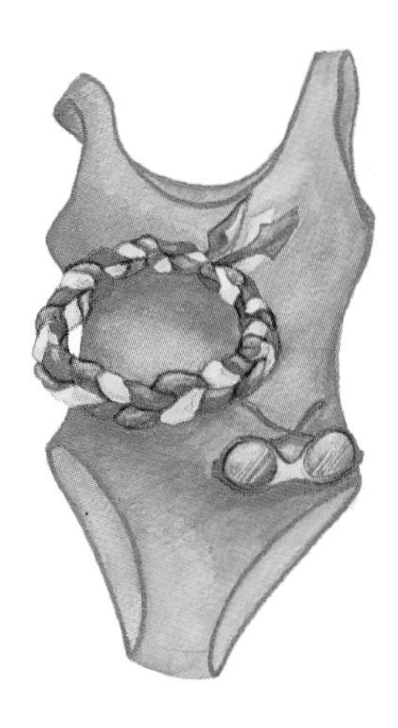

LEOTARD

REQUIREMENTS
80 cm-1 m (¾-1 yd) cotton or nylon Lycra
1.5-2 m x 1 cm-wide (1⅝-2¼ yd x ½ in) brief leg elastic
Matching polyester cotton thread
Floss
Stitch sealant (see page 19)
4.0 mm stretch twin needle

SEAM ALLOWANCE
6 mm (¼ in) seam allowance on all seams

STITCHES
Straight stitch, length 4
Three-thread overlocking
Four-thread overlocking

PATTERNS
Patterns 65 and 66

METHOD
1. Enlarge pattern pieces on page 98 onto graph paper and cut out.

2. Pin pattern pieces onto fabric and cut out 1 x back (on fold) and 1 x front (on fold).

3. With RS together, pin and sew one shoulder seam together using overlocker and four-thread overlocking and stitch length 2-2½.

4. Lay leotard on a flat surface and measure the front and back neck opening. Cut elastic to three-quarters of this measurement.

5. Place elastic on WS of fabric, insert the elastic and fabric into overlocker and secure elastic by sewing a few stitches using overlocker and three-thread overlocking and stitch length 3-3½.

6. **Quarter pin mark** neck opening and elastic (Fig. 6, p. 24). Pin elastic to fabric, matching up the pins.

7. Continue sewing, attaching elastic to fabric. Hold fabric and elastic in front and at back and keep elastic next to blade, cutting 1 mm (1/16 in) off fabric (Fig. 7, p. 24).

8. Fold elastic over to the WS, and on RS, sew using sewing machine, twin needle and straight stitch, keeping the edge of the foot in line with the folded edge.

9. With RS together, pin and sew the other shoulder seam together using overlocker and four thread overlocking and stitch length 2-2½.

10. Lay leotard on a flat surface and measure the armhole opening.

11. Cut elastic to three-quarters of this measurement.

12. Place elastic on WS of fabric, insert elastic and fabric into overlocker. Secure elastic by sewing a few stitches using overlocker and three-thread overlocking, stitch length 3-3½.

13. **Quarter pin mark** armhole opening and elastic (Fig. 6, p. 24). Pin elastic to fabric, matching up pins.

14. Continue sewing, attaching the elastic to fabric. Hold the fabric and the elastic in front and at the back, and keep the elastic next to the blade, cutting 1 mm (1/16 in) off the fabric (Fig.7, p. 24).

15. Fold elastic over to the WS, and on RS, sew using sewing machine, twin needle and straight stitch, keeping the edge of the foot in line with the folded edge.

16. Repeat for the other armhole.

17. With RS together, pin and sew both side seams together using overlocker and four-thread overlocking and stitch length 2½.

18. Lie leotard on a flat surface and measure leg opening. Cut elastic to three-quarters of this measurement.

19. Place elastic on WS of fabric, insert the elastic and fabric into overlocker, and secure elastic by sewing a few stitches using overlocker and three-thread overlocking and stitch length 3-3½.

20. **Quarter pin mark** leg opening and elastic (Fig. 6, p. 24). Pin elastic to fabric, matching up the pins.

21. Continue sewing, attaching elastic to fabric. Hold the fabric and the elastic in front and at the back, and keep elastic next to the blade, cutting 1 mm (1/16 in) off fabric (Fig. 7, p. 24).

22. Fold elastic over to the WS, and on RS, sew using sewing machine, twin needle and straight stitch, keeping the edge of the foot in line with the folded edge.

23. Repeat for the other leg opening.

24. With the RS together, pin and sew front and back together at the gusset seam using overlocker and four-thread overlocking and stitch length 2½.

25. Secure all loose ends by hand or with stitch sealant.

GYM TOP WITH EMBROIDERY THREAD OR FLOSS

REQUIREMENTS
40 cm (16 in) cotton or nylon Lycra
1.5-2 m x 1 cm-wide (1⅝-2¼ yd x ½ in) brief leg elastic
Matching polyester cotton thread
Floss
Embroidery thread
Stitch sealant (see page 19)
4.0 mm stretch twin needle

SEAM ALLOWANCE
6 mm (¼ in) seam allowance on all seams

STITCHES
Straight stitch, length 4
Three-thread overlocking

Flatlocking with floss or embroidery thread
Four-thread overlocking

PATTERNS
Patterns 67, 68 and 69

METHOD
1. Enlarge pattern pieces on page 99 onto graph paper and cut out.

2. Pin pattern pieces onto fabric and cut out 1 x back (on fold), 1 x centre front (on fold) and 2 x side fronts.

3. With WS together, pin both side fronts to centre front and sew together using overlocker and **flatlocking with floss or embroidery thread**, stitch length 2-3.

4. With WS together, pin and sew one shoulder seam together using overlocker and **flatlocking with floss or embroidery thread**, stitch length 2-3.

5. Lay the top on a flat surface and measure front and back neck opening. Cut elastic to three-quarters of this measurement.

LEOTARDS, P. 66

6. Place elastic on WS of fabric, insert the elastic and fabric into overlocker, and secure elastic by sewing a few stitches using overlocker and three-thread overlocking and stitch length 3-3½.

7. **Quarter pin mark** neck opening and elastic (Fig. 6, p. 24). Pin elastic to fabric, matching up the pins.

8. Continue sewing, attaching elastic to fabric. Hold the fabric and the elastic in front and at the back, and keep elastic next to the blade, cutting 1 mm (1/16 in) off fabric (Fig. 7, p. 24).

9. Fold elastic over to the WS, and on RS, sew using sewing machine, twin needle and straight stitch, keeping the edge of the foot in line with the folded edge.

10. With WS together, pin and sew the other shoulder seam together using overlocker and **flatlocking with floss or embroidery thread,** stitch length 2-3.

11. Lay top on a flat surface and measure the armhole opening.

12. Cut elastic to three-quarters of this measurement.

13. Place the elastic on WS of fabric, insert elastic and fabric into overlocker, and secure elastic by sewing a few stitches using overlocker and three-thread overlocking and stitch length 3-3½.

14. **Quarter pin mark** armhole opening and elastic (Fig. 6, p. 24). Pin elastic to fabric, matching up the pins.

15. Continue sewing, attaching elastic to fabric. Hold fabric and elastic in front and at back, and keep elastic next to the blade, cutting 1 mm (1/16 in) off the fabric (Fig. 7, p. 24).

16. Fold elastic over to the WS, and on RS, sew using sewing machine, twin needle and straight stitch, keeping the edge of the foot in line with the folded edge.

17. Repeat for the other armhole.

18. With RS together, pin and sew one side seam together using overlocker and four-thread overlocking and stitch length 2½.

19. Measure under bust. Cut elastic to three-quarters of this measurement.

20. Place elastic on WS of fabric, insert the elastic and fabric into overlocker, and secure elastic by sewing a few stitches using overlocker and three-thread overlocking, stitch length 3-3½.

21. **Quarter pin mark** the under bust opening and elastic (Fig. 10, p. 24). Pin the elastic to fabric, matching up the pins.

22. Continue sewing, attaching the elastic to fabric. Hold the fabric and the elastic in front and at the back, and keep the elastic next to the blade, cutting 1 mm (1/16 in) off the fabric (Fig. 7, p. 24).

23. Fold elastic over to the WS, and on RS, sew using sewing machine, twin needle and straight stitch, keeping the edge of the foot in line with the folded edge.

24. With RS together, pin and sew the other side seam using overlocker and four-thread overlocking and stitch length 2½.

25. Secure all loose ends by hand or with stitch sealant.

HIGH-CUT GYM PANTS

REQUIREMENTS
50 cm (20 in) cotton or nylon Lycra
1 - 1.5 m x 1 cm-wide (1 - 1⅝ yd x ½ in) brief leg elastic
Matching polyester cotton thread
Floss
Stitch sealant (see page 19)
4.0 mm stretch twin needle

SEAM ALLOWANCE
6 mm (¼ in) seam allowance on all seams

STITCHES
Straight stitch, length 4
Three-thread overlocking
Four-thread overlocking

PATTERNS
Patterns 70 and 71

METHOD
1. Enlarge the pattern pieces on page 100 onto the graph paper and cut them out.

2. Pin pattern pieces onto fabric and cut out 1 x back (on fold) and 1 x front (on fold).

3. With the RS together pin the front and the back together at the crotch seam and sew using the overlocker and four-thread overlocking and stitch length 2-2½.

4. Lay pants on a flat surface and measure leg opening. Cut elastic to three-quarters of this measurement.

5. Place elastic on WS of fabric, insert the elastic and fabric into overlocker, and secure elastic by sewing a few stitches using overlocker and three-thread overlocking and stitch length 3-3½.

6. **Quarter pin mark** leg opening and elastic (Fig. 6, p. 24). Pin elastic to fabric, matching up the pins.

7. Continue sewing, attaching elastic to fabric. Hold the fabric and the elastic in front and at the back, and keep the elastic next to the blade, cutting 1 mm (1/16 in) off the fabric (Fig. 7, p. 24).

8. Fold elastic over to the WS, and on RS, sew using sewing machine, twin needle and straight stitch, keeping the edge of the foot in line with the folded edge.

9. Repeat for the other leg opening.

10. With RS together, pin and sew the one side seam together using the overlocker and four-thread overlocking and stitch length 2-2½.

11. Lay pants on a flat surface and measure the waist opening.

12. Cut elastic to three-quarters of this measurement.

13. Place elastic on WS of fabric, insert the elastic and fabric into overlocker, and secure elastic by sewing a few stitches using overlocker and three-thread overlocking and stitch length 3-3½.

14. **Quarter pin mark** the waist opening and elastic (Fig. 6, p. 24). Pin the elastic to the fabric, matching up the pins.

15. Continue sewing, attaching the elastic to fabric. Hold the fabric and the elastic in front and at the back, and keep the elastic next to the blade, cutting 1 mm (1/16 in) off the fabric (Fig. 7, p. 24).

16. Fold elastic over to the WS, and on RS, sew using the sewing machine, twin needle and straight stitch, keeping the edge of the foot in line with the folded edge.

17. With the RS together, pin and sew the other side seam together using the overlocker and four-thread overlocking and stitch length 2-2½.

18. Secure all loose ends by hand or with stitch sealant.

GYM OR BICYCLE TIGHTS WITH EMBROIDERY THREAD

REQUIREMENTS
50 cm (20 in) cotton or nylon Lycra
70-80 cm x 2 cm-wide (¾ yd x ¾ in) nylon elastic
Matching polyester cotton thread
Floss
Embroidery thread
Stitch sealant (see page 19)

SEAM ALLOWANCE
6 mm (¼ in) seam allowance on all seams

STITCHES
Straight stitch, length 3-4
Overcasting stitch, width 4 and length 1
Flatlocking with embroidery thread
Flatlocked hem with floss
Four-thread overlocking

PATTERNS
Patterns 74 and 75

METHOD

1. Enlarge pattern pieces on page 102 onto graph paper and cut out.

2. Pin pattern pieces onto fabric and cut out 2 x back and 2 x front.

3. With WS together pin and sew both outer leg seams together using the overlocker and **flatlocking with embroidery thread** and stitch length 2-3.

4. Fold the hem of the legs over 3 cm (1¼ in) to WS and press. Fold over 3 cm (1¼ in) to WS again and press once more.

5. Sew both hems on folded edge using overlocker and **flatlocked hem with floss** and stitch length 2-3.

6. With RS together, pin front and back together at the inner leg seam and sew together using overlocker and four-thread overlocking and stitch length 2-2½.

7. Turn one leg inside out. With RS together, pin and sew the crotch seam together using overlocker and four-thread overlocking and stitch length 2-2½.

8. Finish the waist edge using overlocker and four-thread overlocking and stitch length 2-2½.

9. Measure waist and cut waist elastic to this measurement.

10. Overlap **elastic to form a circle** (p. 9) and secure using sewing machine and overcasting stitch.

11. Using the sewing machine with zipper foot and straight stitch, insert the elastic in WS of the waist and fold over.

12. Sew all round, pulling the elastic at back to ensure that elastic lies flat in front of the foot, and gathers in at the back.

13. Secure all loose ends by hand or with stitch sealant.

ALL-IN-ONE GYM OR BICYCLE TIGHTS

REQUIREMENTS
70-80 cm (¾ yd) cotton or nylon Lycra
70-80 cm x 2 cm-wide (¾ yd x ¾ in) nylon elastic
Polyester cotton thread
Floss
Stitch sealant (see page 19)

SEAM ALLOWANCE
6 mm (¼ in) seam allowance on all seams

STITCHES
Straight stitch, length 3-4
Overcasting stitch, width 4 and length 1
Flatlocked hem with floss
Four-thread overlocking

PATTERNS
Pattern 76

METHOD

1. Enlarge pattern piece on page 103 onto graph paper and cut out.

2. Pin pattern piece onto fabric and cut out 2 x front and back.

3. Fold the hem of legs over 3 cm (1¼ in) to WS and press. Fold over 3 cm (1¼ in) to WS again and press once more.

4. Sew both the hems on folded edge using overlocker and **flatlocked hem with floss** and stitch length 2-3.

GYM TOP WITH FLOSS, P. 66, AND GYM OR BICYCLE TIGHTS, P. 68

5. With RS together, pin front and back together at the inner leg seam and sew together using overlocker and four thread overlocking and stitch length 2-2½.

6. Turn one leg inside out. With RS together, pin and sew the crotch seam together using overlocker and four-thread overlocking and stitch length 2-2½.

7. Finish the waist edge using overlocker and four-thread overlocking and stitch length 2-2½.

8. Measure waist and cut waist elastic to this measurement.

9. Overlap elastic to form a circle and secure by using sewing machine and overcasting stitch.

10. Using sewing machine with zipper foot and straight stitch, insert the elastic in the WS of the waist and fold over.

11. Sew all round, pulling the elastic at the back to ensure that the elastic lies flat in front of the foot, and gathers in at the back.

12. Secure all loose ends by hand or with stitch sealant.

ALL-IN-ONE THREE-QUARTER LEGGINGS

REQUIREMENTS
70-80 cm (¾ yd) cotton or nylon Lycra
70-80 cm x 2 cm-wide (¾ yd x ¾ in) nylon elastic
Matching polyester cotton thread
Floss
Stitch sealant (see page 19)

SEAM ALLOWANCE
6 mm (¼ in) seam allowance on all seams

STITCHES
Straight stitch, length 3-4
Four-thread overlocking
Overcasting stitch, width 4 and length 1
Flatlocked hem with floss

PATTERNS
Pattern 76

METHOD
1. Enlarge pattern pieces on page 103 onto graph paper and cut out.

2. Pin pattern pieces onto fabric and cut out 2 x front and back.

3. Fold hem of legs over to WS 3 cm (1¼ in) and press. Fold over 3 cm (1¼ in) to WS again and press.

4. Sew both the hems on the folded edge using overlocker and **flat-locked hem with floss** and stitch length 2-3.

5. With RS together, pin the front and back together at the inner leg seam and sew using overlocker and four-thread overlocking and stitch length 2 - 2½.

6. Turn one leg inside out. With RS together, pin and sew the crotch seam together using overlocker and four-thread overlocking and stitch length 2-2½.

7. Finish the waist edge using overlocker and four-thread overlocking and stitch length 2-2½.

8. Measure waist and cut waist elastic to this measurement.

9. Overlap **elastic to form a circle** (p. 9) and secure using sewing machine and overcasting stitch.

10. Using sewing machine with zipper foot and straight stitch, insert the elastic in the waist and fold over.

11. Sew all round, pulling the elastic at the back to ensure that the elastic lies flat in front of the foot, and gathers in at the back.

12. Secure all loose ends by hand or with stitch sealant.

G-STRING GYM PANTS

REQUIREMENTS
50 cm (20 in) cotton or nylon Lycra
1-1.5 m x 1 cm-wide (1-1⅝ yd x ½ in) brief leg elastic
Matching polyester cotton thread
Floss
Stitch sealant (see page 19)
4.0 mm stretch twin needle

SEAM ALLOWANCE
6 mm (¼ in) seam allowance on all seams

STITCHES
Straight stitch, length 4
Three-thread overlocking
Four-thread overlocking

PATTERNS
Patterns 72 and 73

METHOD
1. Enlarge pattern pieces on page 101 onto graph paper and cut out.

2. Pin pattern pieces onto fabric and cut out 1 x back (on fold) and 1 x front (on fold).

3. With RS together, pin front and back together at crotch seam and sew using overlocker and four-thread overlocking and stitch length 2-2½.

4. Lay pants on a flat surface and measure leg opening. Cut elastic to three-quarters of this measurement.

5. Place elastic on WS of fabric, insert the elastic and fabric into overlocker, and secure elastic by sewing a few stitches using overlocker and three-thread overlocking and stitch length 3-3½.

6. **Quarter pin mark** leg opening and elastic (Fig. 6, p. 24). Pin elastic to fabric, matching up the pins.

7. Continue sewing, attaching elastic to fabric. Hold the fabric and the elastic in front and at the back, and

keep the elastic next to the blade, cutting 1 mm (1/16 in) off the fabric (Fig.7, p. 24).

8. Fold elastic over to the WS, and on the RS, sew using the sewing machine, twin needle and straight stitch, keeping the edge of the foot in line with the folded edge.

9. Repeat for the other leg opening.

10. With the RS together, pin and sew the one side seam together using the overlocker and four-thread overlocking and stitch length 2-2½.

11. Lay pants on a flat surface and measure the waist opening.

12. Cut elastic to three-quarters of this measurement.

13. Place elastic on WS of fabric, insert the elastic and fabric into overlocker, and secure elastic by sewing a few stitches using overlocker and three-thread overlocking and stitch length 3-3½.

14. **Quarter pin mark** waist opening and elastic (Fig. 6, p. 24). Pin elastic to waist, matching up pins.

15. Continue sewing, attaching the elastic to the fabric. Hold the fabric and the elastic in front and at the back, and keep elastic next to the blade, cutting 1 mm (1/16 in) off fabric (Fig. 7, p. 24).

16. Fold elastic over to the WS, and on RS, sew using sewing machine, twin needle and straight stitch, keeping the edge of the foot in line with the folded edge.

17. With RS together, pin and sew the other side seam together using overlocker and four-thread overlocking and stitch length 2-2½.

18. Secure all loose ends by hand or with stitch sealant.

NOTE: A high-cut legline, as illustrated in the G-string gym pants, flatters all shapes and lengthens the legs.

GYM TOP, P. 66, ALL-IN-ONE TIGHTS, P. 69, GYM TOP, P. 66, G-STRING GYM PANTS, P. 70, AND TIGHTS P. 68

Sewer's Companion
Finny - Solingen
Stainless
Solingen
Germany

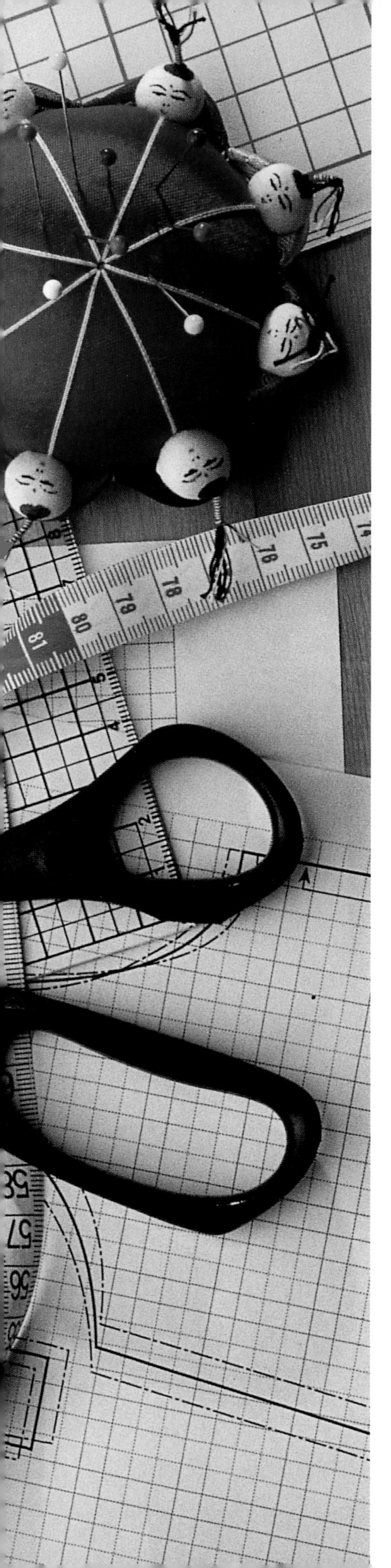

PATTERNS

This section contains the full collection of patterns referred to under each project. Every pattern is numbered and will have to be enlarged according to the scale given on that particular page. On full sized graph paper, one square = 1 cm x 1 cm (½ in x ½ in).

Ensure that you enlarge the pattern pieces accurately – not doing so will result in an ill-fitting garment! In the Introduction on page 15, a step-by-step guide is given on how to scale up a graph pattern. Various products are described on page 19 which will assist you in this, and refer to the instructions on page 14 (Taking Measurements to Determine Size) before beginning. Once this stage is completed, the fun and enjoyment of sewing your own garments begins!

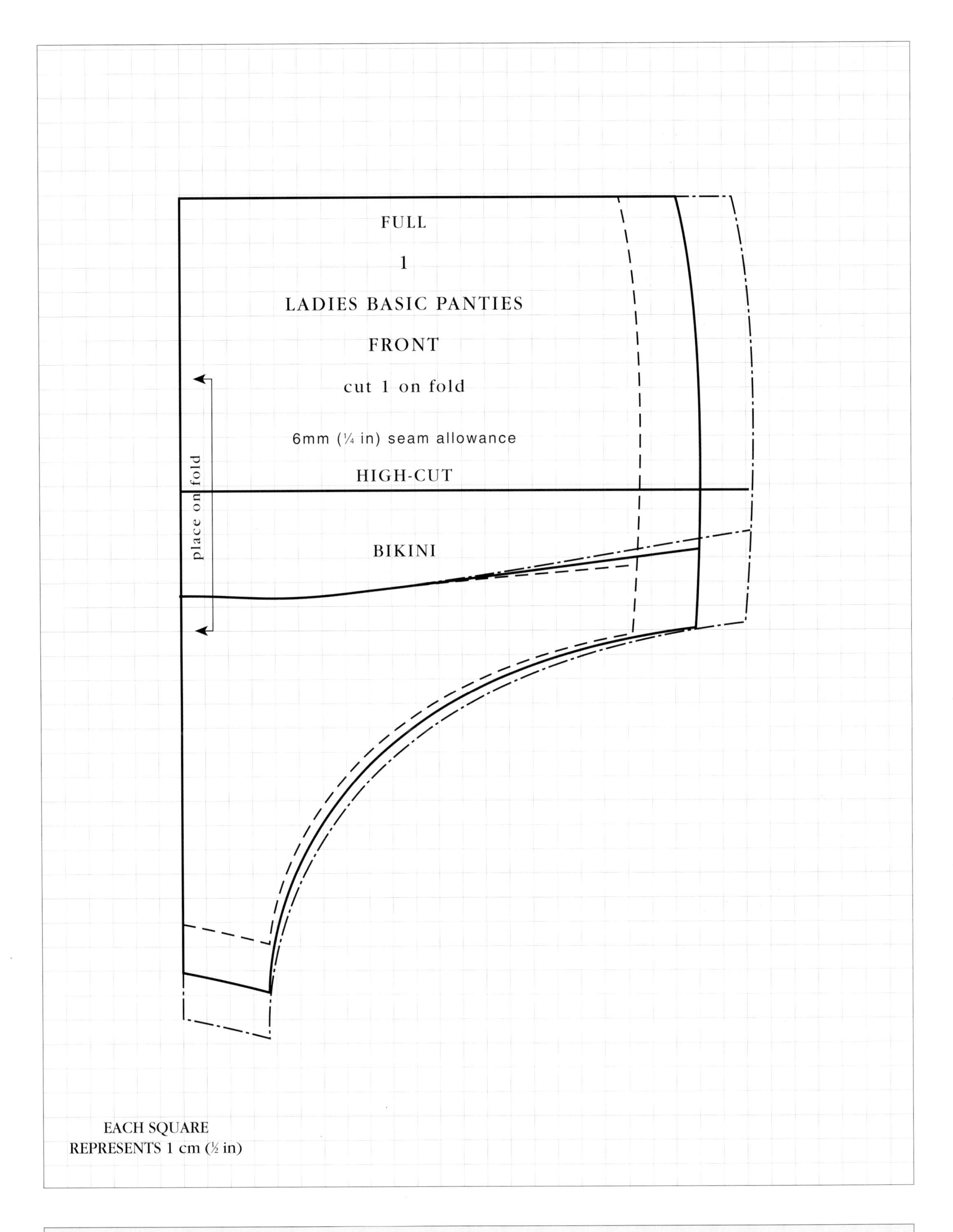
FULL
1
LADIES BASIC PANTIES
FRONT
cut 1 on fold
6mm (¼ in) seam allowance
HIGH-CUT
place on fold
BIKINI
EACH SQUARE
REPRESENTS 1 cm (½ in)

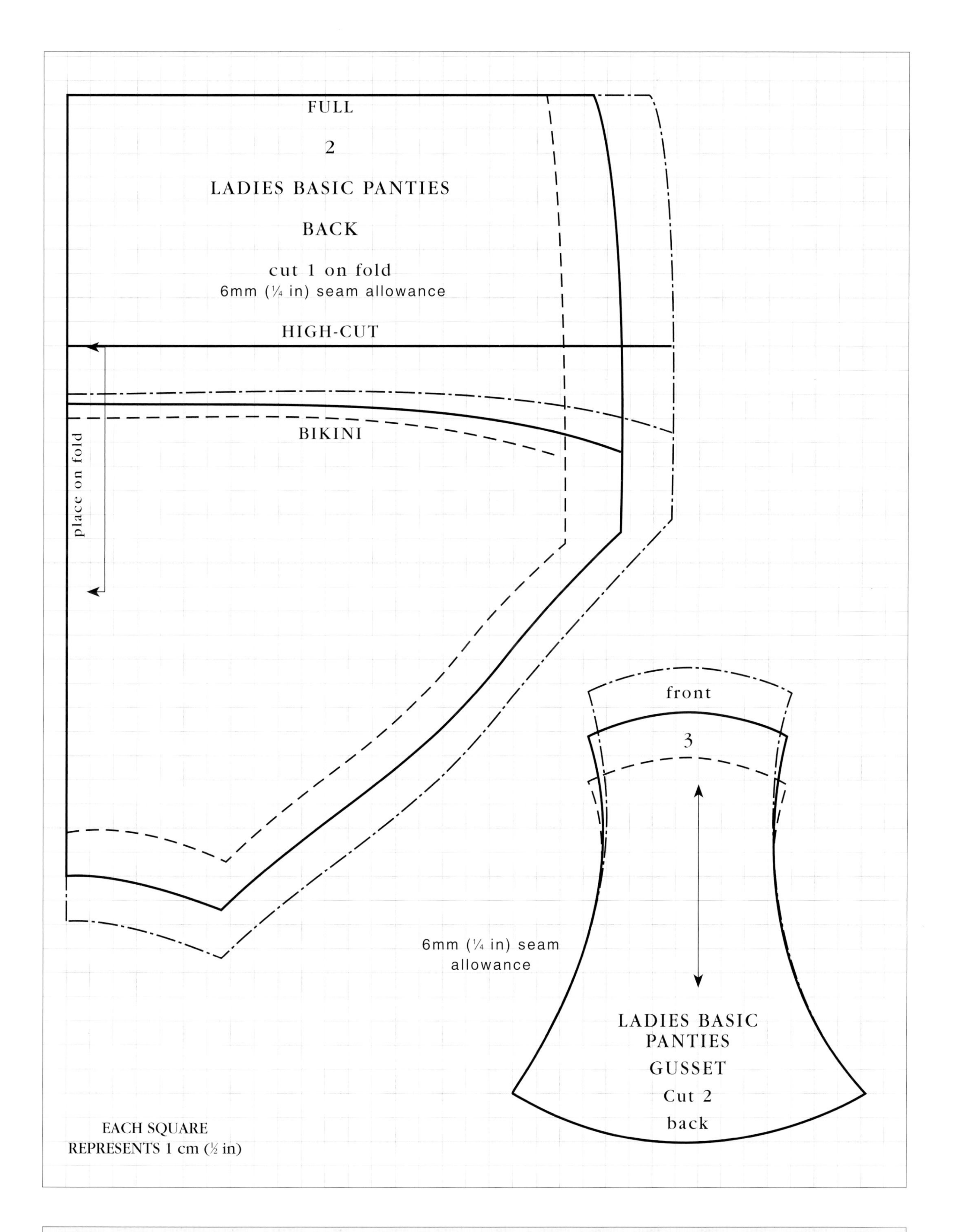
FULL
2
LADIES BASIC PANTIES
BACK
cut 1 on fold
6mm (¼ in) seam allowance
HIGH-CUT
BIKINI
place on fold
front
3
6mm (¼ in) seam
allowance
LADIES BASIC
PANTIES
GUSSET
Cut 2
back
EACH SQUARE
REPRESENTS 1 cm (½ in)

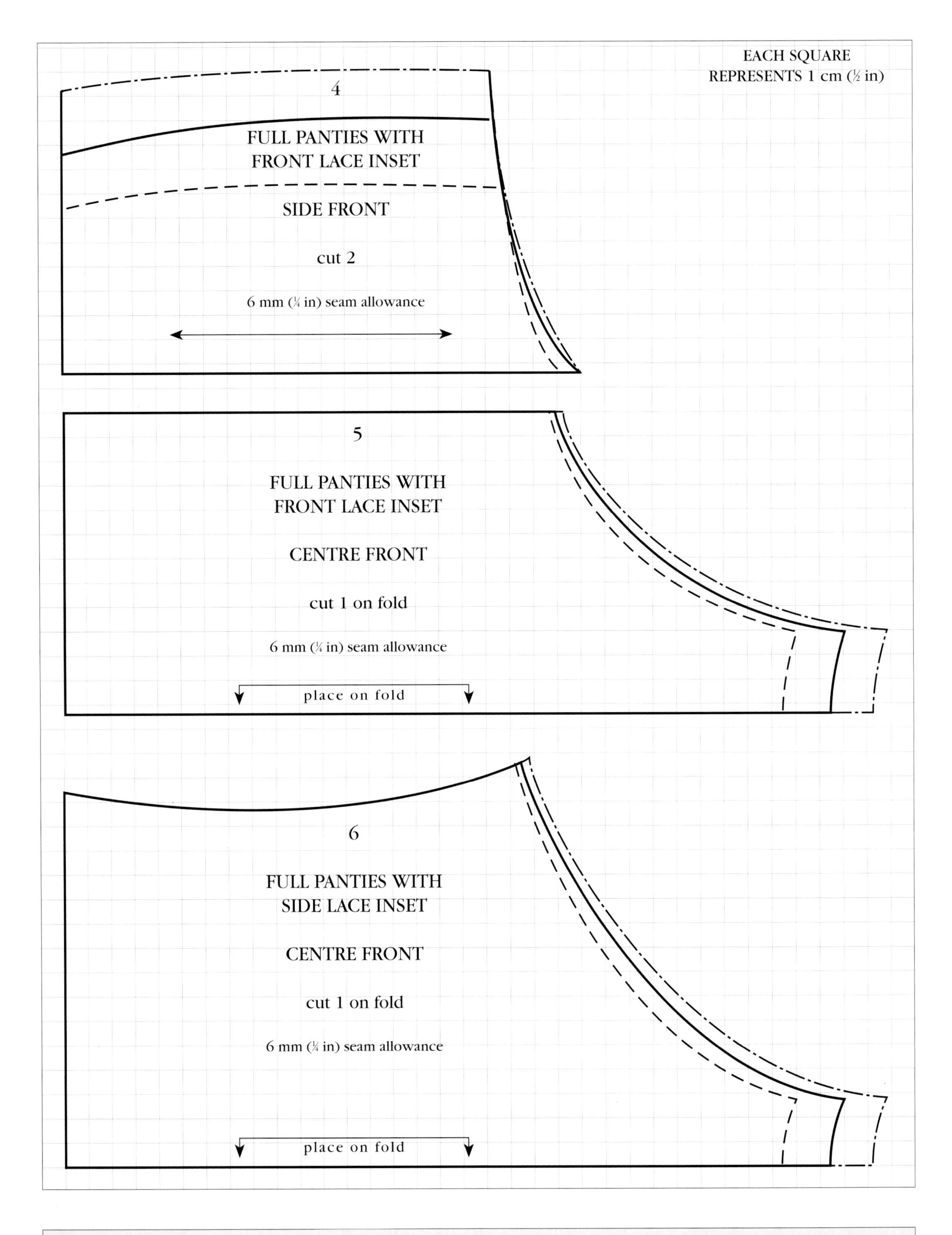
EACH SQUARE
REPRESENTS 1 cm (½ in)
4
FULL PANTIES WITH
FRONT LACE INSET
SIDE FRONT
cut 2
6 mm (¼ in) seam allowance
5
FULL PANTIES WITH
FRONT LACE INSET
CENTRE FRONT
cut 1 on fold
6 mm (¼ in) seam allowance
place on fold
6
FULL PANTIES WITH
SIDE LACE INSET
CENTRE FRONT
cut 1 on fold
6 mm (¼ in) seam allowance
place on fold

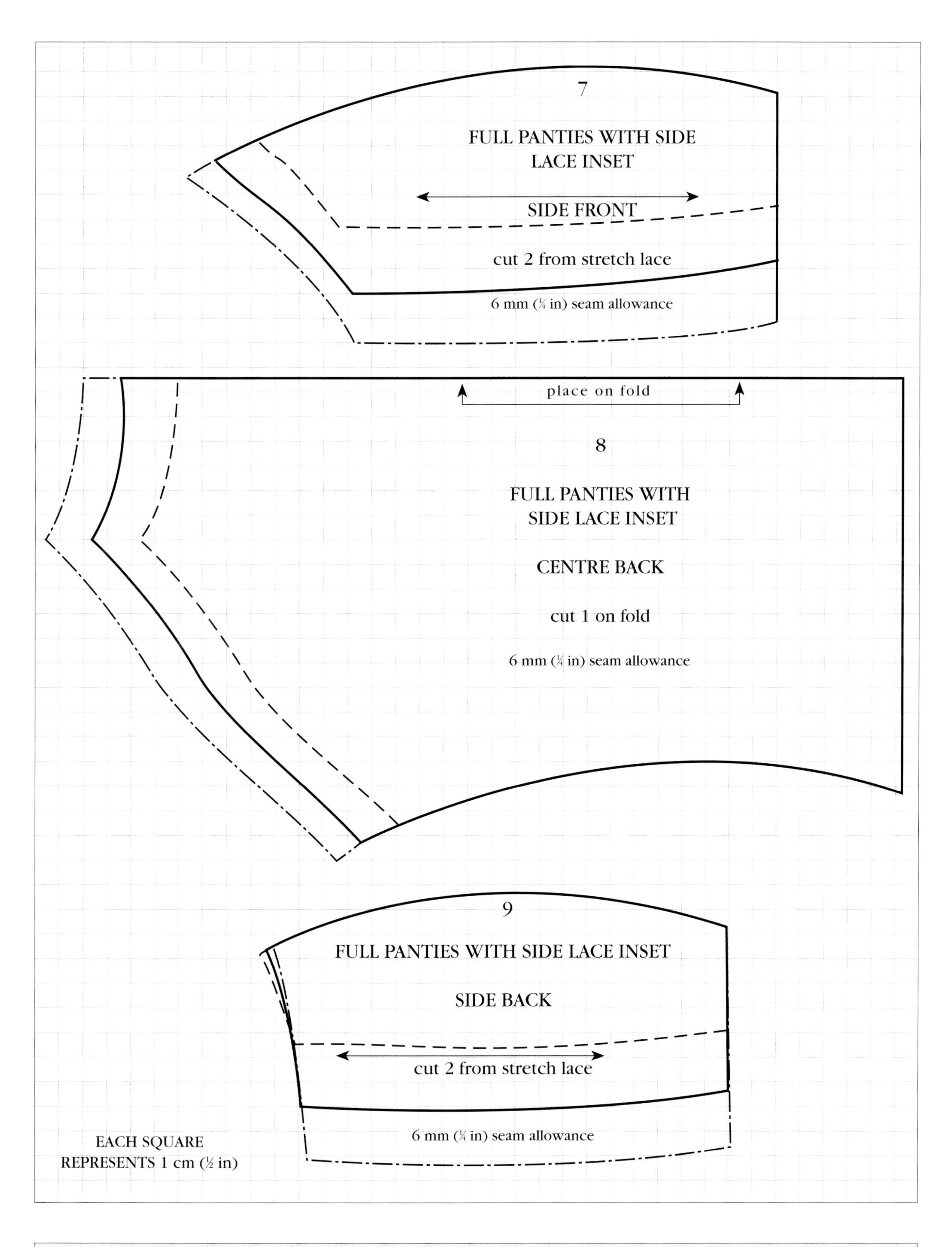
7
FULL PANTIES WITH SIDE
LACE INSET
SIDE FRONT
cut 2 from stretch lace
6 mm (¼ in) seam allowance
place on fold
8
FULL PANTIES WITH
SIDE LACE INSET
CENTRE BACK
cut 1 on fold
6 mm (¼ in) seam allowance
9
FULL PANTIES WITH SIDE LACE INSET
SIDE BACK
cut 2 from stretch lace
6 mm (¼ in) seam allowance
EACH SQUARE
REPRESENTS 1 cm (½ in)

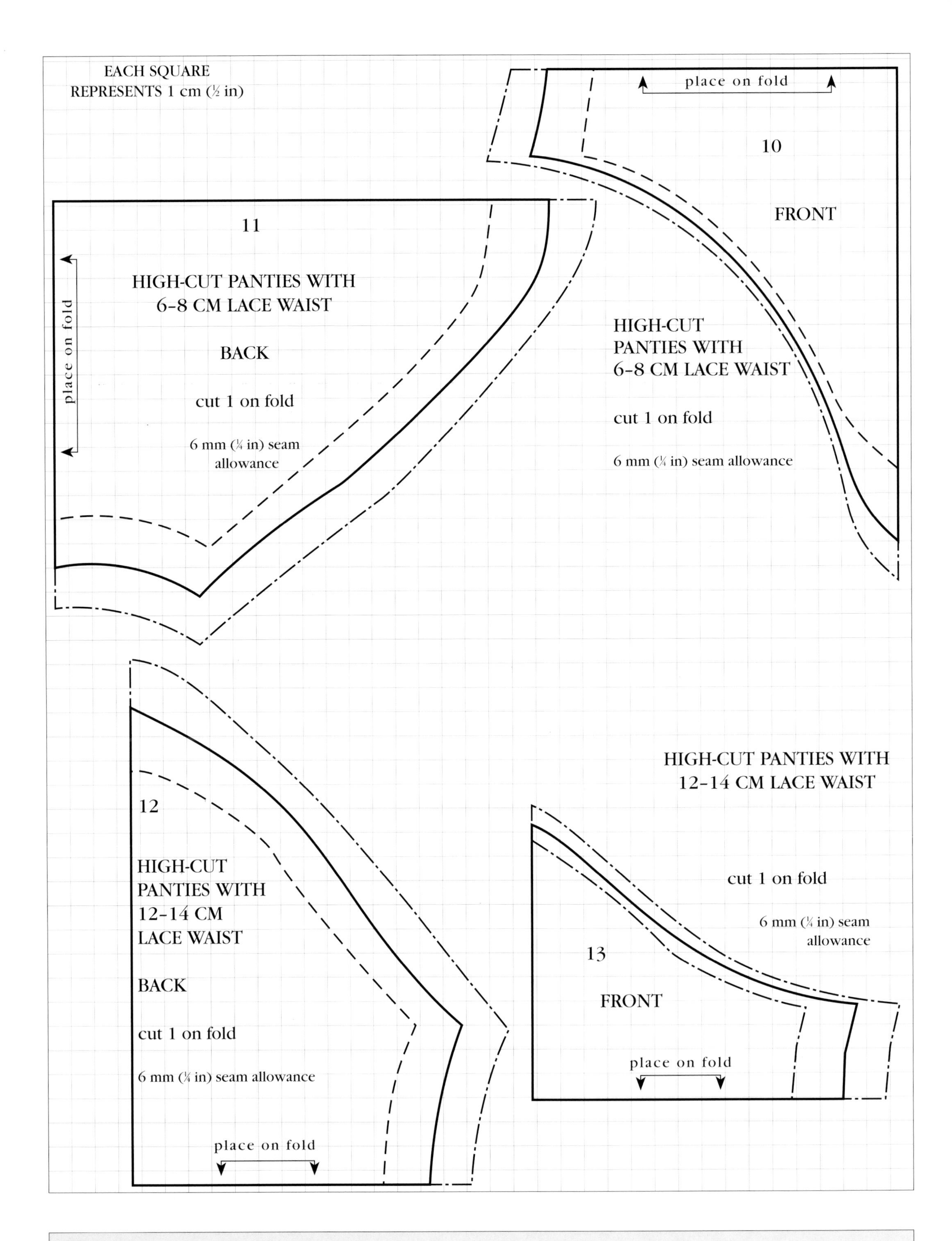
EACH SQUARE
REPRESENTS 1 cm (½ in)
place on fold
10
FRONT
HIGH-CUT
PANTIES WITH
6-8 CM LACE WAIST
cut 1 on fold
6 mm (¼ in) seam allowance
11
HIGH-CUT PANTIES WITH
6-8 CM LACE WAIST
BACK
cut 1 on fold
6 mm (¼ in) seam
allowance
place on fold
12
HIGH-CUT
PANTIES WITH
12-14 CM
LACE WAIST
BACK
cut 1 on fold
6 mm (¼ in) seam allowance
place on fold
HIGH-CUT PANTIES WITH
12-14 CM LACE WAIST
cut 1 on fold
6 mm (¼ in) seam
allowance
13
FRONT
place on fold

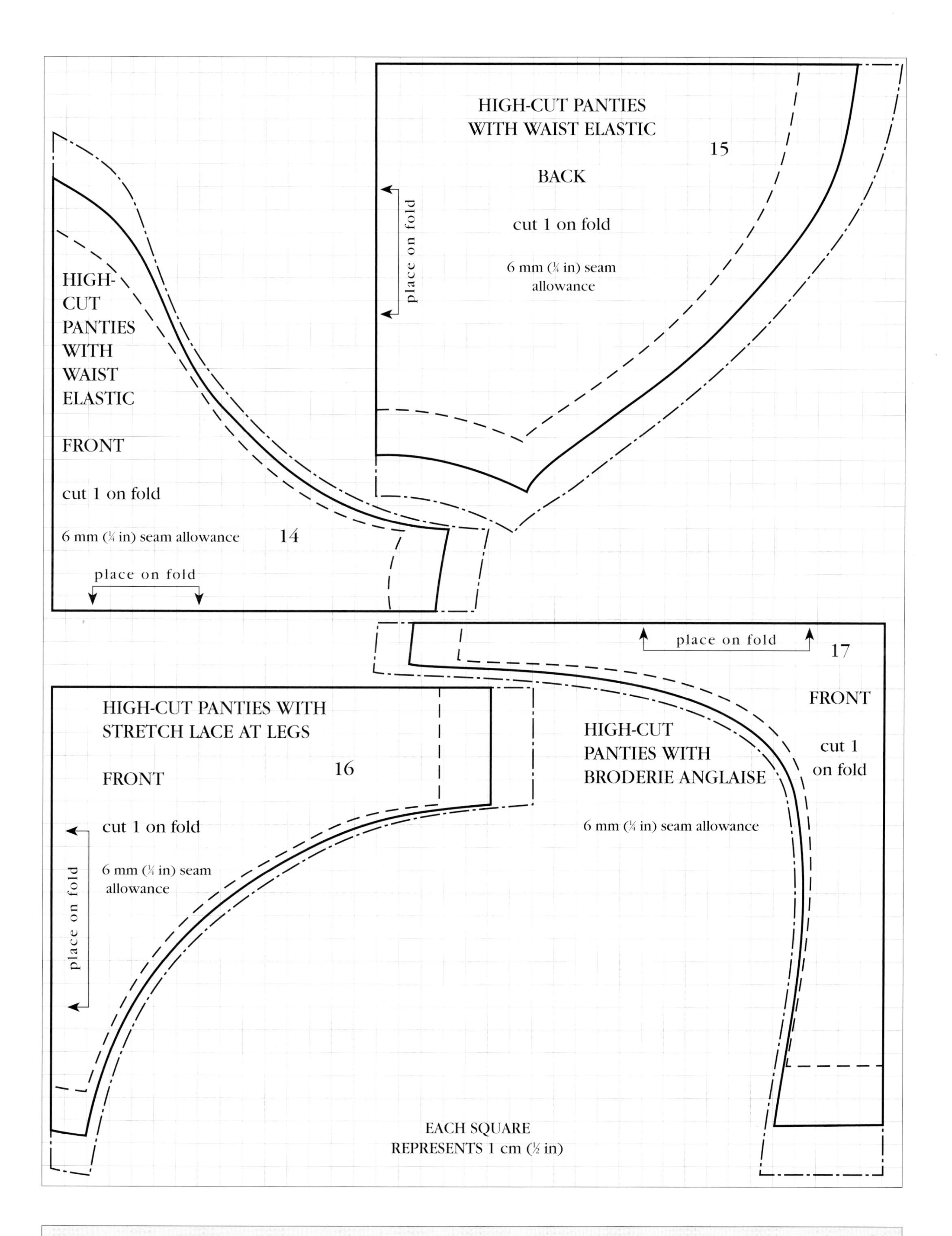
HIGH-CUT PANTIES
WITH WAIST ELASTIC
15
BACK
cut 1 on fold
6 mm (¼ in) seam
allowance
place on fold
HIGH-
CUT
PANTIES
WITH
WAIST
ELASTIC
FRONT
cut 1 on fold
6 mm (¼ in) seam allowance
14
place on fold
place on fold
17
FRONT
cut 1
on fold
HIGH-CUT PANTIES WITH
STRETCH LACE AT LEGS
16
FRONT
cut 1 on fold
6 mm (¼ in) seam
allowance
place on fold
HIGH-CUT
PANTIES WITH
BRODERIE ANGLAISE
6 mm (¼ in) seam allowance
EACH SQUARE
REPRESENTS 1 cm (½ in)

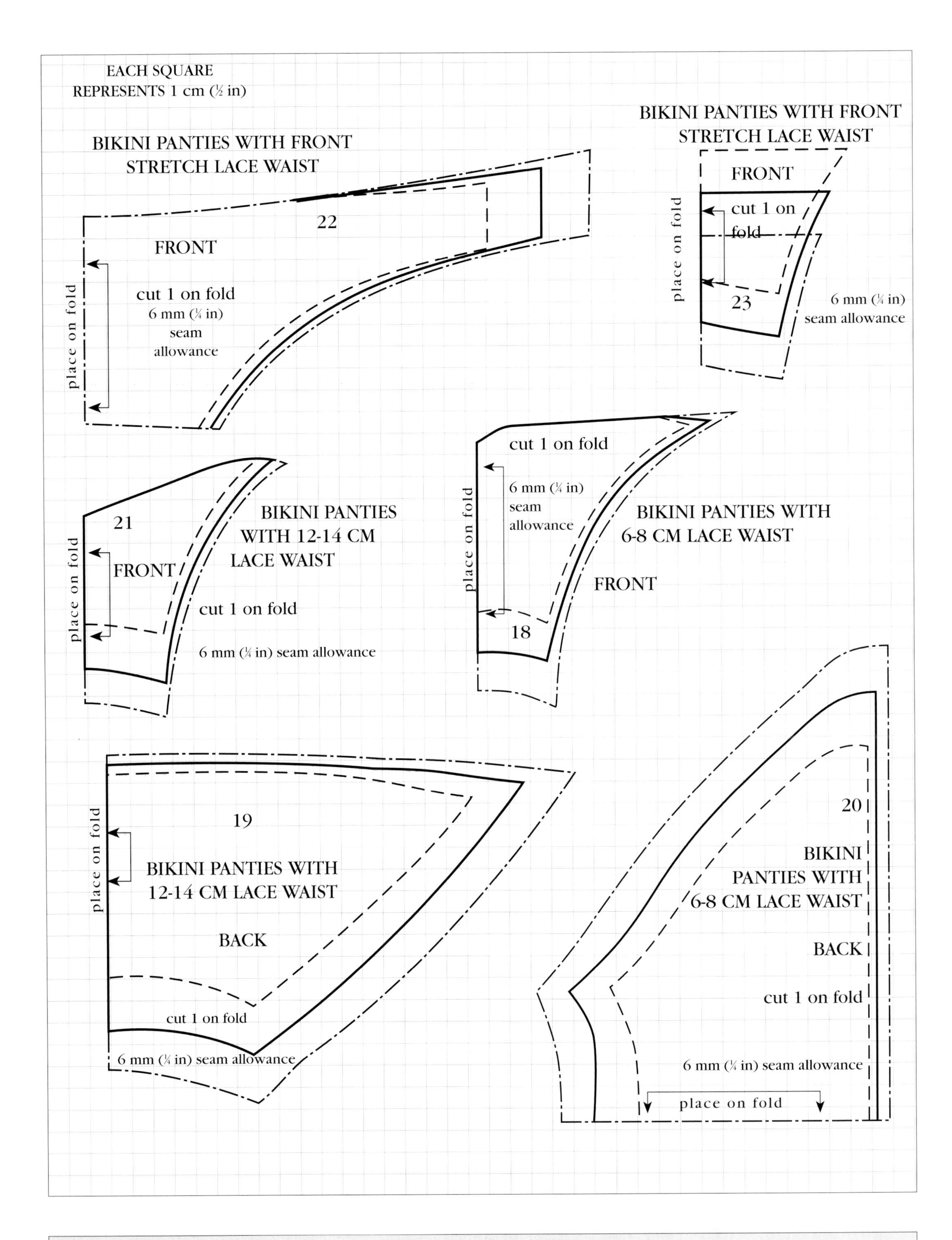
EACH SQUARE
REPRESENTS 1 cm (¼ in)
BIKINI PANTIES WITH FRONT
STRETCH LACE WAIST
22
FRONT
place on fold
cut 1 on fold
6 mm (¼ in)
seam
allowance
BIKINI PANTIES WITH FRONT
STRETCH LACE WAIST
FRONT
cut 1 on
fold
place on fold
23
6 mm (¼ in)
seam allowance
21
place on fold
FRONT
BIKINI PANTIES
WITH 12-14 CM
LACE WAIST
cut 1 on fold
6 mm (¼ in) seam allowance
cut 1 on fold
6 mm (¼ in)
seam
allowance
place on fold
BIKINI PANTIES WITH
6-8 CM LACE WAIST
FRONT
18
19
place on fold
BIKINI PANTIES WITH
12-14 CM LACE WAIST
BACK
cut 1 on fold
6 mm (¼ in) seam allowance
20
BIKINI
PANTIES WITH
6-8 CM LACE WAIST
BACK
cut 1 on fold
6 mm (¼ in) seam allowance
place on fold

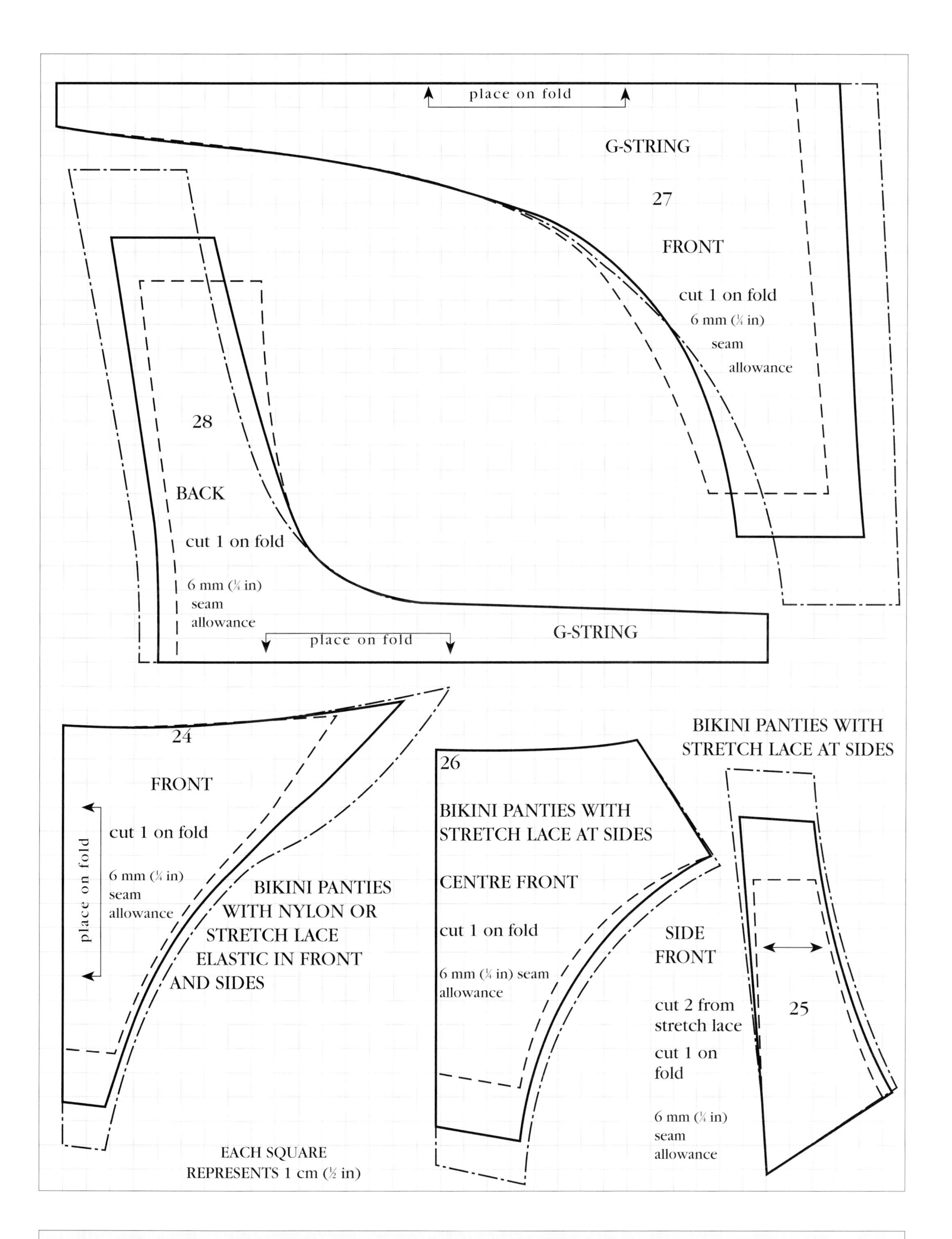
place on fold
G-STRING
27
FRONT
cut 1 on fold
6 mm (¼ in)
seam
allowance
28
BACK
cut 1 on fold
6 mm (¼ in)
seam
allowance
place on fold
G-STRING
24
FRONT
place on fold
cut 1 on fold
6 mm (¼ in)
seam
allowance
BIKINI PANTIES
WITH NYLON OR
STRETCH LACE
ELASTIC IN FRONT
AND SIDES
26
BIKINI PANTIES WITH
STRETCH LACE AT SIDES
CENTRE FRONT
cut 1 on fold
6 mm (¼ in) seam
allowance
BIKINI PANTIES WITH
STRETCH LACE AT SIDES
SIDE
FRONT
25
cut 2 from
stretch lace
cut 1 on
fold
6 mm (¼ in)
seam
allowance
EACH SQUARE
REPRESENTS 1 cm (½ in)

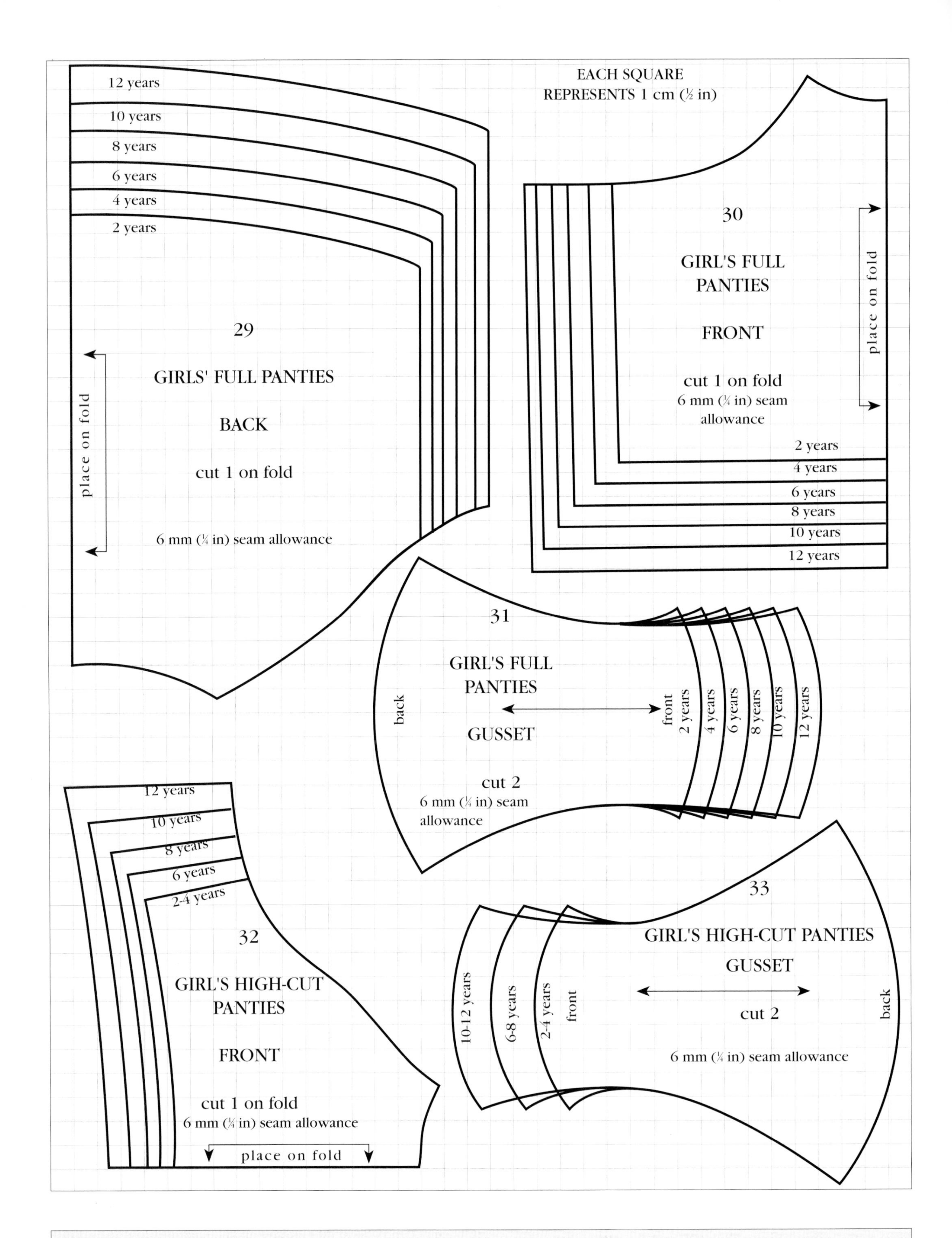
EACH SQUARE
REPRESENTS 1 cm (½ in)
12 years
10 years
8 years
6 years
4 years
2 years
29
GIRLS' FULL PANTIES
BACK
cut 1 on fold
6 mm (¼ in) seam allowance
place on fold
30
GIRL'S FULL
PANTIES
FRONT
cut 1 on fold
6 mm (¼ in) seam
allowance
place on fold
2 years
4 years
6 years
8 years
10 years
12 years
31
GIRL'S FULL
PANTIES
GUSSET
cut 2
6 mm (¼ in) seam
allowance
back
front
2 years
4 years
6 years
8 years
10 years
12 years
12 years
10 years
8 years
6 years
2-4 years
32
GIRL'S HIGH-CUT
PANTIES
FRONT
cut 1 on fold
6 mm (¼ in) seam allowance
place on fold
33
GIRL'S HIGH-CUT PANTIES
GUSSET
cut 2
6 mm (¼ in) seam allowance
10-12 years
6-8 years
2-4 years
front
back

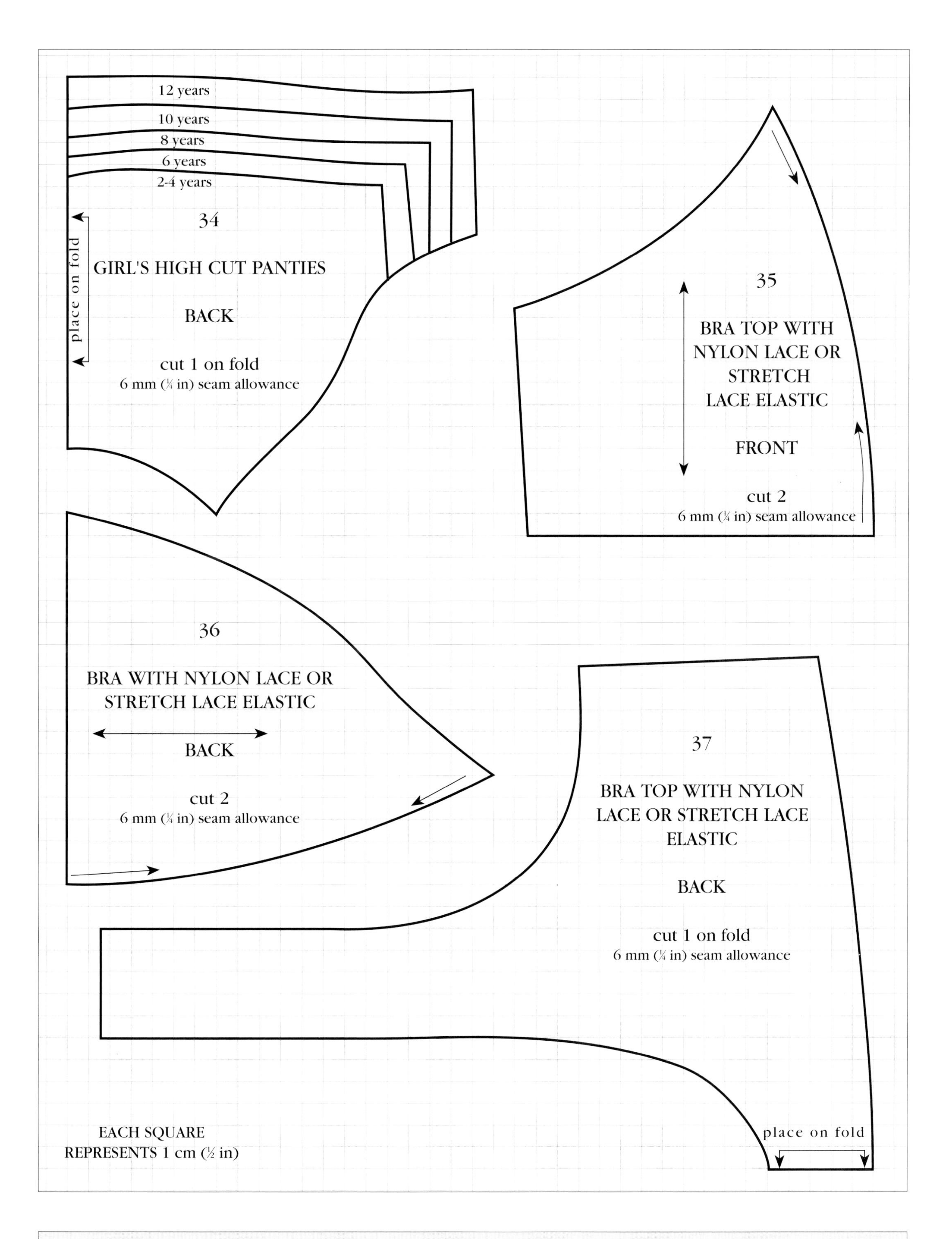
12 years
10 years
8 years
6 years
2-4 years
34
place on fold
GIRL'S HIGH CUT PANTIES
BACK
cut 1 on fold
6 mm (¼ in) seam allowance
35
BRA TOP WITH
NYLON LACE OR
STRETCH
LACE ELASTIC
FRONT
cut 2
6 mm (¼ in) seam allowance
36
BRA WITH NYLON LACE OR
STRETCH LACE ELASTIC
BACK
cut 2
6 mm (¼ in) seam allowance
37
BRA TOP WITH NYLON
LACE OR STRETCH LACE
ELASTIC
BACK
cut 1 on fold
6 mm (¼ in) seam allowance
place on fold
EACH SQUARE
REPRESENTS 1 cm (½ in)

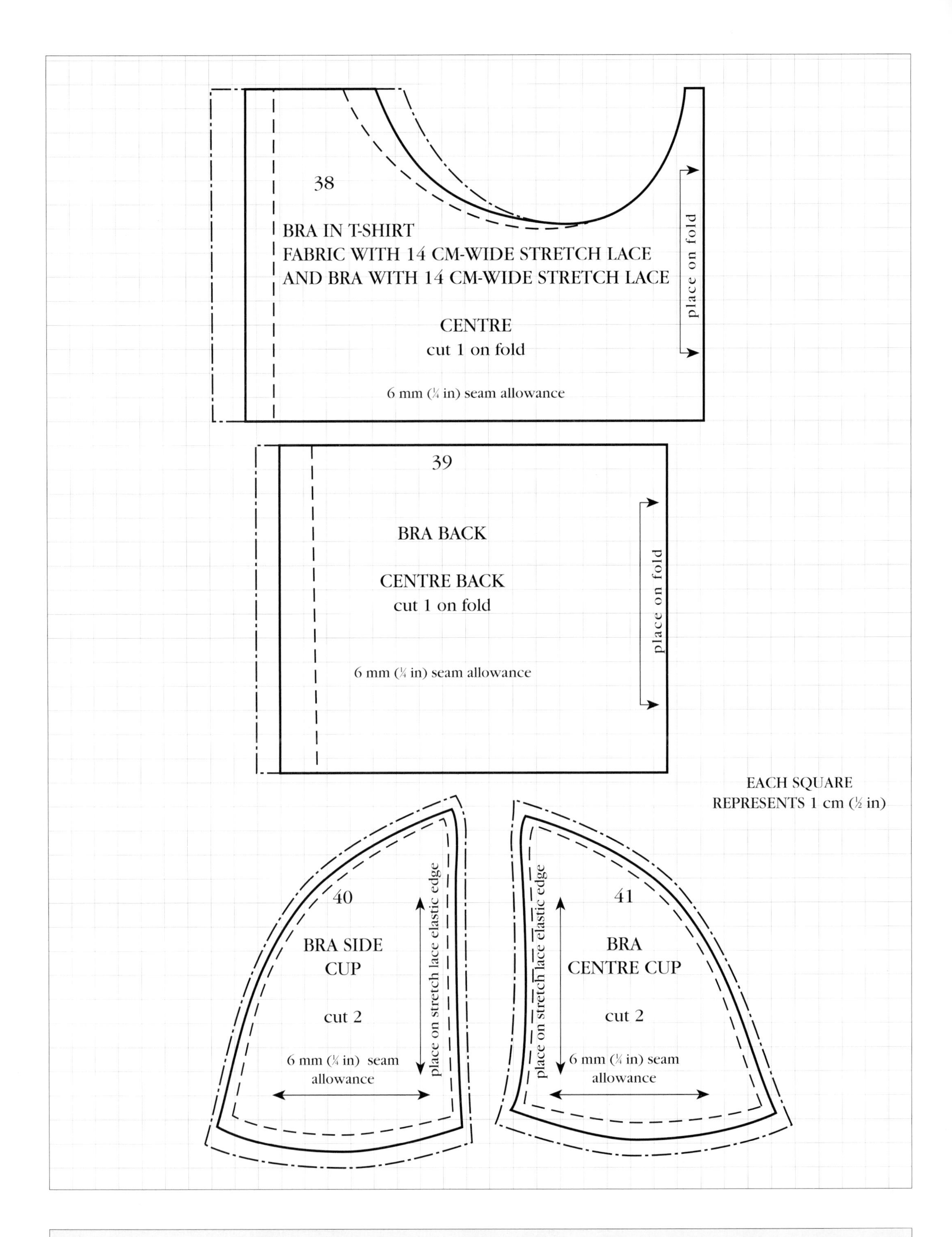
38
BRA IN T-SHIRT
FABRIC WITH 14 CM-WIDE STRETCH LACE
AND BRA WITH 14 CM-WIDE STRETCH LACE
CENTRE
cut 1 on fold
6 mm (¼ in) seam allowance
place on fold
39
BRA BACK
CENTRE BACK
cut 1 on fold
6 mm (¼ in) seam allowance
place on fold
EACH SQUARE
REPRESENTS 1 cm (½ in)
40
BRA SIDE
CUP
cut 2
6 mm (¼ in) seam
allowance
place on stretch lace elastic edge
41
BRA
CENTRE CUP
cut 2
6 mm (¼ in) seam
allowance
place on stretch lace elastic edge

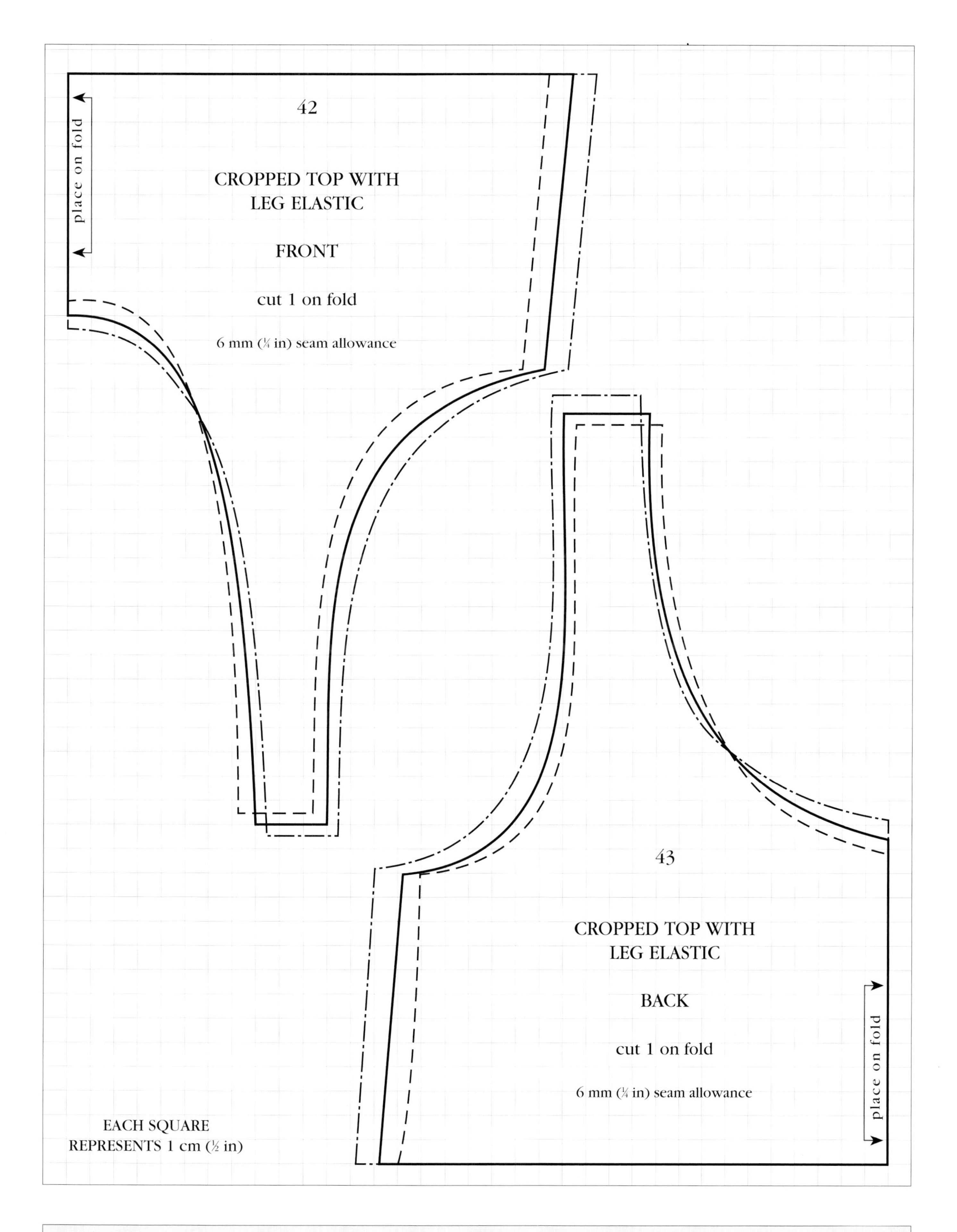
42
place on fold
CROPPED TOP WITH
LEG ELASTIC
FRONT
cut 1 on fold
6 mm (¼ in) seam allowance
43
CROPPED TOP WITH
LEG ELASTIC
BACK
cut 1 on fold
6 mm (¼ in) seam allowance
place on fold
EACH SQUARE
REPRESENTS 1 cm (½ in)

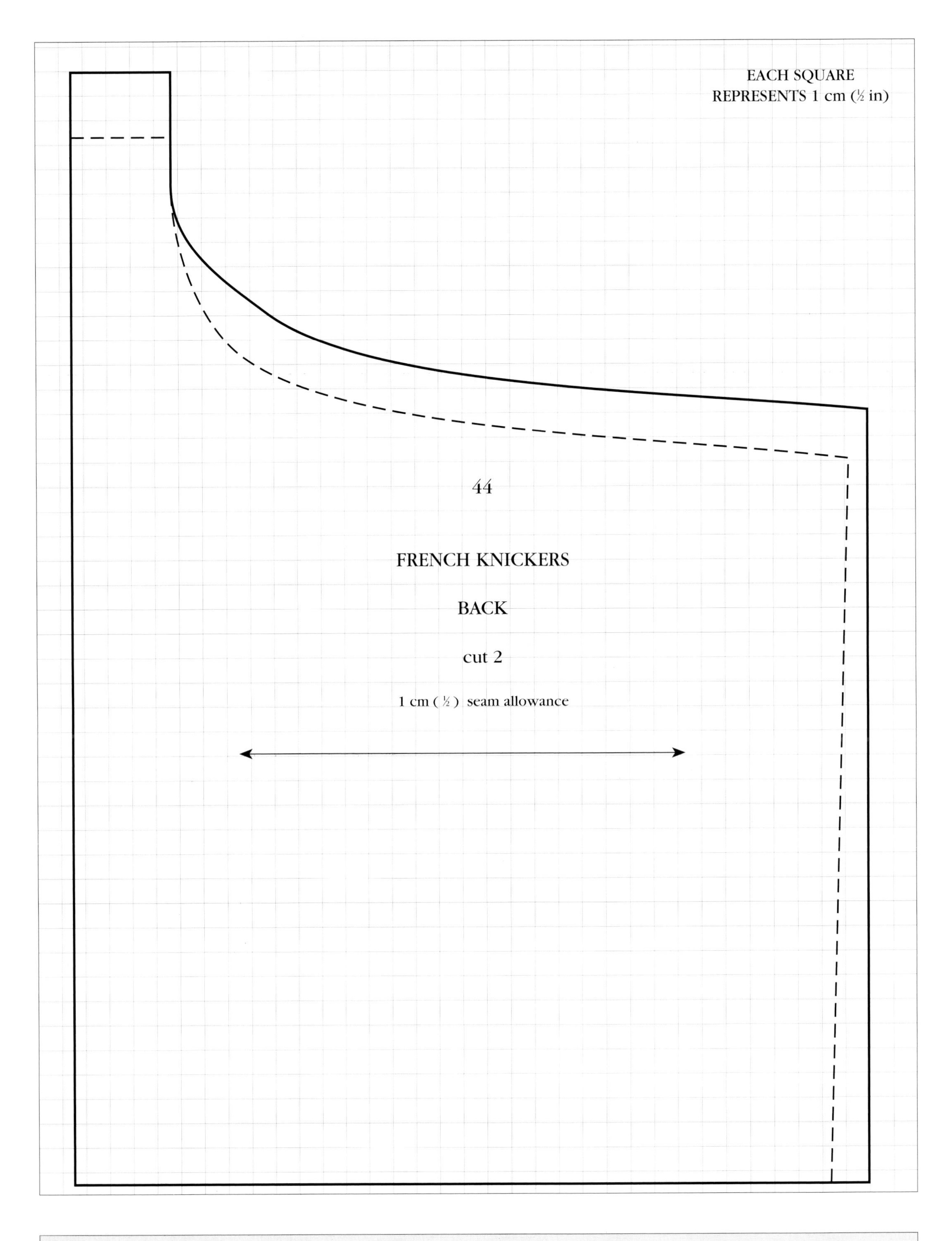
EACH SQUARE
REPRESENTS 1 cm (½ in)
44
FRENCH KNICKERS
BACK
cut 2
1 cm (½) seam allowance

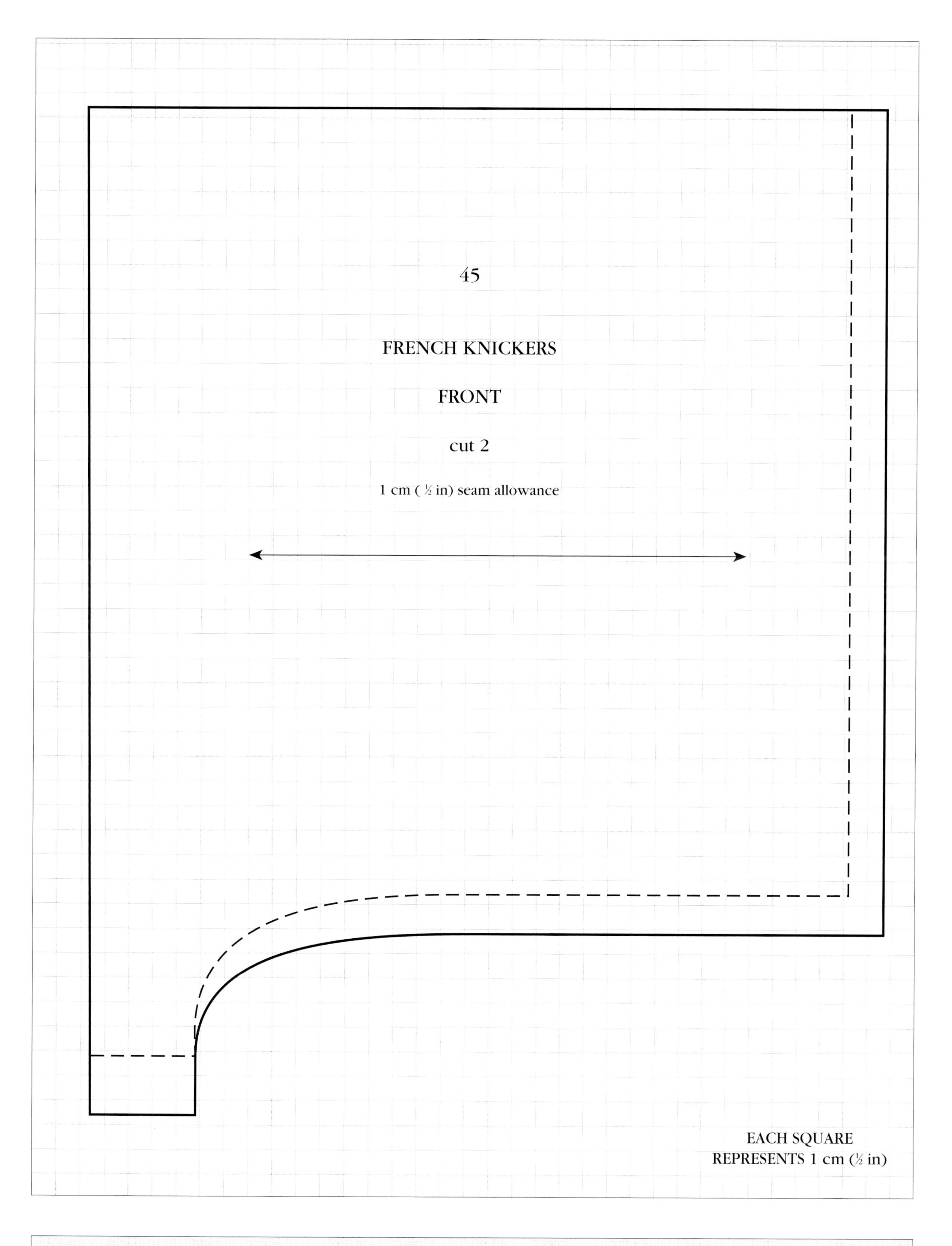
45
FRENCH KNICKERS
FRONT
cut 2
1 cm (½ in) seam allowance
EACH SQUARE
REPRESENTS 1 cm (½ in)

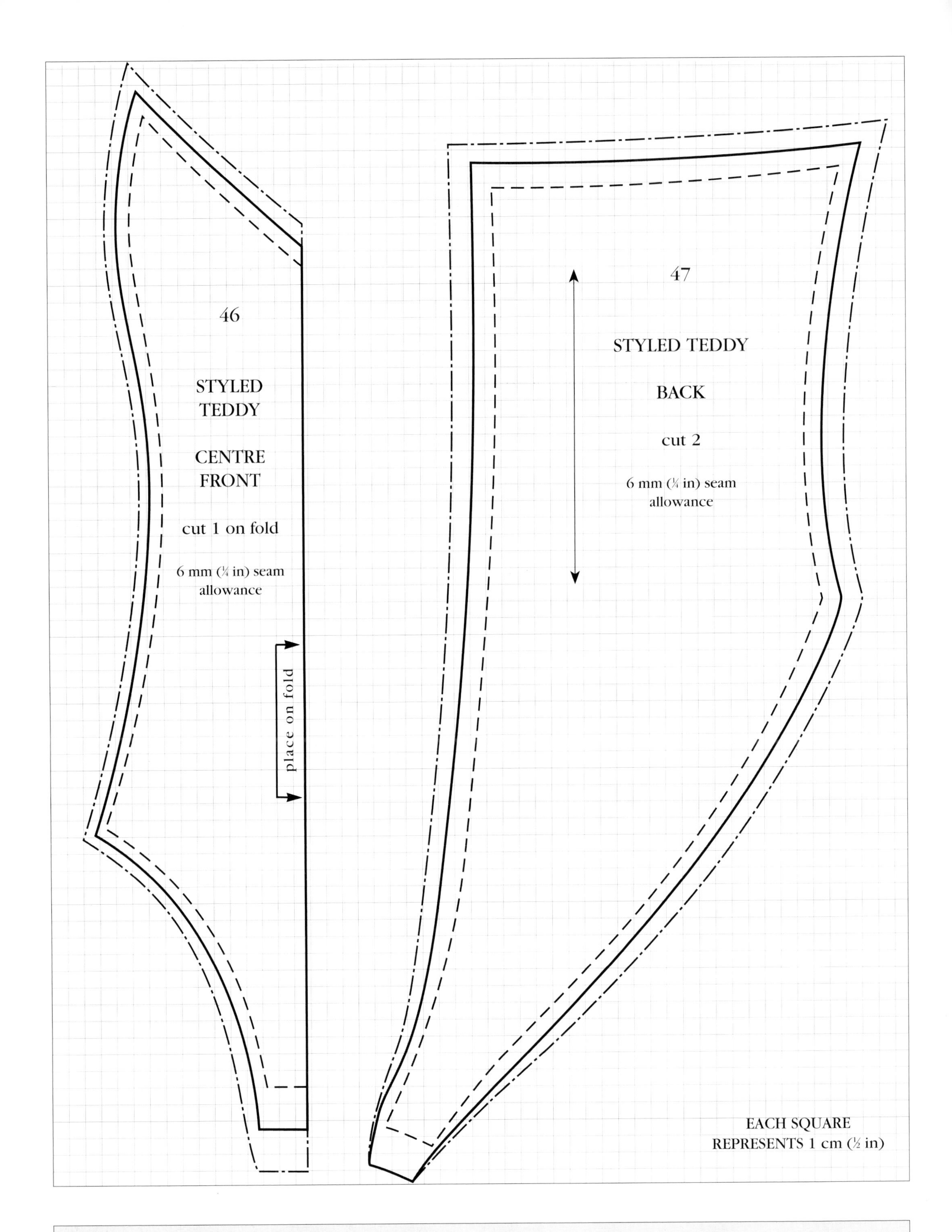
46
STYLED
TEDDY
CENTRE
FRONT
cut 1 on fold
6 mm (¼ in) seam
allowance
place on fold
47
STYLED TEDDY
BACK
cut 2
6 mm (¼ in) seam
allowance
EACH SQUARE
REPRESENTS 1 cm (½ in)

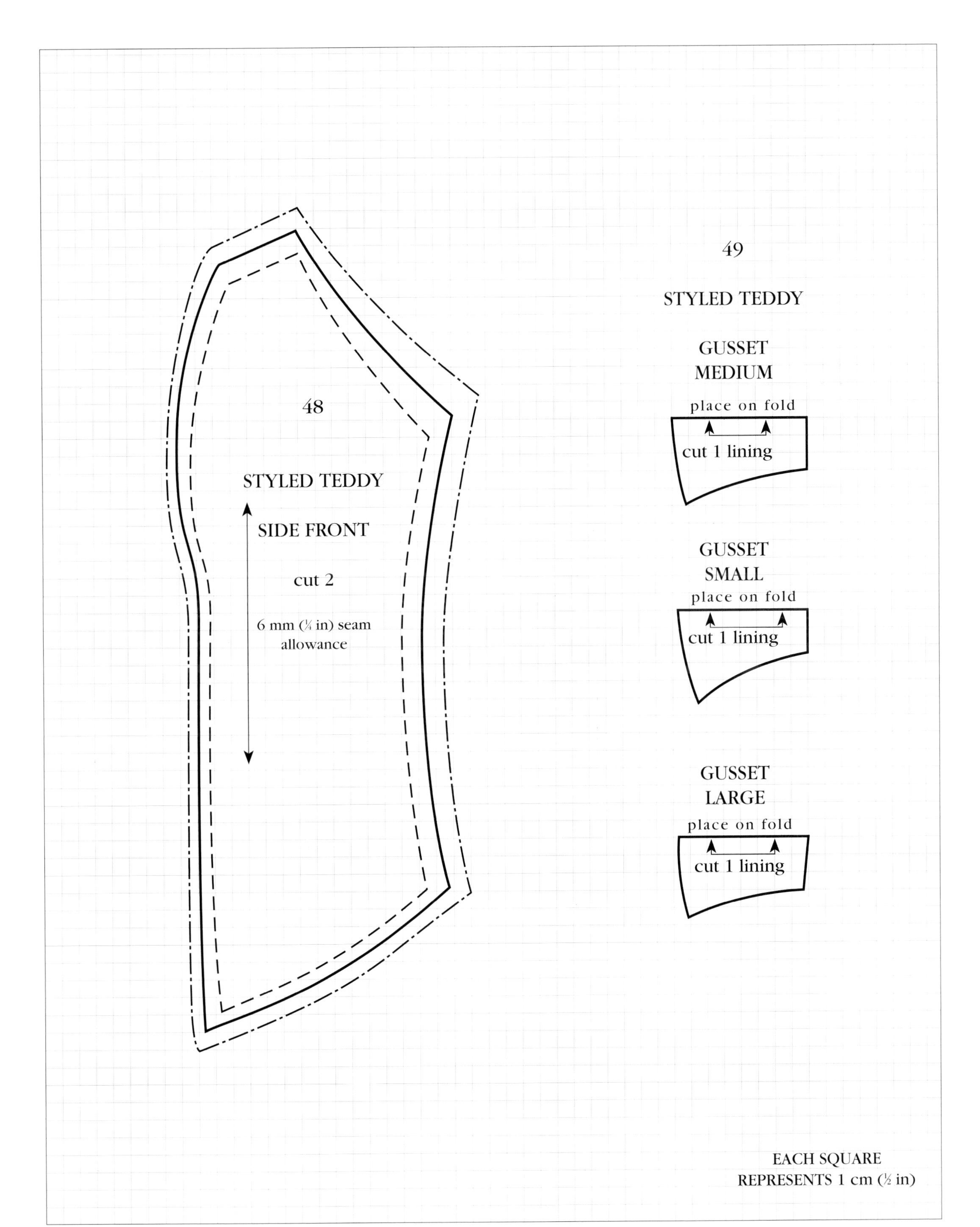
48
STYLED TEDDY
SIDE FRONT
cut 2
6 mm (¼ in) seam
allowance
49
STYLED TEDDY
GUSSET
MEDIUM
place on fold
cut 1 lining
GUSSET
SMALL
place on fold
cut 1 lining
GUSSET
LARGE
place on fold
cut 1 lining
EACH SQUARE
REPRESENTS 1 cm (½ in)

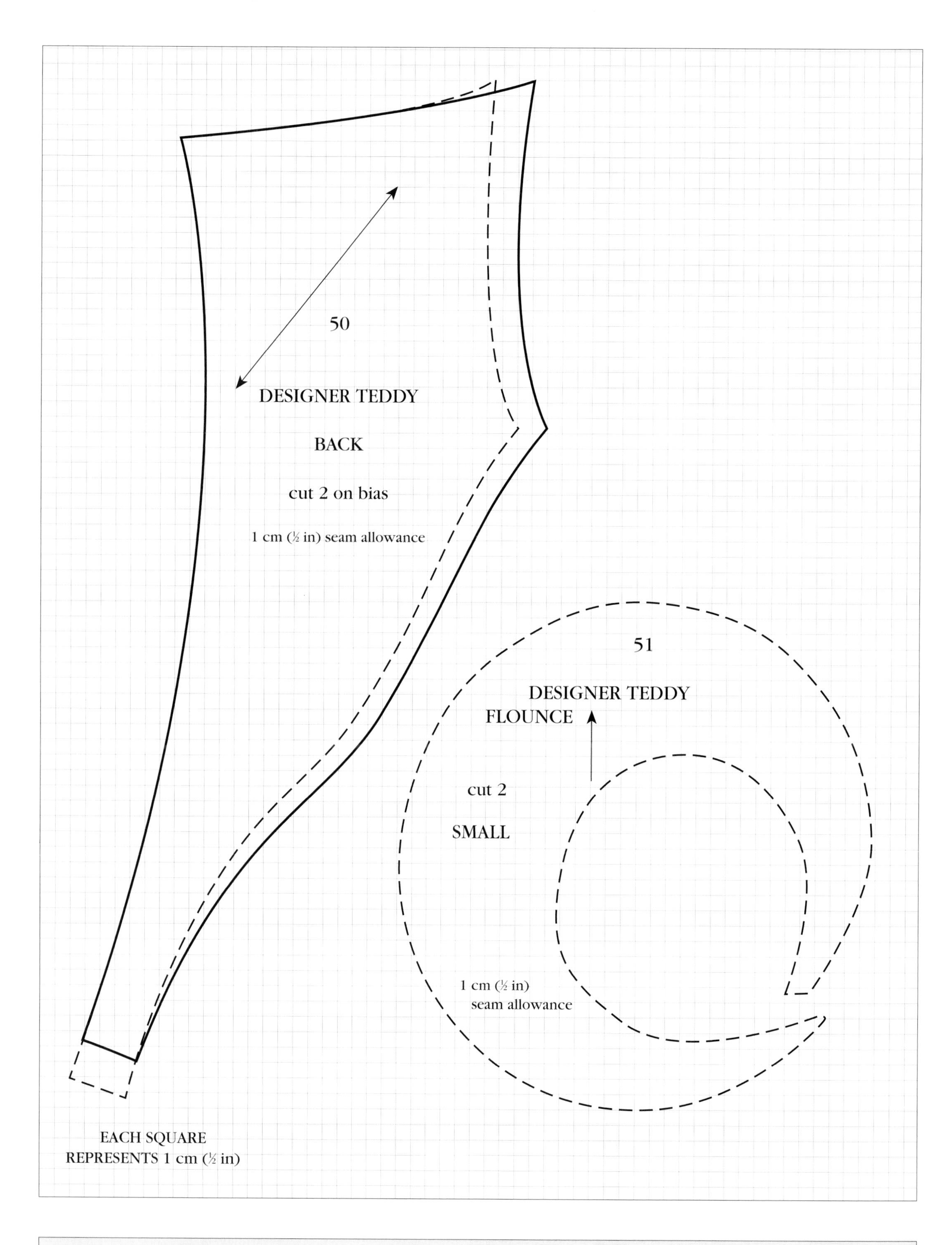
50
DESIGNER TEDDY
BACK
cut 2 on bias
1 cm (½ in) seam allowance
51
DESIGNER TEDDY
FLOUNCE
cut 2
SMALL
1 cm (½ in)
seam allowance
EACH SQUARE
REPRESENTS 1 cm (½ in)

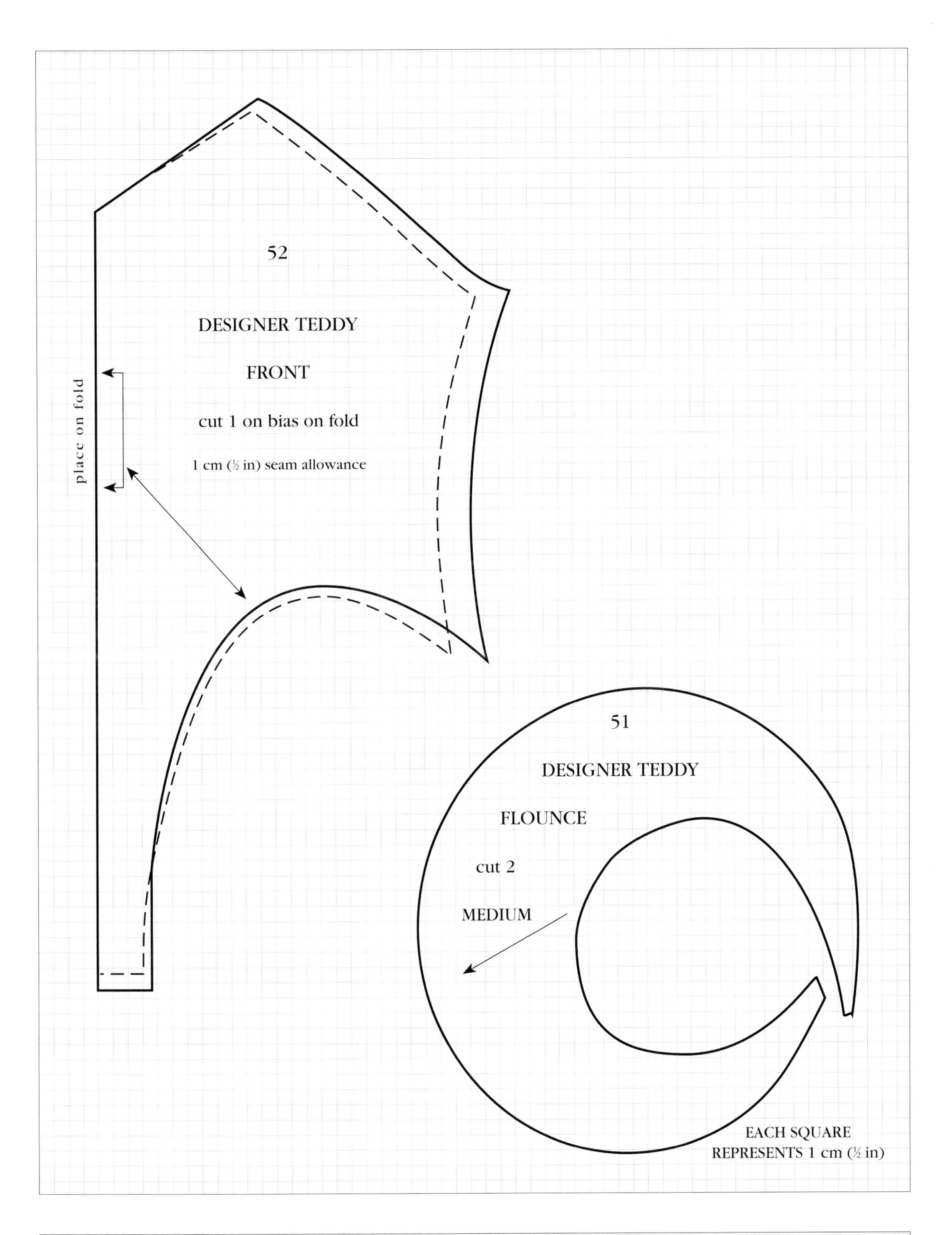
52
DESIGNER TEDDY
FRONT
cut 1 on bias on fold
1 cm (½ in) seam allowance
place on fold
51
DESIGNER TEDDY
FLOUNCE
cut 2
MEDIUM
EACH SQUARE
REPRESENTS 1 cm (½ in)

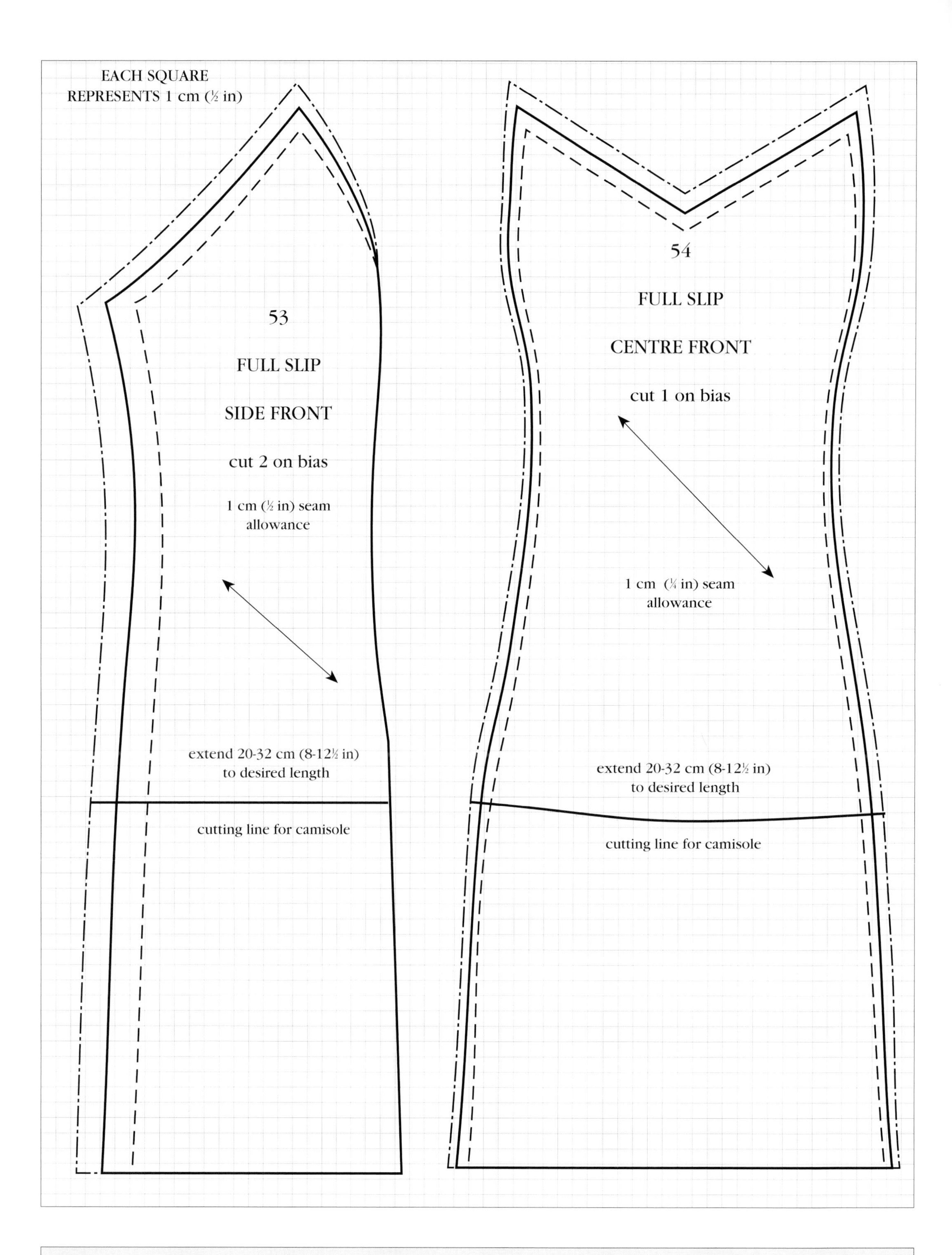
EACH SQUARE
REPRESENTS 1 cm (½ in)
53
FULL SLIP
SIDE FRONT
cut 2 on bias
1 cm (½ in) seam
allowance
extend 20-32 cm (8-12½ in)
to desired length
cutting line for camisole
54
FULL SLIP
CENTRE FRONT
cut 1 on bias
1 cm (¼ in) seam
allowance
extend 20-32 cm (8-12½ in)
to desired length
cutting line for camisole

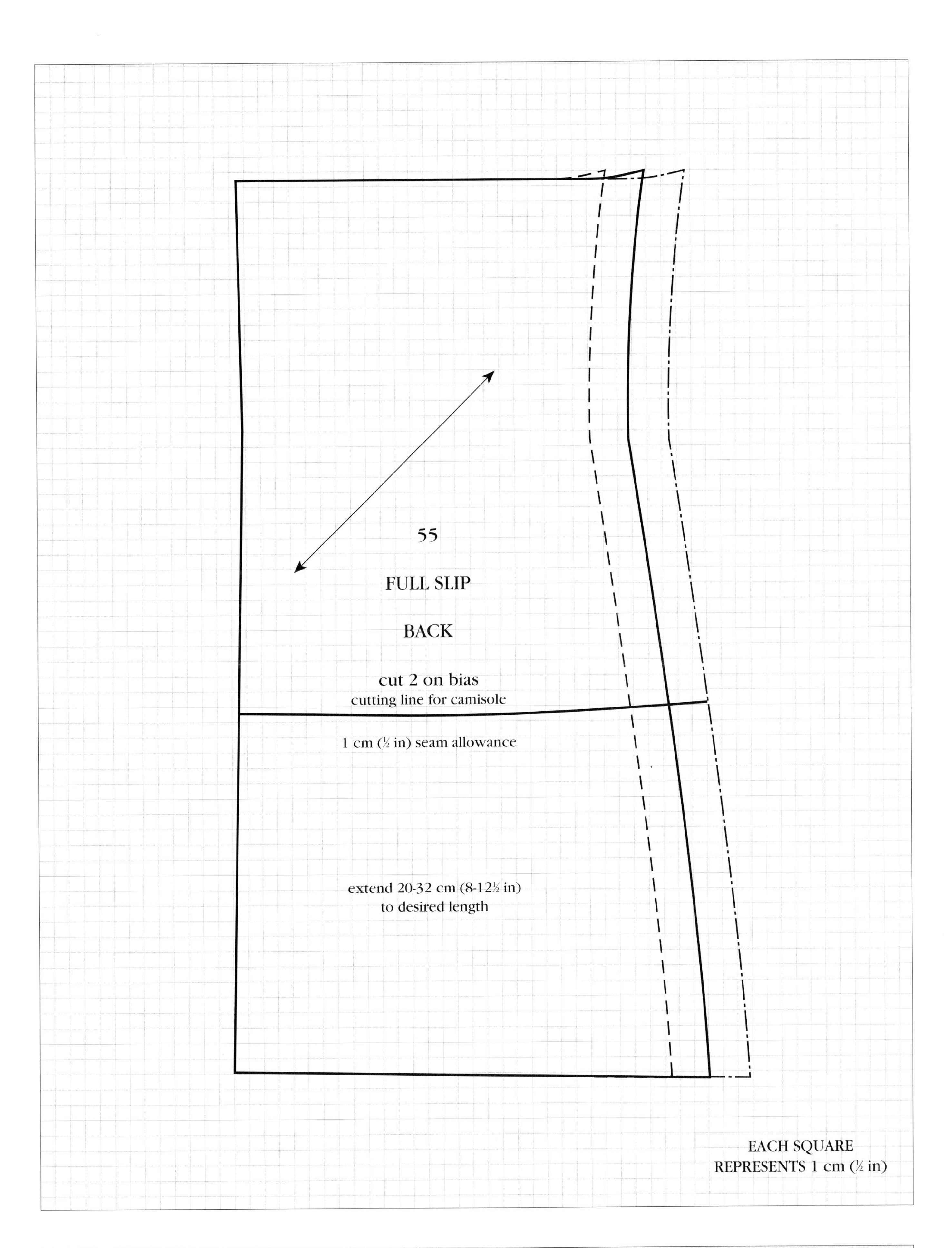
55
FULL SLIP
BACK
cut 2 on bias
cutting line for camisole
1 cm (½ in) seam allowance
extend 20-32 cm (8-12½ in)
to desired length
EACH SQUARE
REPRESENTS 1 cm (½ in)

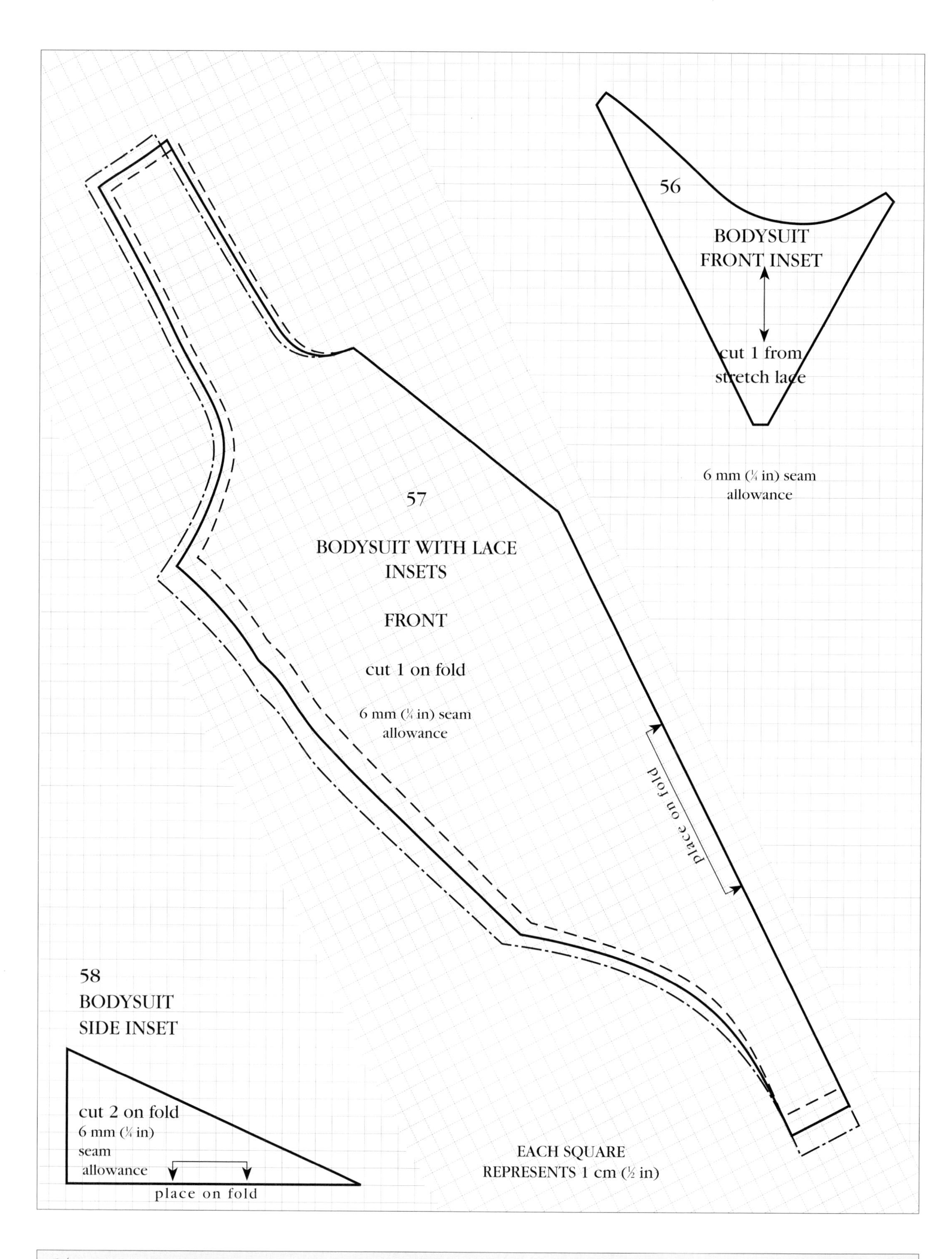
56
BODYSUIT
FRONT INSET
cut 1 from
stretch lace
6 mm (¼ in) seam
allowance
57
BODYSUIT WITH LACE
INSETS
FRONT
cut 1 on fold
6 mm (¼ in) seam
allowance
place on fold
58
BODYSUIT
SIDE INSET
cut 2 on fold
6 mm (¼ in)
seam
allowance
place on fold
EACH SQUARE
REPRESENTS 1 cm (½ in)

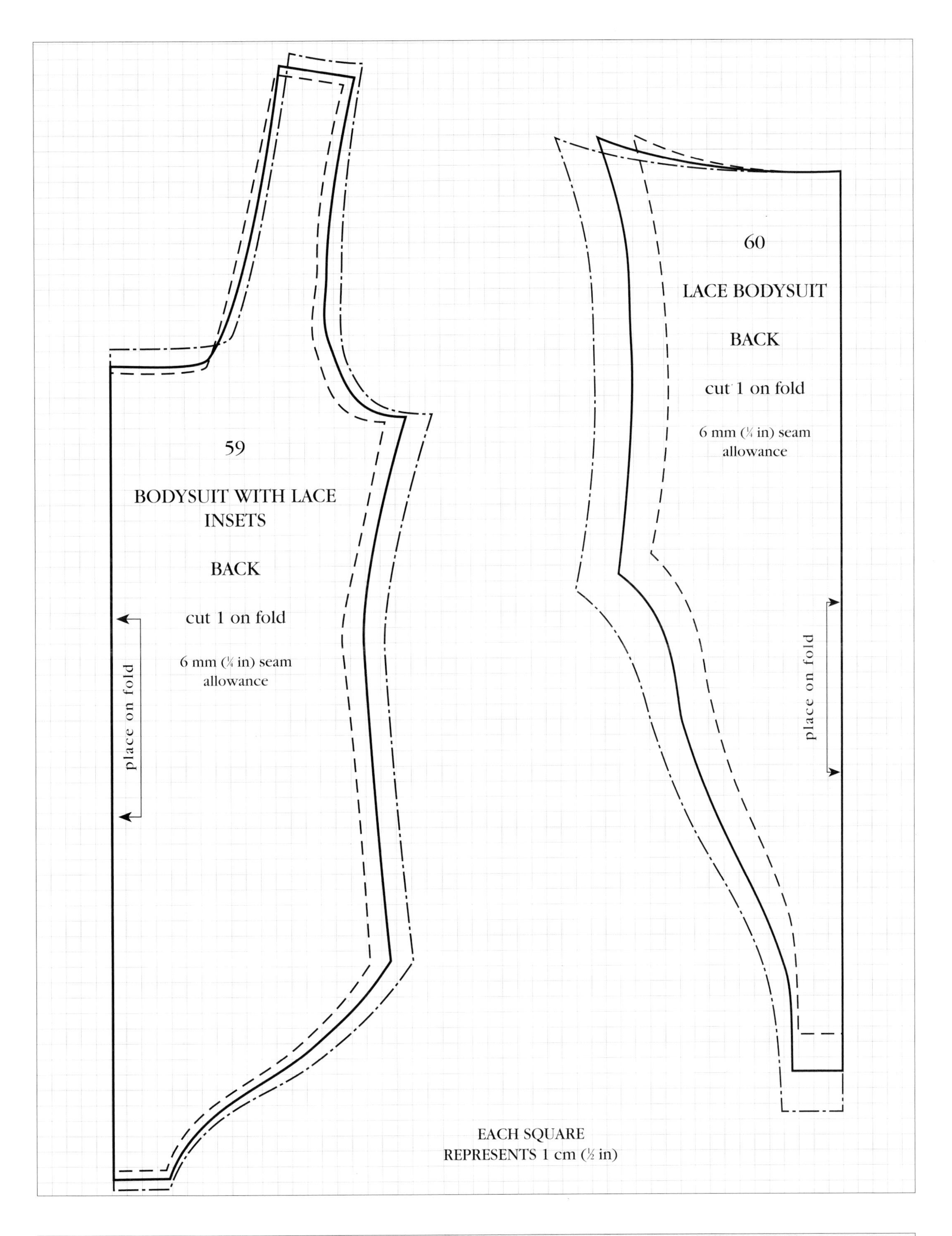
59
BODYSUIT WITH LACE INSETS
BACK
cut 1 on fold
6 mm (¼ in) seam allowance
place on fold
60
LACE BODYSUIT
BACK
cut 1 on fold
6 mm (¼ in) seam allowance
place on fold
EACH SQUARE
REPRESENTS 1 cm (½ in)

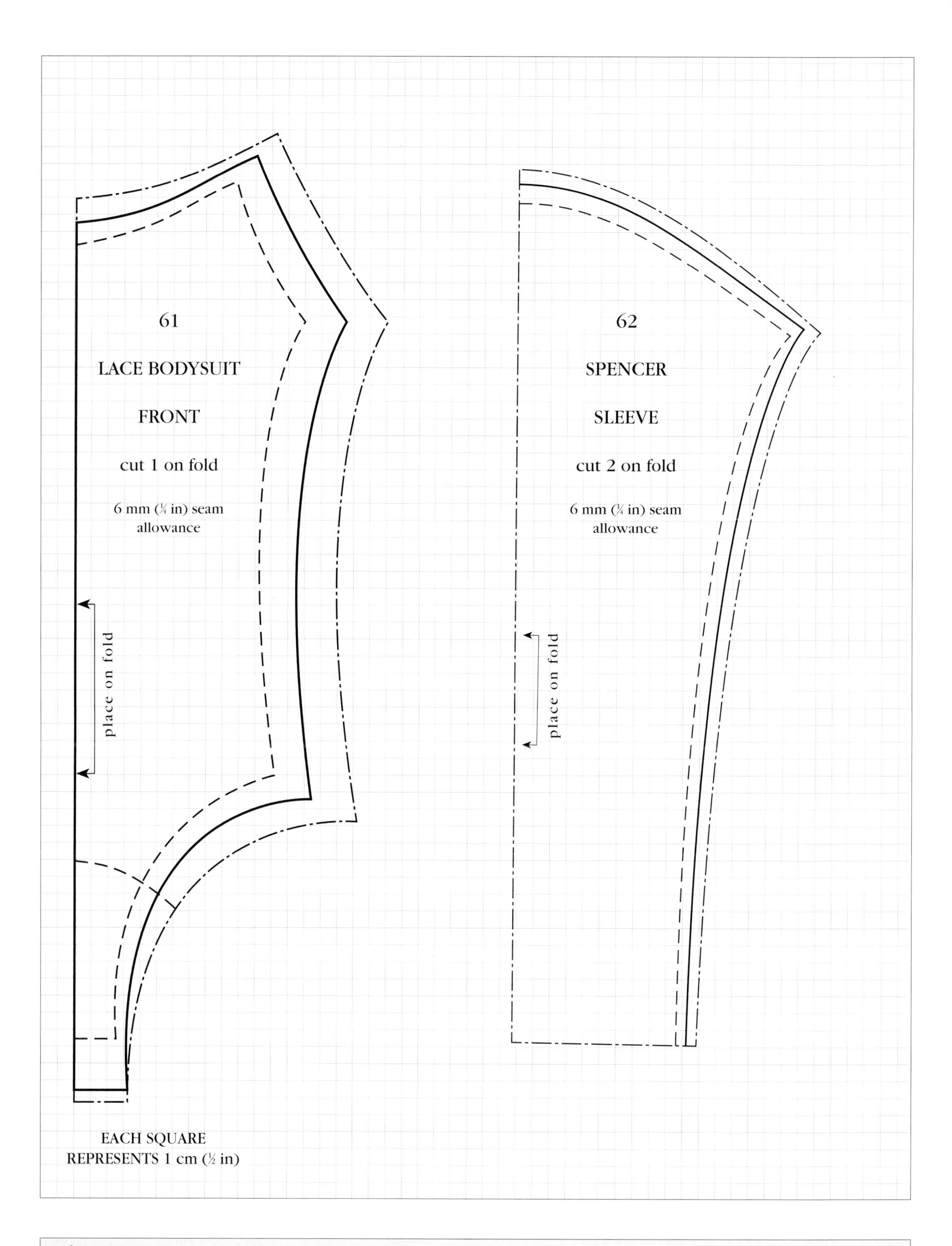
61
LACE BODYSUIT
FRONT
cut 1 on fold
6 mm (¼ in) seam
allowance
place on fold
62
SPENCER
SLEEVE
cut 2 on fold
6 mm (¼ in) seam
allowance
place on fold
EACH SQUARE
REPRESENTS 1 cm (½ in)

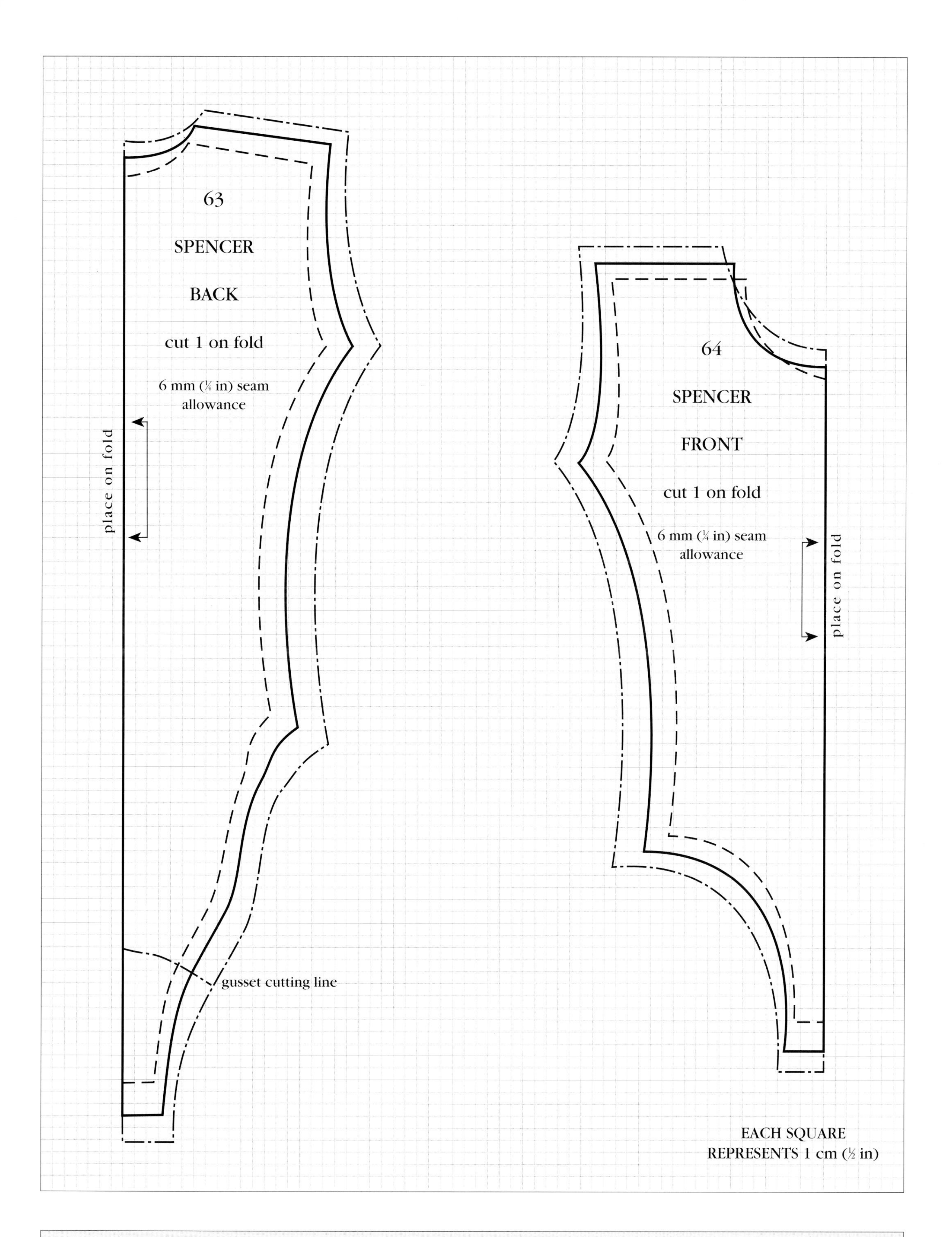
63
SPENCER
BACK
cut 1 on fold
6 mm (¼ in) seam
allowance
place on fold
gusset cutting line
64
SPENCER
FRONT
cut 1 on fold
6 mm (¼ in) seam
allowance
place on fold
EACH SQUARE
REPRESENTS 1 cm (½ in)

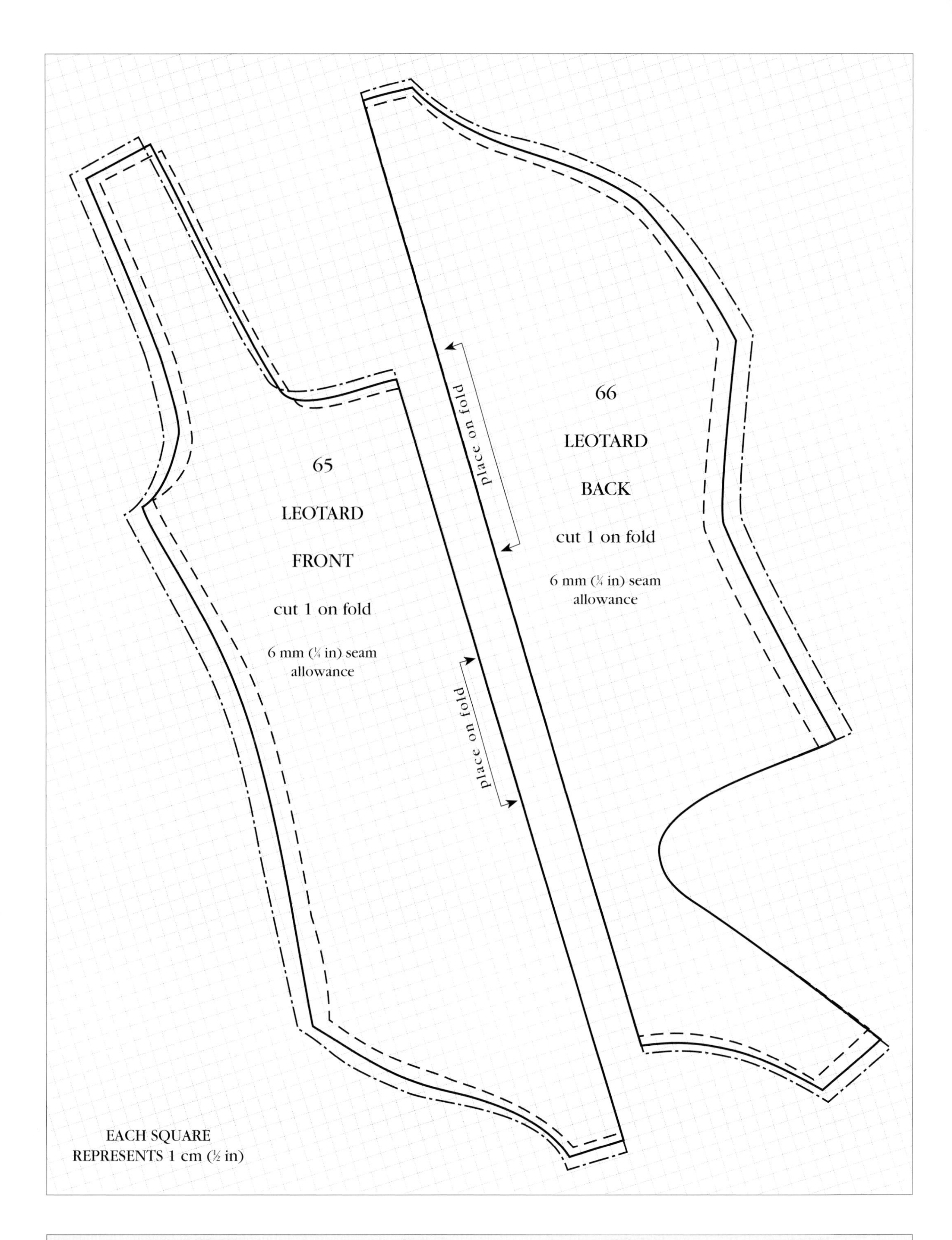
65
LEOTARD
FRONT
cut 1 on fold
6 mm (¼ in) seam
allowance
place on fold
place on fold
66
LEOTARD
BACK
cut 1 on fold
6 mm (¼ in) seam
allowance
EACH SQUARE
REPRESENTS 1 cm (½ in)

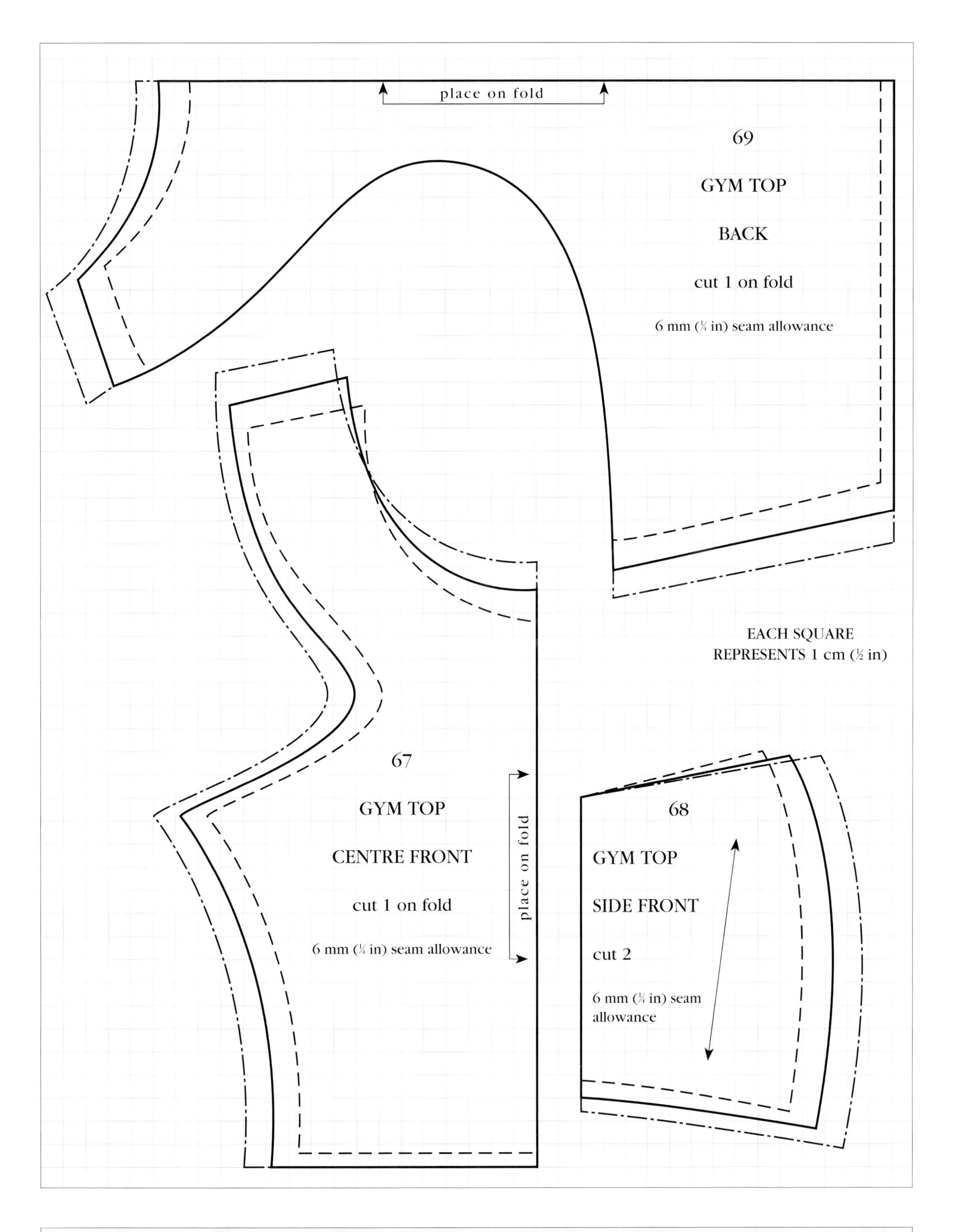
place on fold
69
GYM TOP
BACK
cut 1 on fold
6 mm (¼ in) seam allowance
EACH SQUARE
REPRESENTS 1 cm (½ in)
67
GYM TOP
CENTRE FRONT
cut 1 on fold
6 mm (¼ in) seam allowance
place on fold
68
GYM TOP
SIDE FRONT
cut 2
6 mm (¼ in) seam
allowance

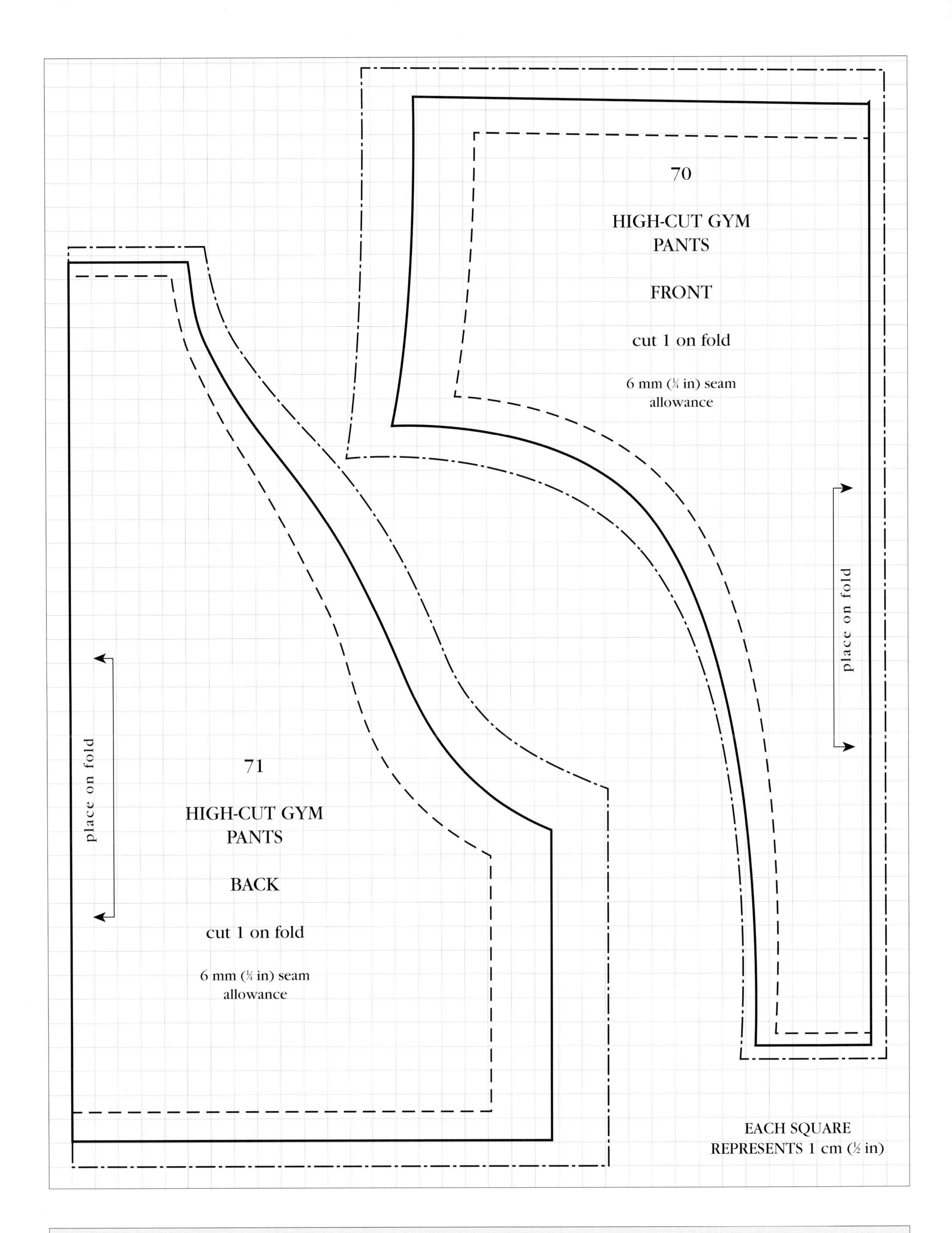
70
HIGH-CUT GYM
PANTS
FRONT
cut 1 on fold
6 mm (¼ in) seam
allowance
place on fold
71
HIGH-CUT GYM
PANTS
BACK
cut 1 on fold
6 mm (¼ in) seam
allowance
place on fold
EACH SQUARE
REPRESENTS 1 cm (½ in)

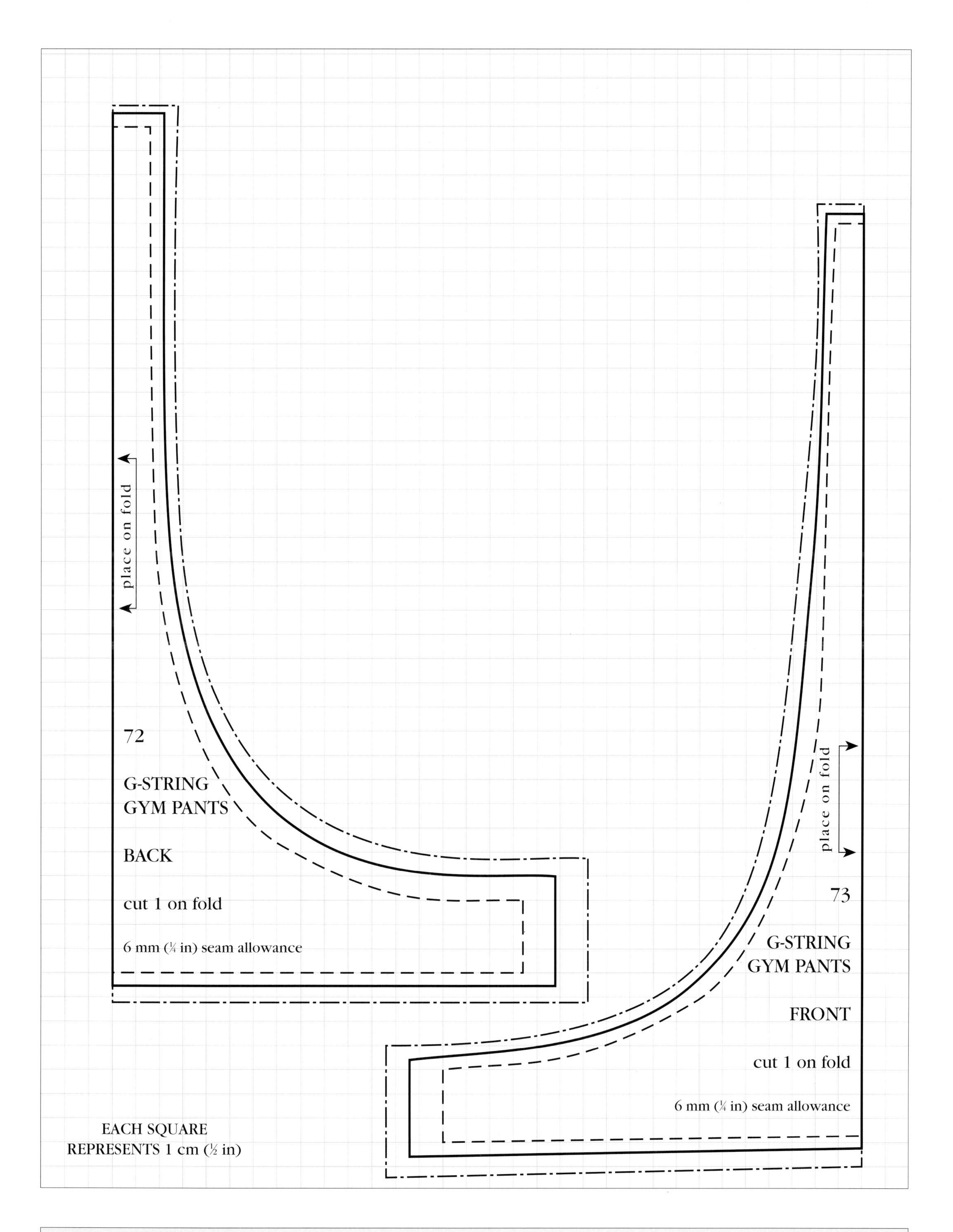
place on fold
72
G-STRING
GYM PANTS
BACK
cut 1 on fold
6 mm (¼ in) seam allowance
place on fold
73
G-STRING
GYM PANTS
FRONT
cut 1 on fold
6 mm (¼ in) seam allowance
EACH SQUARE
REPRESENTS 1 cm (½ in)

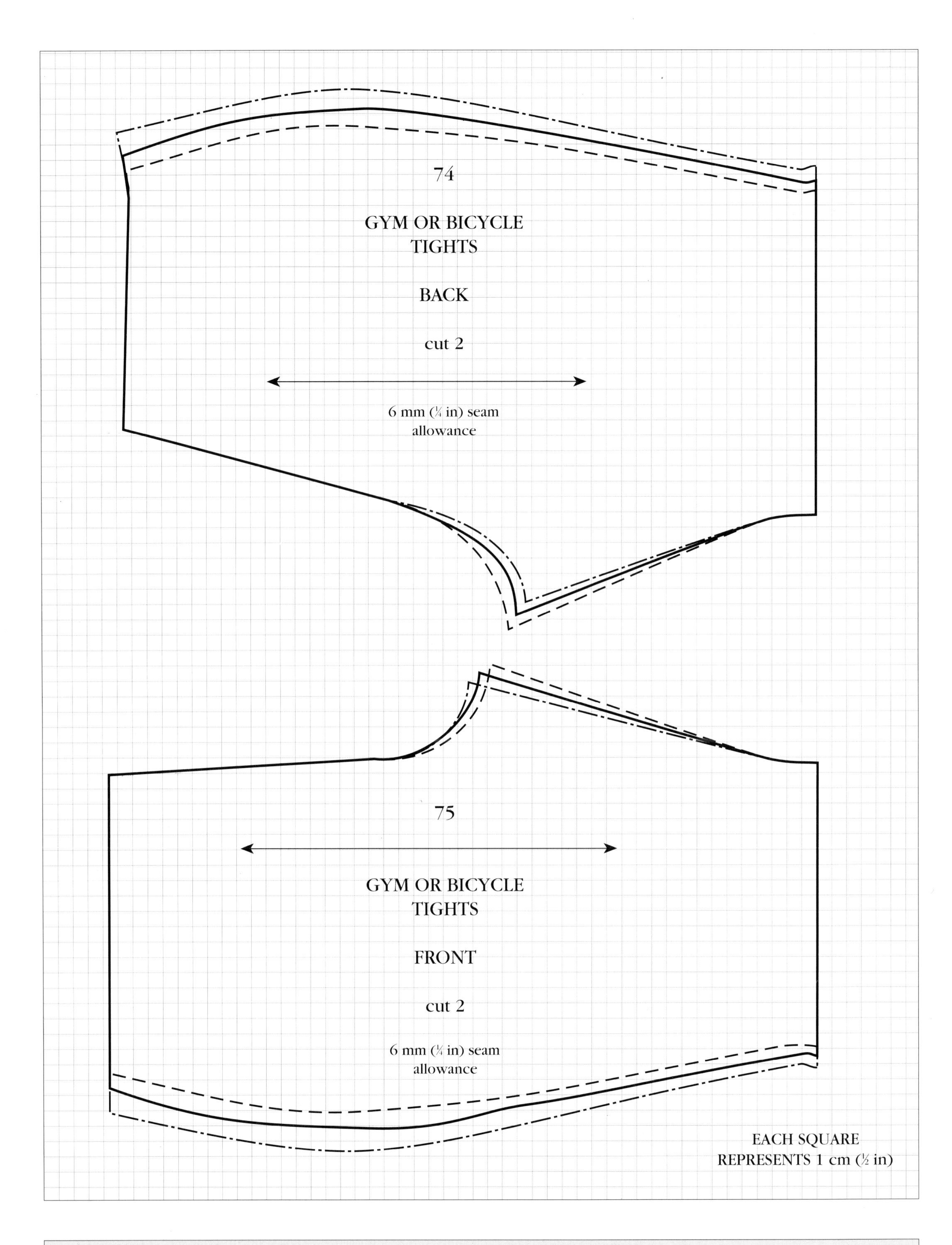
74
GYM OR BICYCLE
TIGHTS
BACK
cut 2
6 mm (¼ in) seam
allowance
75
GYM OR BICYCLE
TIGHTS
FRONT
cut 2
6 mm (¼ in) seam
allowance
EACH SQUARE
REPRESENTS 1 cm (½ in)

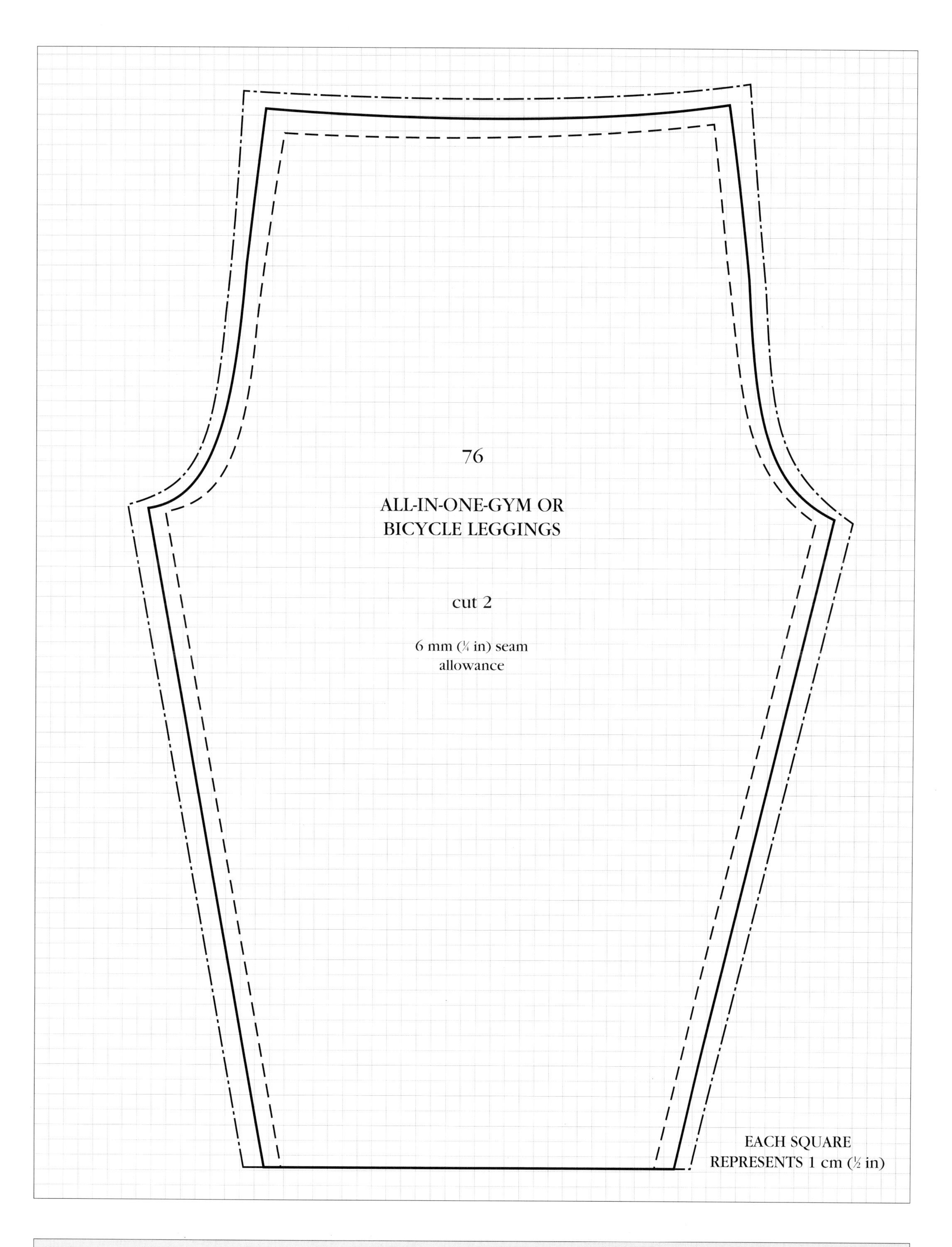
76
ALL-IN-ONE-GYM OR
BICYCLE LEGGINGS
cut 2
6 mm (¼ in) seam
allowance
EACH SQUARE
REPRESENTS 1 cm (½ in)

INDEX